Absurdistan

Absurdistan

a bumpy ride through some of the
world's scariest, weirdest places

Eric Campbell

HarperCollins*Publishers*

HarperCollins*Publishers*

First published in Australia in 2005
by HarperCollins*Publishers* Australia Pty Limited
ABN 36 009 913 517
A member of the HarperCollins*Publishers* (Australia) Pty Limited Group
www.harpercollins.com.au

HarperCollins*Publishers*
25 Ryde Road, Pymble, Sydney NSW 2073, Australia
31 View Road, Glenfield, Auckland 10, New Zealand
77–85 Fulham Palace Road, London W6 8JB, United Kingdom
2 Bloor Street East, 20th Floor, Toronto, Ontario M4W 1A8, Canada
10 East 53rd Street, New York NY 10022, United States of America

National Library of Australia Cataloguing-in-Publication data:

Campbell, Eric James, 1960– .
  Absurdistan: a bumpy ride through some
  of the world's scariest, weirdest places.
  ISBN 0 7322 7980 1.
  1. Campbell, Eric James, 1960– . 2. Foreign correspondents
  – Australia – Biography. 3. Foreign correspondents –
  Australia – Anecdotes. I. Title.
070.4332092

Cover design and map design by de Luxe & Associates
Cover illustration by Katherine Angove
Internal design by Katy Wright, HarperCollins Design Studio
Typeset in 11.5 on 16.5pt Bembo by Kirby Jones
Printed and bound in Australia by Griffin Press on 79 gsm Bulky White

13 12 11 10   06 07 08 09

To Kim and Nicholas,
who make everything possible,
and to Sebastian and Paul,
who were too young to die.

Contents

Part Two — Further East

Acknowledgements

Many journalists have a book in them and some believe that's the best place to keep it. Those who helped me get mine out include Maeve O'Meara, Sally Sussman, Michael Carey, Julie Lewis, Xiao Li, John Taylor, Nadia Rodova, Eve Conant, Peter Scougall, Alicia Hannan, Lindsay Simpson, John Amy, Gabrielle Deakin, Amruta Slee and above all Kim Traill. Thanks also to Paquita Sabrafen and Joaquin Hernandez, who kindly let us stay in their village in La Mancha to write the first draft; to David Nel-lo for casting a novelist's eye over it; to Carol and Alastair Traill for giving Kim and me precious time to write; to Deanna Medina for navigating the ABC's archives; and to Jill Gardner for helping me remember things I had tried to forget.

As a television correspondent, you spend much of your life being followed by a giant camera and tape recorder. Where possible, I have gone back to camera tapes to check quotes and descriptions. For the parts lived off-camera, I've tried to check my recollections with the people I mention. But apologies in advance to any Siberian coal miners or Arctic reindeer herders who have wound up shorter, fatter or more belligerent than they really were.

All prices quoted in the book are in US dollars, the unofficial currency of choice in the former Soviet empire. When writing Russian words, I have used the Russian plural 'i' rather than the English 's' except for words that have come into common English usage. In the chapters on the former Yugoslavia, 'Serbian' refers to the state of Serbia, and 'Serb' to ethnicity, whether in Serbia/Kosovo, Macedonia or Bosnia.

There are no endnotes. This is not an academic treatise. It is a book about the places I saw, the events I experienced and the people I met. I was both fortunate and cursed to be in extraordinary places at extraordinary times. I hope you find the journey as intriguing, if at times as dark, as I did.

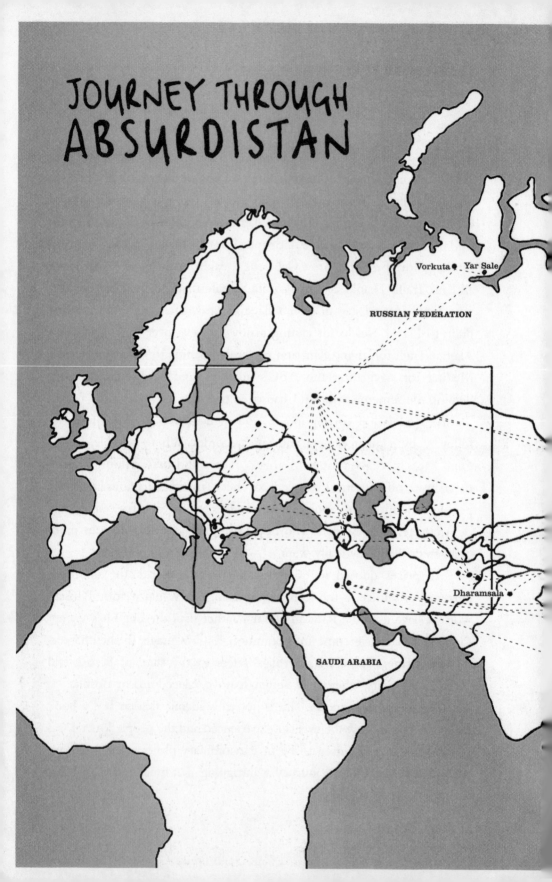

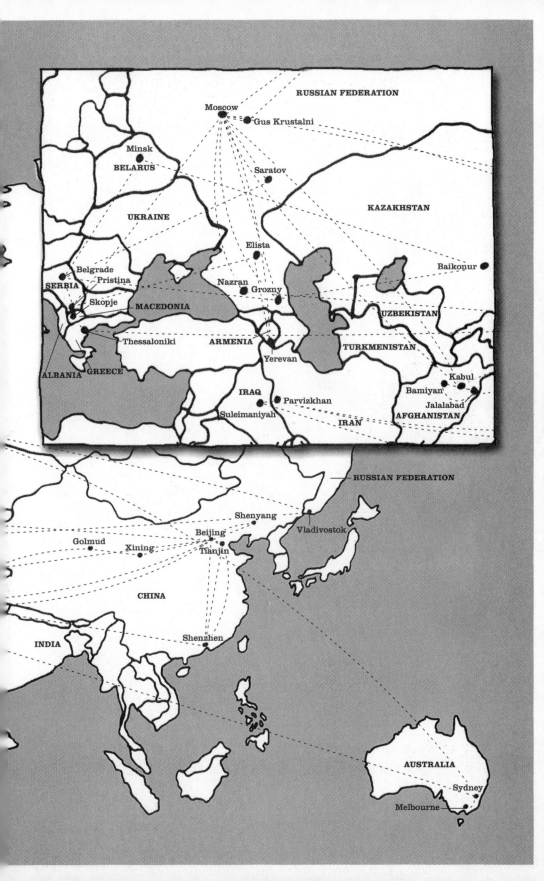

Prologue, 2003

The cameraman was filming *me*. He must have thought I was one of *them*. I didn't look as badly wounded as the others so he didn't linger long, moving off to the next room where people were more photogenic because they were lying in their own blood.

I had done it often myself — walked round war zone hospitals looking for shots with the most pathos. Too much injury was bad: you couldn't show it. Blood without the gore usually got through. Screaming or moaning was best: it gave viewers a feeling of the pain and horror and they could imagine the wounds that caused it.

The moaning today was different. I wasn't sure if it was the woman with the mutilated leg, or the man with the wounded stomach, or the other man who'd been shredded by shrapnel, or my neighbour lying on the floor beside me. The explosion had wrecked my hearing and everything sounded muffled, even someone wailing just a body's length away.

There was a voice in my head, too. It was my own, trying to tell me I wasn't here. *This isn't real. We don't get hurt. It's not our world. We both have babies. Paul has a little girl.*

It was only the third day of the Iraq war and the fighting had barely begun. I was in Kurdistan, the part that was supposed to be relatively safe. We had brought gas masks, thinking there might be chemical weapons strikes, but I wasn't supposed to be lying bleeding in a hospital near the body of my friend. *This wasn't supposed to happen.*

I looked up and the cameraman was filming me again. I recognised him as the BBC's shooter. I looked straight into his lens and he glanced up startled. 'I'm a journalist,' I said. 'I met you yesterday. Do you remember my cameraman, Paul? He's dead.' He said something about being sorry and asked if he could help me but I was seeing the explosion again and it overpowered everything.

We had been the last to drive to the militants' base after the Americans bombed it because we wanted to be sure it was safe. That made us the last ones there. In another minute we would have been gone. Paul was getting some last shots of civilians driving out. He walked a few steps in front of me following some action when a car pulled up beside him and blew up.

For a moment I couldn't understand what was happening. I saw the car explode into a ball of flame. I felt the blast wash over me. I watched as parts of the car flew towards me and struck me in the chest. I heard the ringing in my ears and felt the blood all over me. I saw the people around me dead and dying. I felt shock greater than anything I'd ever known. Then I saw Paul's body on the road and I knew the worst thing in the world had just happened.

A doctor was beside me now; he spoke some English. 'How are you feeling?' he asked. I just nodded. 'We have a special room for you upstairs.' I didn't feel deserving of anything special but I wanted to get away from the moaning and I knew I had to make some more phone calls to tell people I was alive. The doctor helped me up the stairs.

There had been nobody to call for help after the car blew up and I couldn't have called anyway because the blast had melted my satellite phone. As soon as I'd reached the nearest town, I'd borrowed a satphone from the first journalist I saw. She'd had to dial the number because my hands were covered in blood and shaking badly. The first person I rang was the ABC's Head of International Operations, John Tulloh. I wanted to sound in control but I was sinking into a black hole and could barely get the words out.

'I have terrible news,' I said, sobbing. 'Paul . . . Paul's dead.'

Then I rang my wife Kim. She was staying at her parents' house in Melbourne. It was one in the morning and the answering machine cut in, so I kept saying, 'I'm OK, but Paul's dead,' until she came on the line and started crying too. Later I rang my father and asked him to call my sisters, because I couldn't say any more to anyone.

I was in the special room upstairs now and it was full of people staring at me. Most of them were journalists; genuinely shocked, wanting to help, feeling it could have been them, but still working, still getting quotes. I told them I had a three-month-old son and Paul had had a six-week-old daughter. I asked them not to mention Paul's name yet because the ABC couldn't reach his wife, Ivana, and I didn't want her to learn her husband was dead by hearing it on the radio.

I was feeling nauseous again and wanted to vomit. The doctor came in and insisted that I have an injection. I remembered the battlefield first-aid courses where they told us to carry our own syringes because war zone hospitals sometimes reused them and you could catch HIV. But the other journalists said the syringe was new and clean, so I let him shoot me up with antibiotics, painkiller and Valium.

I told them what had happened at the checkpoint and how Paul had talked so much about his daughter. But the question none of the journalists asked, because they all knew the answer, was why we had left our children to come to Iraq.

On my last night in Australia, my wife and father and sisters had asked again and again why I was going. I told them it was my job and I was expected to go, but the truth was that I'd pushed to go and the thing that had scared me most was that I could miss out on covering the world's biggest story. I had been a foreign correspondent for seven years and it was a competitive, all-consuming business. If you weren't covering the major events, like wars or revolutions, you felt left behind. There was nothing worse than sitting in a bureau doing nothing while your friends and colleagues flew off to the latest trouble spot. I'd reached a stage where I no longer thought it strange to leave a wife and baby to go to a war.

I assumed Paul had felt the same but we hadn't got round to discussing it. I had come to think of him as a friend, as happens quickly in intense situations, but I had known him only four days. That's how long we'd been in Iraq.

The voice came back to me. *I shouldn't be here.*

I had reported on conflicts from Chechnya to Kosovo to Afghanistan and never been hurt. They had shocked me and depressed me but they had also exhilarated me. Big stories, intense experiences, strange cultures, misadventures, physical danger, isolation, tension, fear; moving on, always moving on, had become my idea of what passed for a good life.

Now I could only wonder how I became this way and why I had chosen to live and work in a world that normal people tried to flee. I could only marvel that I'd once thought covering wars would be fun.

Part One

EAST

Chapter 1
Sydney to Moscow, 1995

Leaving

Some people become television journalists to shine light in the darkness, making films to expose injustice and build understanding. More do it just for the money. Many see television as glamorous; a few hope it will make them famous. But to my knowledge, nobody ever became a television reporter to film caravan parks in East Gippsland.

It was just how things worked out for me.

In 1990, as the first Gulf War was about to get under way, I was working for a TV travel program, planning a shoot about budget holidays in Victoria. I had always had a vague plan to become a foreign correspondent, but some unwise career choices had trapped me in the dimmest recesses of Australian television.

When a revolution overthrew the dictator Ferdinand Marcos in the Philippines in 1986, I was comparing toasters for a consumer-affairs program. When the Berlin Wall came down three years later, I was profiling a stripper who also worked as a horse strapper ... 'She's the Stripper Strapper!' ... for a tabloid current-affairs program. Now, as Saddam Hussein's forces pillaged Kuwait, I was getting ready to report on 'adventure weekends' in Bairnsdale.

What began as a fuzzy aim to work overseas was becoming a gnawing obsession. I wanted desperately to be reporting great moments of history rather than watching them on television like everyone else. And in one dark hour, lost between horse-drawn caravan trips in Bendigo and child-friendly walking tours in the Grampians, I swore I would become a foreign correspondent, no matter what the cost.

It took me another five years to make it happen. I switched to lower paid but serious current-affairs programs at the ABC and started applying for postings in its overseas bureaus. I read prodigiously about Asia in a bid to become the Hong Kong reporter, but came third. I studied Japanese for a year, hoping to be sent to Tokyo, but was pipped at the last moment by a former correspondent who decided to go back. I studied all things Chinese for six months thinking I was a certainty for Beijing, and came second. I decided to give it one last try, applying to be the television correspondent in Moscow. By now, I was so despondent I didn't bother learning any Russian. It was the job I was least prepared for. I got it.

It wasn't a dream destination. The city's reputation was coloured by a decade's perestroika-era images of food shortages, queues, civil strife and mafia crime. My wife Meredith was so thrilled by the prospect that she planned to stop off indefinitely in London on the way. But I didn't care if it was every bit as extreme as people warned. I was now 35 and bored rigid with life in Australia. If the price of escape was living somewhere cold, hard and mean, I was happy to pay it. At least that's what I thought sitting in the February sunshine in Sydney.

It was early afternoon but already dark when the plane thudded onto the ice in Moscow. The passengers broke into spontaneous applause as if to congratulate the pilot for not crashing.

Russia looked just as I'd imagined: horrible. The international airport, Sheremetyevo, had been built for the 1980 Olympics and had all the charm and efficiency of Soviet central planning. Dimly lit corridors and cracked concrete stairs led to long queues in front of rude officials.

I handed my documents to the Immigration officer, a woman with a beehive hairdo, false eyelashes, thick blue eyeshade and a short military uniform. She looked like an extra from a 1960s James Bond film. But instead of pouting at me, she snarled.

'*Fotokopie!*'

I stared blankly. She raised her voice.

'*Fotokopie nyeto?*'

'I'm sorry, I don't speak Russian,' I said in English. She stared blankly at me.

'*Fotokopie u vas yest!?*' she shouted. '*Vi Russki ne panimaiti!?*'

I had come to cover the complex politics and societies of the former Soviet Union and I was having trouble getting through the airport. The person behind me explained that the officer wanted a photocopy of my visa to save her the trouble of entering the details. Of course. It had taken me an hour to get to the front of the queue and she was angry with me for wasting *her* time.

'*Nyet,*' I replied, using one of the 25 words I knew in Russian. '*Izviniti,*' I added — Sorry — using one of the other 24.

Frowning, she looked from my face to my photo, back to my face then to the photo, again to my face and back to the photo, before grudgingly accepting that it was my face in the photo. Then, with painstaking deliberation, she copied out my details, stamped my passport and waved me through. I was finally in Russia. Or at least in the luggage hall.

It was a dirty room full of porters spitting on the floor and smoking. Dozens of passengers suffering withdrawal symptoms from the four-hour flight from London were also puffing greedily. There were No Smoking signs all around the hall but someone had thoughtfully placed a large ashtray under each of them. To comply with regulations, No Smoking stickers were plastered on the ashtrays.

Half the luggage carousels were broken. I waited 40 minutes for my bags to appear, surrounded by pot-bellied Russian businessmen with slender peroxide-blonde girlfriends shouting into tiny mobile phones. All of them seemed to be wearing Versace, Armani or Hugo Boss. There was obviously some serious money in Moscow, even if it wasn't being spent on the airport.

I joined the queue for Customs, filling in yet more declaration forms that were headed Союз Советских Социалистических Республик (Union of Soviet Socialist Republics). It was 1996, five years after the USSR had disintegrated, and they were still using up the old forms.

The Customs officers eyed my television equipment greedily. Self-interest had taught them some English. 'How much these?' an official demanded, pointing to my boxes of camera tapes. 'You must pay money.' I had no idea what to say. They let me go with a $100 fine (cash only, no receipt) and I walked through the exit into a mob of shifty-looking men in fur hats and leather jackets shouting '*Taksi! Taksi!*' The ABC driver, Volodja, was among them. He was about 40 years old with an alcoholic complexion, thick glasses and no English. He helped carry my bags outside into a wall of freezing air. We trudged through the slush and ice to the office car, a Volvo station wagon that looked like a wreck after just two years of Moscow roads in Moscow weather.

Volodja pointed to the headlights to show they weren't working. Then he gestured that it didn't matter. We drove down the freeway in darkness, Volodja weaving across the ice and slush trying not to be hit by other cars.

Moscow looked like a black-and-white movie; the snow turning to grey sleet as we passed kilometre after kilometre of drab high-rise apartment blocks. There were splashes of colour as we neared the city centre; neon signs proclaiming what I guessed was Cyrillic for 'casino', and giant, illuminated billboards advertising Marlboro, Jack Daniels and lingerie. Eventually we stopped at what was my new home.

I tried to ignore the smell of dog urine as the lift shuddered to the sixteenth floor. Volodja gave me a large, old-fashioned key and I clanked open the heavy metal door to my flat. It was bigger than I had expected, with three small bedrooms and a lounge and dining room. There was faded pink carpet, tattered beige furniture and leftover ashtrays, ornaments and *Teach Yourself Russian* books from previous correspondents.

The ABC had a large network of foreign bureaus but little money with which to run them. While some Western media groups could give prospective correspondents six months' full-time training in language, politics, history and culture, the ABC had reimbursed me for the cost of some Russian language tapes. I'd also brought a bundle of press clippings for research.

I read them again. The essence of being a foreign correspondent is to be able to parachute into a foreign country and report on any aspect of it with confidence and certainty. Nobody watching television wants to hear correspondents say they're as clueless about the place as the viewers are. Having come all this way, you have to at least pretend you know what you're doing.

The next day, I woke early and looked out at my new view. The building was surrounded on three sides by identically bland white-tiled concrete high-rises. From the rear, through the grey, wintry pall, there was a view of a police station, an army barracks, a small forest and an expanse of snow and ice. It felt like a crummy suburb on the far edge of town. I would later find it was one of the most prestigious addresses in Moscow.

The ABC bureau was on the tenth floor of the tower block next door. Or at least half of it was. The radio correspondent, Michael Brissenden, worked there with the radio staff. But my job would be reporting for television. For reasons I never quite understood, the TV staff all worked in another office on the other side of town. The ABC had a talent for expanding bureaucracy but I was about to learn it had nothing on the Russians.

I walked into the (radio) bureau to introduce myself to the local staff and found the office manager, Ira, almost crying into the phone. 'I cannot believe this,' she said to me, after pleading to an obscure official on the other end of the line. 'It's even worse than *Soviet* bureaucracy. They change the rules every day. But sometimes they will tell you money can solve the problem.'

Among other battles, Ira was now into her third month of trying to get me a multiple-entry visa. She explained that the Foreign Ministry was refusing to issue a new visa in Russia, meaning that I would have to fly to London just to get a new visa from the Russian embassy so I could fly back to Moscow.

Volodja arrived to take me to the TV office. It was a terrifying 30-minute trip down icy highways, weaving through an avalanche of lumbering trucks and cars. It was impossible to see lane markings under the snow and almost as hard to see out the windscreen because of the mush flying up from the road. On the plus side, it was daylight, so we didn't have to worry about not having lights.

The (television) bureau was in a business centre in an allegedly five-star hotel called the Radisson Slavyanskaya. The hotel had lured foreign media groups including the BBC, NBC and Reuters with cheap starting rents and was now bleeding them dry. But it had the only on-site transmission point for satelliting stories, so everyone was obliged to stay.

Our tiny office had two assistants: Robert Gutnikov, an Uzbek-American trying to take a backdoor route into journalism; and Slava Zelenin, a Moscow translator who seemed to look down on the job but enjoyed the part-time work and easy money. Robert, who spoke Russian with a thick American accent, was designated the producer, and Slava was supposed to be the sound-recordist as well as translator, but neither of them had been doing much of anything since the previous television correspondent left four months earlier. I hoped my arrival wouldn't be an unwelcome intrusion into their otherwise perfect working arrangement.

The only other person in the bureau was the cameraman, Tim Bates, who was crammed into a tiny edit suite at the end of the room. Like almost all the camera operators the ABC posted to Moscow, he was Tasmanian. They had all joked that they weren't scared of the cold, but like many who grew up on the southern tip of Australia, they just wanted to get as far away as possible. Tim was quietly spoken and generally positive about the world. But two years in Russia had given him a laconically brutal view of the place. 'World's biggest rubbish dump,' he called it. Still, he preferred it to Hobart.

The Radisson Slavyanskaya was an odd place to have a bureau. It was mafia central. The hotel's shopping arcade was lined with luxury stores catering to the tasteless new rich. Impossibly tall and cosmetically enhanced women perused furs and designer jewellery, while toadlike men in gangster suits waddled along the hallway past thick-necked security guards with walkie-talkies.

The hotel's corridors were also full of what appeared to be paramilitaries patrolling with Kalashnikov assault rifles. Tim explained there was an ongoing armed standoff between two of the hotel owners. An American entrepreneur, Paul Tatum, claimed a stake in the business centre from which we leased our office. But a well-connected Chechen businessman, Umar Dzhabrailov, who had close ties to the Moscow City government, was trying to force him out and seize his share. Both sides had rival armed guards roaming the hotel.

'The nicest thing about working here is having so many thugs wandering around with machine guns,' Tim said.

I was staggered by the ostentatious wealth of the Russians who lounged round the hotel's cafés and restaurants. Even their bodyguards seemed to wear Armani suits. 'We call them *Novi Russki*, New Russians,' Ira told me. 'You can't imagine how much money they have. And they stole it all. Most of them are in their thirties. When Yeltsin privatised everything, it all went to the children of the *nomenklatura*, the old party leadership. They paid almost nothing for it.'

The centre of Moscow was full of them; bright young spivs who just happened to own hugely valuable former State assets, like oil fields, coal mines or gold mines worth tens of millions of dollars.

The richest of the rich were known as the 'oligarchs': well-connected crooks who had managed to amass billions. They were the chief winners from five years of turbulent reforms under the first post-Communist president, Boris Yeltsin. Western apologists for Yeltsin's reforms called them 'robber barons', as if they were no different from the ruthless industrialists who built America's railways and steelyards. In fact, they were just robbers. They hadn't built anything; they'd taken Soviet-built industry through rigged privatisations which were closed to public scrutiny or foreign competition. Most were stripping the assets of their new holdings and funnelling the proceeds into bank accounts in Cyprus and Switzerland. This was what was widely known as 'economic reform'. At least that's what I'd read in the press clippings.

Further down the scale were obscenely rich thugs who had muscled their way into privatised factories, sports complexes or entertainment venues. They called themselves *biznesmen*. Ordinary people called them *mafia*.

It wasn't just criminals who had prospered. The money swilling around Moscow had inevitably created a new middle class of office workers and traders. But even in this relatively rich capital, there was shocking poverty. Old people sat outside metro stations begging, their savings wiped out by hyperinflation and their pensions nearly worthless. The saddest were the *babushki*, the ubiquitous term for any women over 55.

This was not a good time for Yeltsin to be standing for re-election. I had arrived just in time to see the launch of his campaign. We watched on the edit-suite television as he hauled himself up to a podium in his home city of Yekaterinburg and declared his readiness to stand in the June presidential poll. It was hard to imagine he would even live that long. The once inspiring leader looked as potent as mouldy cabbage. His eyes were glazed and his speech was painfully slow and slurred.

Nobody was quite sure what was wrong with him. Rumours ranged from alcohol poisoning to heart failure to terminal cancer. What was certain was that hardly anyone planned to vote for him. His approval rating was just 8 per cent.

The man who seemed assured of victory was the leader of the Communist Party, Gennady Zyuganov. He was a dull, porcine party hack but had a huge lead in the opinion polls. 'People have already forgotten how bad things were under the Communists,' Ira said ruefully.

A few days later we headed out for my first shoot: a campaign march of Russia's unreformed, anti-Semitic, discredited Communists. Thousands of Zyuganov's supporters were assembling in October Square beneath a giant statue of Vladimir Lenin. It was one of the most imposing Lenin statues in Russia: the father of the Bolshevik Revolution pointing his right arm towards a glorious future, his cloak flapping behind him as if filled with the winds of change.

'We call this one Farting Lenin,' Tim said.

The crowd was an unimpressive sight — mostly toothless pensioners with war medals and ageing mid-level bureaucrats with bad suits and worse haircuts. Five years earlier the Communists had been written off as a spent force. Now they had the cocky manner of winners already planning to settle scores.

We followed their march for an hour down the wide boulevards of the city centre as they chanted abuse at Yeltsin and sang revolutionary songs, holding banners painted with crude caricatures of big-nosed Jews and capitalist bankers. The crew were anxious to go before they froze but I wanted to do a 'piece to camera', the ubiquitous sign-off to news stories, where the reporter looks into the camera and says something authoritative. I had been in Russia less than a week, but after waiting so long to get overseas I wasn't about to let inexperience get in the way of being an expert.

'The Communists here can almost taste victory,' I said in my serious voice. 'And time is running out for Boris Yeltsin to stop them. History hangs in the balance,' I concluded ominously.

Two weeks after arriving in Moscow, I flew to England to collect a multiple-entry visa and to attend a British Army course on surviving in war zones. I spent three days watching videos of horrific war injuries and practising first aid for wounds like severed legs, with a dozen other journalists from the BBC and ITN. Every one of them had covered wars before. I was the only virgin.

Meredith flew back with me from London. She seemed strangely tense and unexcited about seeing our new home. I put it down to culture shock but was too busy with work to give it much thought.

As bleak as Moscow seemed, it was paradise compared to what lay outside. My first field trip was to the town of Gus Krustalni, a four-hour drive east from Moscow. It was famous for producing Russia's finest crystal, but like 80 per cent of Russian industrial towns, this one was effectively bankrupt. The state no longer bought the crystal so the factories couldn't afford to pay wages. Instead, they gave their workers crystal — everything from chandeliers to sets of glassware to elaborate (and hideous) sculptures.

Unable to eat it, wear it or pay their bills with it, the workers set up an open-air market where they tried to sell the crystal to each other. When Tim and I arrived to film, we were mobbed by hungry craftsmen waving pink glass flamingoes and horse-shaped paperweights.

It was the same story throughout Russia. Workers were being paid with the second-rate unsaleable products they made. Siberian matchstick makers were taking home cartons of matches in lieu of wages, tyre makers were wheeling out car tyres at the end of each month, and children's toy makers were being paid in plastic animals. I once saw a group of men standing in the snow holding up bath towels with Hawaiian beach scenes. If workers were lucky, they could sell enough of the goods their factories produced to get drunk. On a really good day, they could feed their families as well.

The further you went from Moscow, the bleaker life became. After two months in Russia, I flew north to the bleakest place I had ever seen.

Chapter 2
Vorkuta and Yar Sale, April 1996

Life in the Freezer

Pavel Ivanovich Negretov was lucky to be alive. Or unlucky, considering the life he'd led. For ten years of his youth he had been imprisoned on a remote speck of the Russian Arctic watching tens of thousands die around him. 'I don't fear death or hell,' he told me as our feet crunched on the frozen tundra. 'Why should I? I've lived through hell on Earth.'

We were walking around the ruins of the labour camp where he had been abused, starved, beaten and nearly worked to death for 3652 days. The remains of barbed-wire fences and wooden watchtowers still protruded from the deep snow. A bitterly cold wind was blowing from the north, sending flecks of ice into the pale spring sunshine. Pavel shivered in his thin overcoat. 'After Stalin's death there were strikes at all the mines,' he said. 'The troops just opened fire on us. The first to die were those who were ready to go to work and those who were holding them back.'

Pavel Ivanovich was one of perhaps 25 million Soviet citizens sent between the 1920s and the 1950s to the labour camps known as gulags. His camp at Vorkuta was among the worst of the worst. Men, women and children were forced to work in unimaginable cold to build coal mines and a railway line to transport the coal south. 'Malingerers' were shot or sent to exposed punishment cells where death was certain.

He was never sure what his 'crime' was. Most people were sent to camps for unwise gossip or on trumped-up allegations. They were used as human workhorses to build the glorious Soviet Union. Even when his sentence ended, the terms of his release required him to work in the new city built beside the gulag. Now 72, with ruined health and failing eyesight, he knew he would die here, trapped by his past and without hope of redemption. And he was appalled that many of his fellow survivors were planning to vote for the leader of the party that had sent them here as slaves. Even former gulags like Vorkuta were expected to choose Gennady Zyuganov over Boris Yeltsin in the June presidential election. Support for the Communists was soaring in places that had every reason to hate them.

'All our people have to wander in the desert for 40 years, just like Moses and the Jews, so that we can get rid of the slave mentality,' Pavel Ivanovich said bitterly. 'The whole generation must die. Only in 40 years will we enter democracy.'

I had come here with Tim, Robert and Slava to profile Vorkuta as a symbol of Yeltsin's failed revolution. But the city looked more of a testament to old-style Soviet folly. Built on the bones of forced labour, it had the same centrally planned apartment blocks, public squares, wide boulevards, snaking power lines and belching smokestacks as any Soviet-built city. Yet it was closer to the North Pole than to Moscow, meaning that the cost of digging and transporting the coal was greater than its value. But Communist expansionism had always triumphed over common sense. Even when the gulag was closed in the 1960s, the state continued to bring people here to work the mines, luring them with high salaries and benefits, though it cost more to heat the buildings than could ever be recovered from coal sales.

Now that Russia was capitalist the folly was unsustainable. The subsidies had disappeared and the mines were bankrupt. The city that housed the workers and their families had no reason for being, but its 120,000 residents had nowhere else to go. And the likely winner was the political party that had created the whole mess.

Vorkuta was a miserable place, but its resident Communist apparatchiks were in high spirits. They met every Saturday morning in a schoolroom with a social realist mural of a mineshaft on the back wall. The venue was a comedown from the days when they ran the city, but they knew their fortunes were changing. The party secretary, Vladislav Asadov, had the relaxed confidence of a man who would soon be back in charge. He was in his late forties, balding, with a stocky miner's build gone soft from desk sitting. His assistants fussed round him as he sorted through the agenda for the meeting.

The main item was signing up new members. People applied to join every week, and today half a dozen men had come to lodge their applications. The first candidate was a young newspaper journalist. He made a speech denouncing Yeltsin's administration as 'bureaucrats who call themselves democrats but don't even know what democracy is'. His application was accepted unanimously.

Later I asked him why he was joining a party that had never allowed free media: 'It is no different under Yeltsin. My editor tells me what to write.'

There was a sense of decay in the city, with cracked buildings, giant potholes, broken streetlights, and frozen rubbish dumped on the footpaths. The streets were made even gloomier by the coal dust that settled on each snowfall and turned it black. But it was the only place that most of the community had ever known. There was even a hint of civic pride, with a miners' orchestra, community theatre groups and a local television station.

A reporter with big hair, a flouncy dress and shoulder pads came to interview us about our first impressions of Vorkuta. I thought of saying it had a lot of snow, but this didn't seem polite enough.

'The warmth of the people is as delightful as the cool of the snow,' I said. Slava translated.

'Is it like Australia?' the reporter asked.

'Uh, yes,' I said. 'It's very similar to a mining town called Broken Hill. Except it has lots of snow.'

She pressed me further for similarities. Ever more desperate I said, 'Australia was also founded as a prison colony. But we have developed our own civilisation; therefore we feel great empathy with places like Vorkuta.'

That night, as we watched the black-and-white television set in the hotel room, we found that we led the news bulletin. We'd even pushed news of the winner of Mine Number Five's ski contest into second place.

Most of the miners had not been paid for six months. But they still went to work. It was partly because there was nothing else to do and partly because they hoped one day to be paid their back wages. Fatalism and hope were the twin conditions that kept them going.

The next day we joined a group of miners kitting up for a shift. They wound cloth around their feet instead of socks and queued up for headlamps and oxygen canisters. The shift leader was Volodja Miller, a middle-aged gulag descendant. His father and grandfather had been sent to the camps in World War II for nothing more than being ethnic Germans. Their ancestors had settled on the Volga River more than two centuries earlier, at the time of Peter the Great. But when the Nazis invaded in 1941, Stalin regarded anyone with a German surname as suspect.

Volodja had little interest in the past. He just wanted to feed his family. 'Our mine is not so bad; we only wait for two months for our salaries. Different mines pay their workers on different days, and we borrow money from each other. That's how we live.'

The miners turned on their headlamps and we crammed into a steel cage at the top of a lift shaft. The door closed and we plunged 250 metres into darkness. The cage clunked to a stop and we poured out into a passageway, illuminated only by the faint glow of our lamps. I assumed we were walking to the coal seams but, after decades of excavation, they were now many kilometres away. We stopped at an underground railway.

Volodja and the other miners climbed into box-like metal containers. I felt a stab of claustrophobia as I climbed in after them, Tim squeezing in beside me with his camera. The doors clanged shut and the train screeched off into pitch-black darkness. I closed my eyes and tried to imagine I was somewhere else.

After 10 kilometres it finally stopped. We set off on foot again, sloshing through puddled water on the mineshaft floor. The air was dank and cold. I had to fight against a feeling of being buried. For Volodja and his workmates it was just another day.

Ninety minutes after leaving the surface, we finally reached the spot they would be clearing. A huge and dangerous-looking drill was tunnelling into the wall. Volodja's team loaded up large chunks of coal into rail carts. It was arduous work and they did it slowly and without enthusiasm. The coal would probably never be sold.

Five years earlier Boris Yeltsin had passed through Vorkuta, campaigning for Russia's first presidential election. Volodja and his mates had been impressed. Now they felt cheated.

'Yeltsin didn't keep his promises,' Volodja told me. 'He promised us golden mountains. He said we'd live better, we'd get higher wages but none of this happened. I can't say how all the miners will vote, but most of them will be supporting Communists. They are promising better and we lived better under Communism than now. There is no trust in Yeltsin.'

We left them working to begin our journey back to the surface. By the time we reached the lift, our faces were black from coal dust. Most miners were invalids by the age of 50. For a brief time, in the 1970s and early '80s, they had been among the highest paid workers in the Soviet Union. The state gave them bonuses to live here and flew them south each year for holidays in the sun. Now they worked for nothing, like the prisoners who came before them.

Back on the surface, a group of ex-miners had set up a protest group in a small apartment. Aged from 20 to 50, they'd been left unable to work through accidents or ill health. It had been months since they had received their pensions so they had just begun a hunger strike. Ten of them were sitting around watching a small television set when we arrived. Boris Yeltsin was on the screen outlining a new plan to end the war in Chechnya. They sneered at him.

'At least he's not drunk today but what he's saying is rubbish,' one complained. 'He drinks and we don't even eat, let alone drink. Why should we listen to a drunk man?'

The speaker's name was Vladimir Polishny and he was the organiser of the hunger strike. He was a big man with a big moustache who still had a miner's muscles. A back injury from a mine accident had left him unemployable. But he hadn't lost a black sense of humour. The small kitchen, which had become his office, was dominated by a large bust of Lenin. Vladimir had stuck a German army helmet on its head and painted its face with the stars and stripes of the US flag. Unlike many of the miners, he hated the Communists as much as he hated Yeltsin.

'There's no difference between them. Eighty-six per cent of Yeltsin's administration are former Communist Party members,' he said. 'The smartest of the meanest people have come to power.'

I wanted to give something to Vladimir and his friends. They were proud men and wouldn't take money so I offered them a souvenir from Australia. I had brought hundreds of kitschy miniature soft-toy clip-on koalas to Russia on the advice of the ABC's first correspondent, John Lombard. It didn't quite seem appropriate to give a toy koala to a tough ex-miner but Vladimir was touched.

'I have heard of this animal and I envy it,' he said. 'It can live on nothing but leaves.'

Democracy and economic reform were also coming to the indigenous people of the Arctic, who lived on nothing but reindeer. Before Stalin sent prisoners here, the only inhabitants were nomadic reindeer herders. Called Nentsi, they had been roaming the tundra around Vorkuta and across the far north for centuries. Now, as well as having a chance to cast their votes in the presidential elections, they found Western energy companies eyeing off their untapped oil and gas resources. It was an exciting time to be a reindeer herder.

We had planned to hire a helicopter in Vorkuta to take us across the Ural Mountains on the first leg of a journey to the Yamal Peninsula, where hundreds of Nentsi were gathering for an annual reindeer festival. However, the week before we arrived we heard that the helicopter had crashed, killing all eleven passengers. There were no commercial flights across the Urals so we asked the Vorkuta city administration for advice. They suggested we try to hire a plane from a nearby army base. This would have been unthinkable in Soviet times, but it seemed even the military was going entrepreneurial.

I went down to the base with Slava and Robert and asked the commander if there was any chance they were flying in that direction and could offer us a lift. 'How much can you pay us?' he asked. We settled on $1600.

The next morning we returned to the base to find a border patrol plane with a dozen armed soldiers waiting for us. I wasn't sure if the soldiers were part of the package but they climbed on with us and sat silently with their weapons stowed as we flew towards our destination, the small town of Yar Sale (pronounced Yar Sulay), where the festival would be held. The plane skidded onto an ice landing strip as a herd of reindeer ran a short distance in front of us.

Yar Sale was from a time before concrete. Wooden cottages lined snow-covered streets on which the only traffic was reindeer-drawn sleds. A statue of Lenin in the town square was the only visible sign that this was an outpost of the former Soviet empire. Yar Sale was once used as a base from which to explore the area's huge gas reserves, but the isolation had defeated all previous attempts to build a viable industry. It was now a sleepy administrative centre and trading post for the mainly nomadic population. A few ethnic Russians lived here as teachers, bureaucrats or merchants, but most people were Nentsi.

To our surprise, there was also an American. We heard a voice cry out, 'Hey, where'd you guys come from?'

Sven Haakonson was a young anthropologist doing a field study of the Nentsi. He had a personal interest in the work. He was an ethnic Inuit from Alaska and felt a strong affinity with the Nentsi, who had a similar culture and lifestyle to traditional Inuit. He was scared that that lifestyle was in danger of coming to an end, as it had in so many communities in Alaska. The reason was a multibillion-dollar plan by Amoco to build a gas pipeline to the west. While the royalties would go to the state, Sven feared the injection of such massive investment would change the Nentsi forever.

'I think it could destroy them,' he said sadly. 'Once you start bringing money into an area where people have never had it before, they're going to want foreign goods, they're going to want snow machines, the women are going to want a house, they're going to want things that make them seem like the rest of the world. Alcoholism, violence, all that will probably increase once more Nentsi decide they want to live in the villages.'

Sven suggested we go out of town to see how the tundra Nentsi lived. The festival was still two days away and our plan had been to do just that. However, nobody in town could tell us where any nomads were camped. 'They don't have addresses,' one official told us sardonically. 'They're nomads.'

We knew that many were heading towards Yar Sale for the festival but, staring out at the white nothingness surrounding the town, it didn't seem like a smart idea to wander out to find some. The next day, though, a group of nomads came to us. We found them in the general store, buying supplies for their camp, about 10 kilometres outside town. They were stocking up on tea, condensed milk and vodka, the three luxuries for late twentieth-century reindeer herders.

Their headman, Timofei, was taken aback when Robert asked if we could go back to their camp with them. 'It's going to be twenty below zero tonight,' he said. 'And we sleep on the ground.'

Robert explained that we were filming a story about them and wanted to see how they lived. But Timofei had been through this before. 'We had an Englishman come out to study us once,' he said. 'He didn't speak a word of Russian. He was an idiot.'

This wasn't quite the welcome we were hoping for. 'We can pay you,' Robert said.

They were the magic words. Timofei agreed.

We went back to the guesthouse and put on every item of thermal clothing we had. I layered up with two sets of neck-to-knee underwear, two pairs of woollen socks, one jumper, two fleeces, a thick down jacket, gloves, mittens and a fur hat.

Tim handed each of us a camera battery half the size of a house brick. 'Put these in your underpants,' he ordered. 'It's the only way to keep them warm. If the batteries die I can't shoot.'

We walked back to the trading store looking like Michelin men with genital mumps.

Timofei had found two snowmobiles to take us out, not trusting us with reindeer. We loaded our gear into two wooden sleds hitched behind them and squeezed in. With a shout from Timofei, the reindeer and snowmobiles pulled forward and we lurched after them, gliding across the snow towards the late afternoon sun. The town soon disappeared behind us and I felt swallowed up by the tundra. It was like being in the middle of a white ocean, but Timofei's men knew exactly where to go, navigating by wind flurries and small outcrops of rock.

The sun was dipping behind the horizon as we reached the camp. The snowmobiles were the only sign of modernity. There were six large tepee-shaped tents, called *choomi,* made from reindeer hide wrapped around long wooden poles. A herd of more than a thousand reindeer gambolled around the *choomi* or stood pawing the snow to get at the lichen just under the surface. Children were playing in the fading light wearing smaller versions of the adults' reindeer-hide outfits. The temperature was dropping fast and Timofei was anxious to get us inside. He pointed out the *choom* we would sleep in and directed us into another to eat.

We stepped through the reindeer-hide flap. My glasses and Tim's camera lens instantly fogged up from the warmth. There was a small potbelly stove with a chimney leading up to a hole in the peak of the *choom.* A dozen people sat around on wooden boards laid on the snow, eating the last of a pot of reindeer stew. They seemed remarkably relaxed about having a Western television crew crash their dinner.

Robert briefly explained what we were doing and an older woman named Nadia invited us to sit down and have some reindeer. It was a

little tough, but pleasantly warming after a two-hour ride. Dessert was a frozen fish. 'Eat it before it thaws,' Nadia advised us.

It was dark by the time we finished eating. The glowing coals dimly illuminated the faces of the adults and children. Someone passed around a glass of vodka for us to share. Sven had warned us about the high rates of tuberculosis among the Nentsi so I pretended to sip and passed it on. Remembering what Sven had said about the impact of development, I asked how keen the people were for Amoco's money.

Nadia said she just wanted Amoco to go away. 'They will take the land from us, and where will our children live? Not everyone wants to live in town. My son, for example, goes to school now, but when he grows up he won't live in town. He wouldn't want to. He'll have the reindeer he inherits from his father. He wants to live in the tundra, where else? That's why we don't want gas.' She chewed another piece of frozen fish.

It was time to sleep. Timofei took Tim, Robert and Slava to the neighbouring *choom* but indicated that I should stay where I was in a narrow space next to an old man. I assumed he was giving me the honour of sleeping next to the most venerable member of their clan. I took off my boots and climbed into the sleeping bag wearing every item of clothing I had, including my fur hat. Gradually the others fell asleep; the old man started snoring about three centimetres from my face. I tried to move away but the *choom* was packed.

Within an hour the fire had gone out and the temperature inside began to approach the temperature outside. I realised I hadn't been to the toilet; not that there was a toilet between here and Yar Sale. I climbed out of my sleeping bag and felt my way towards the flap, stumbling out onto the snow for an Arctic pee. Hurrying back inside, I pawed around for my rucksack and found my bottle of drinking water. I put it inside my sleeping bag so it wouldn't freeze.

My neighbour was now snoring like an express train. I tried to remember what I'd read about tuberculosis. I was certain that lying next to a wheezing old man was not the recommended way to avoid it. I had plenty of time to ponder this because I was so bloody cold I couldn't sleep. I had bought the sleeping bag in Australia from a camping store salesman who had assured me it was designed for the Antarctic. I imagined going back to Australia and punching him before I sued him. My teeth were chattering, my legs were shaking and there were six hours to go before sunrise. The old man's snoring was growing even louder. As I lay awake until dawn, I kept reminding myself that this was a unique and magical experience in the Arctic tundra.

I had just dozed off when a reindeer stuck its head through the flap and began to snuffle at my feet. I looked up and saw two women combing their daughters' hair. The *choom* had warmed up to a relatively balmy minus ten. I reached for my water bottle and found it had frozen solid *inside* my sleeping bag. I put my boots on and clambered outside. Just by the entrance, a woman was sawing off a hunk of frozen reindeer meat for breakfast. Tim was already up filming.

'How'd you sleep?' I croaked.

'Really well,' he said. 'I was toasty.'

Suddenly, it felt wonderful to be here. The sky was a brilliant blue, the snow pure white. We were in the middle of nowhere in a nomad camp watching Nentsi herders lassoing reindeer. I walked around the camp in awe of what I was seeing, with the snow crunching under my feet.

The most remarkable thing about the Nentsi was how they had managed to preserve their way of life during the brutal conformity of Soviet times. The literature I had read about the Nentsi made for dispiriting reading. Under the forced collectivisation of the 1930s, the Communists rounded them up from their remote grazing lands and herded them into newly established and completely unviable Arctic towns. Their clan leaders and Shamanist holy men were hanged or shot en masse.

To maintain the herds, the Communists soon had no choice but to send some of the Nentsi back onto the tundra to graze the reindeer. They divided them into work units, which gradually melded into the old clan system. For many Nentsi involved with migrating herds across the peninsula, life continued much as it always had. And Timofei did not want Western companies coming in with big money to change things.

'They will take all the gas and leave all their rubbish,' he said. 'They will plough the land and we'll suffer from it, we'll lose our pasture. Nothing good comes from them. There is nothing we can do, they don't listen to us. They decide themselves how it would work but they don't ask us. And the people here are not literate, they can't speak out. It's politics and they don't understand politics.'

We rode back with Timofei's clan into Yar Sale for the start of the festival. By now he'd become quite a camera slut and insisted that Tim ride on his sled to film him as he shouted commands and stood with the wind in his face racing across the ice and snow. Eight sleds drawn by 32 reindeer followed him.

The town was now filling with nomads. Wooden sleds were parked like cars along the edge of town as Nentsi children held their reindeer to stop them mixing with other herds. Everyone looked up as a helicopter hovered overhead and landed on the airstrip 200 metres away. The door opened and a team of Amoco executives clambered out, bearing gifts for the school and prizes for the festival. The head of the proposed gas project, Randy Joseck, seemed less than happy to see a Western camera crew but agreed to give us an interview. He swallowed nervously as I asked him about the environmental implications of building a gas pipeline across the permafrost.

'The pipeline will be installed in the winter when the permafrost is frozen, so there'll be very little damage to the permafrost at that point,' he said. 'With regard to the reindeer, the animals are herded, so the routes will be mapped prior to the development and crossings will be built for the reindeer.' He argued that the benefits would far outweigh any detriment.

There was no doubt the Nentsi needed help. The new Russian authorities had all but abandoned them, cutting back the few benefits they'd enjoyed in the time of the USSR. Helicopters no longer took their sick children to hospital. Social services were being wound back.

The Amoco executives were travelling with a consultant anthropologist, Dr William Fitzhugh, who echoed Randy Joseck's view. 'There's going to be some hard times,' he said. 'I think they've got some bargaining to do. But I think the local people realise that they've got to have economic support. They want their kids to go to school, they want to improve the towns they have. I think it's necessary.'

Walking through Yar Sale's streets, the benefits of development didn't seem so clear cut. The Nentsi living in town were very different from the nomads. Most of the men were alcoholics and, to celebrate the festival, they had gone on blinders and now reeled around drunkenly or lay unconscious in the snow. Life was hard in the tundra, but it was healthier than this.

The festival began with wrestling matches followed by sled races. It was the one chance the nomads had to show off their skills to a wide audience and winning was a matter of fierce pride. Amoco's prospective partner, the state gas monopoly, Gazprom, was supplying much sought-after prizes — snowmobiles and coloured beads.

When it was all over, Timofei told us they were breaking camp the next day to begin the northern migration across the peninsula. Few Westerners had ever seen this: the area had only begun to open to outsiders in the early 1990s. We hired snowmobiles and in the morning rode out before dawn to film it.

The Nentsi were in the final stages of packing up their camp as we arrived. As the men rounded up the herds, the women unwound the reindeer hides of the *choomi*, took down the poles, stacked the wooden boards they slept on and loaded it all on sleds. Their meagre belongings came next — the stoves, some extra clothes, tea and vodka. For the next few months they would live entirely off the land, eating reindeer and fish and moving camp every few days or weeks to graze the herds.

Timofei moved out first, followed by a long line of heavily laden sleds snaking off into the distance. We watched them until they disappeared over the frozen hills. It seemed as improbable a sight in the late twentieth century as a wagon train taking pilgrims across the

American west. Somehow the Nentsi had preserved an ancient way of life throughout the time of Tsarist Russia and Communist dictatorship. I wondered how long that way of life would survive in the free market.

As for the election, all the Nentsi we spoke to said they would vote for Yeltsin if the ballot papers reached them. He was the only candidate any of them had heard of.

It took us five days to get back to Moscow, three of them stuck in a blizzard that closed the airport. We'd all spent our ABC travel allowance by now, so we moved into one hotel room and ate bread and cheese until the weather cleared. I had naively assumed we'd be able to use credit cards in the Arctic. We had trouble even finding a phone we could use to let the office know we were stranded.

I had only been in Russia for three months but I was already exhausted. I had immersed myself in work and travel, trying to get on top of a story I could barely follow in a country I was struggling to understand. And Meredith was still distant and unsettled. Expatriates I met warned me that Moscow was doubly difficult for the partner who wasn't working. There was all the discomfort and culture shock without the excitement and job challenge. There was little joy in being stuck in an apartment on the edge of the city, not speaking the language and having to wrap up in four layers of clothing to go outside. Moscow really didn't offer much to Meredith. She was an actor just starting to get the kind of work she wanted in Australia when we left everything to move here for my sake. I decided it was time for us to take a break from Russia.

Traditionally, the country shuts down in the first week of May. In Soviet days, this was so that everyone could celebrate International Labour Day. In post-Communist Russia, it was so that everyone could stop labouring. We decided to fly to Florence for a week.

After two days in Italy, Meredith told me she had some news. She was in love with a friend of ours and wanted to marry him. She wanted to go back to Australia and she wanted a divorce as soon as possible. I had no idea what to say. I hadn't even noticed what was happening.

Back in Moscow, she organised her return flight to Sydney and we divided up our belongings. We barely spoke. I drove her to the airport, we said goodbye and I went back to my soulless apartment. I slumped on the floor in shock, finally taking in that she had really gone. My marriage was over and I was completely alone on the other side of the world.

I searched the apartment, found a bottle of vodka, drank it all and passed out. The next morning I began my new life.

Chapter 3
Chechnya, May 1996

A Short War

The armoured personnel carrier (APC) blocked the sun as it sped up to pass us. Five Russian soldiers bristling with guns sat on the roof. It was too good a shot to miss and Tim shifted his camera to the car window, discreetly filming as they overtook us. I saw a soldier at the back of the APC notice Tim. He called to his commander who turned to see the camera. I thought he might shout at us to stop filming. Instead, he raised his machine gun and opened fire.

There was a deafening blast of rapid fire about a metre from the windscreen. Our Chechen driver slammed on the brakes and skidded off the road. In the long silence before anyone spoke, all I could hear was a ringing in my ears and my heart pounding. I felt stunned by what had just happened. It was so stupid, dangerous and brutal. The driver smiled mockingly, as if to say, 'Welcome to Chechnya.'

It was two weeks since Meredith had left and Chechnya was the last place in the world I felt like being in. There had been no question of taking time off, as the elections were just weeks away, so I'd buried myself in work. I drove into the office early each morning and stayed until late. Now I had come to my first war.

I was travelling with Tim and Slava, who seemed to be enjoying it as little as I was. We had planned to fly straight to Grozny, the capital of Chechnya, but fresh fighting closed its airport just as we were about to board the plane in Moscow. So we flew to the neighbouring Russian republic of Ingushetia instead and hailed a taxi to Chechnya. Even at the worst times, taxis would do runs to Grozny. The price just escalated depending on the danger: up to $1000 if the fighting was intense. War was becoming a normal state of affairs in the region and, for some people, it was a once-in-a-lifetime chance to make big money from Western journalists.

We saw the aftermath of fighting as soon as we crossed the administrative border into Chechnya. Oil rigs and pipelines were destroyed; Chechnya's only legitimate industry was in ruins.

The first Russian checkpoint was a few kilometres down the road. I hadn't been sure of what to expect of the army but I'd imagined there would be strict military discipline, with officers barking orders and soldiers snapping to attention. The young conscripts blocking the road appeared to have no idea what they were doing. Some were drunk and told us that they hadn't eaten for days. Their uniforms were dishevelled; some wore sneakers rather than boots. Nobody seemed to be in charge.

They wouldn't let us pass unless we allowed them to use our 'satphone' to call their mothers. In those days, satellite phones were portable suitcases with phone sets where the lid served as the satellite dish. They were heavy and unreliable but in good conditions you could call from anywhere in the world. Tim had been to Chechnya before and suggested we limit the soldiers to two calls or we'd never get to Grozny.

He propped open the lid on the car bonnet and turned it until it locked onto the North Atlantic satellite signal. Two of the boys then called home to tell their families they were still alive. They asked them to call the other soldiers' mothers too, rattling off names and phone numbers in provinces across Russia. All were lucky to have survived this long. The Chechen guerilla fighters were vastly outnumbered but they had little trouble picking off the poorly trained and badly led Russian conscripts.

Further down the road we came across a group of Russian soldiers who were every bit as ruthless as the guerillas. They were *kontraktniki*, low-grade mercenaries who had signed up to fight in Chechnya for $50 a month, some because they needed the money and others for the chance to kill. A few of them had shaved their heads and painted camouflage greens and black on their faces. Their Russian uniforms had touches of Rambo action movies — bandanas, tight black singlets, hunting knives strapped to their legs. Another correspondent had advised us to bring alcohol, Marlboro cigarettes and pornographic magazines to ensure our passage to Grozny. It took us most of that, plus the use of our satphone, before they would let us pass.

Chechnya had never been a welcoming place to intruders. When the Tsarist empire swallowed up the Caucasus in the nineteenth century, the fiercely independent Muslim Chechens had been the hardest group to subdue. It took 30 years of fighting before Chechnya was officially incorporated into Russia in 1859. Stalin transported the entire population to Central Asia in the 1940s, accusing them of collaborating with the Germans. More than a third died before Stalin's successor, Khrushchev, allowed the survivors to return in the 1950s.

When the Soviet Union collapsed, the Chechen parliament declared itself independent of the new Russian Federation. While some Chechens were happy to remain part of Russia, most wanted to regain their ancestral lands. But Chechnya quickly descended into violent infighting, drug and arms dealing and black-market smuggling. At the end of 1994, Boris Yeltsin lost patience with the chaos, ordering a military invasion to bring Chechnya back under federal control. He promised it would be a 'short, small-scale war' and that 'force in Chechnya will be employed with due consideration of the principle of humanity'. The Russians began systematically bombing Grozny a week later.

Yeltsin's 'short war' turned into an ongoing bloodbath. He might have hoped that decisive action would bring Chechnya into line, but he hadn't counted on the fierce determination of the Chechens, a clannish mountain people whose blood feuds can go on for generations. Yeltsin was due to fly into Grozny any day to try to boost his image as a peacemaker before the elections. For security, the Kremlin was keeping the exact date of his visit a secret.

We arrived in Grozny late in the afternoon and stared in disbelief. After eighteen months of fighting, the entire city was in ruins. Almost every building had been bombed, shelled or riddled with machine-gun fire. Most of the population had fled but hundreds of thousands still lived amid the rubble. Some had hung tarpaulins over giant holes in the walls of their homes. Children were carrying buckets of water up the stairwells of bombed apartment blocks. Kerosene lamps appeared in the windows of buildings that looked destroyed.

As well as ethnic Chechens, there were sick and elderly Russians who had nowhere else to go. The Russian military occupied Grozny but its grip was tenuous. The conscripts and *kontraktniki* lived in fortified bunkers dotted throughout the city. Every night Chechen fighters sneaked in from the countryside and attacked them.

While morale among the conscripts was at rock bottom, this was just the kind of real-life Hollywood fantasy some of the *kontraktniki* had come for. We filmed a group of them strutting and posing outside their bunker as the light was disappearing over the shelled remains of the university behind them. 'Come back tonight and you'll see some action,' one of them shouted. Another heard we were from Australia and asked us to send a greeting to his brother who was studying in Canberra.

The Russians' intense aerial bombardment had destroyed every hotel. We stayed in a residential compound with a group of British, French and Georgian journalists. Eight small houses shared a dirt courtyard behind a high metal gate. An old woman named Tamara let us sleep in her house. There were bullet holes in her windows and television screen. Tamara cooked a simple dinner for us and filled the bath with buckets of cold water for us to wash in. The war had destroyed the city's sewerage system. The houses shared a single fly-ridden pit toilet in the courtyard.

Tamara would have conversations with herself, sometimes shrieking with laughter for no apparent reason. She told us she had once had gold fillings in her teeth until rebel bandits pulled them out with pliers.

The other journalists in the compound seemed relaxed and unfazed by the chaos around them. They had all covered the siege of Grozny and had made regular trips here since the Russian military took control. They sat around in the evening discussing the safety of roads in and out of various towns and making jokes about past misadventures, while a Georgian cameraman strummed a guitar and flirted with the Chechen women.

After a restless night listening to sporadic gunfights, we drove to the market in the city centre to film some 'colour': random interviews and vignettes that might give a sense of what it was like to live here. Traders had set up vegetable and clothing stalls in the rubble. Women were hanging their washing from the balconies of bombed-out apartment buildings. Children laughed as they played war games amid the ruins.

Twenty minutes after we arrived, there was a burst of gunfire as three Russian soldiers at the other end of the market were ambushed and shot. Their killers fled undetected. There was a brief commotion but people soon went back to their daily routine. A man with an outdoor stove invited us to sit at a table and enjoy his 'restaurant'. A camera crew from Grozny television came up to ask us our impressions of their city. It was as though everyone was pretending things were normal.

The petrol stations had been destroyed so men stood beside the road pouring bottles of home-mixed fuel into cars, cigarettes dangling from their mouths. Down the street, we found a beauty parlour still operating. It had no power or running water and a shell blast had blown out the windows. The women passed in buckets of water through the gaps to wash the customers' hair. The beautician, Madina, felt it was important that women continued to look after their appearance. 'Our men and women never lose their spirit,' she said. 'They always want to look their best. That's the kind of people we have.'

There was little else here that people could control. The Russian soldiers patrolling the city were violent and the Kremlin had installed an administration of equally unpredictable Chechens. They were a mixture of former Communists and opportunistic *biznesmen* — effectively bandits using government connections to drain the budget and continue their smuggling operations. The nominal president, Dogu Zagdayev, was so unpopular he never ventured outside the fortified Russian Air Force base in Grozny, except to fly to Moscow in his private jet.

Most of Grozny saw the pro-Moscow Chechens as collaborators and traitors. If anything, Russia's invasion seemed to have inflamed the desire for independence. Every person we spoke to supported the rebels and was not scared to say so. 'If Yeltsin comes here, I will kill him,' one man shouted as Tim and I filmed him. 'I will pick up a gun and shoot him myself.' A crowd of men around him cheered and clapped.

Guns are an integral part of Chechen culture and boys learn to shoot almost as soon as they can hold one. Every Chechen had access to weapons, even though many had hidden them to evade Russian searches.

There was little to admire in the tactics of either side. The Russian military had acted with extraordinary disregard for civilians. A report prepared by the Memorial Human Rights Center in Moscow described their conduct:

> ... shelling, strafing of streets from armored vehicles, sniper fire
> on streets and in courtyards, execution-style shootings in
> houses and yards; grenades thrown into and exploded in
> cellars, yards and rooms with people present; the burning of
> houses, murders committed while detained people were being
> marched off. Many of the wounded died because the troops
> refused to allow timely, decent medical help to reach them.

The Chechen rebels didn't have the firepower to inflict the same damage as the Russians but their methods were just as brutal. They rarely took prisoners unless it was to hold them to ransom. A common fate for a captured Russian soldier was execution, sometimes after torture. Some rebels mutilated the corpses of their victims, severing their heads as a warning to the next batch of invaders.

Few Russians had much sympathy for the plight of Chechen civilians, whom they derisively called *chorniy* (blacks) for their dark hair and swarthy complexions. They were widely seen to be *banditi*, just like the fighters. The conflict had reached the stage where neither side saw the other as fellow humans.

One of the worst atrocities had taken place the year before in the village of Samashki, about 50 kilometres west of Grozny on a scenic road winding through steep grassy hills. The Russian military moved in to conduct a *zachistka*, meaning cleansing, to search for rebel fighters. Over two days the army killed 103 civilians, including fifteen women and children. In one incident, Russian troops fired into the backs of a group of old men as they walked back to the village after trying to negotiate a ceasefire. The Russian Presidential Human Rights Commissioner, Sergei Kovalyov, witnessed the slaughter and reported it in graphic detail. Despite his account, some Russian media reported that Chechens had killed their own elders.

A few weeks before we arrived in Chechnya, Russian forces carried out yet another assault on Samashki. This time they surrounded the village and threatened to shell it unless the residents handed over Chechen rebels believed to be sheltering there. The army dismissed the village elders' protests that the rebel fighters had already fled but agreed to sell them a 'humanitarian corridor', giving people two hours to flee in exchange for cash before the shelling started.

Some were too sick to get out, others defiantly stayed to protect their homes, while some men and youths were terrified the soldiers would take them to so-called filtration camps. These were prisons for determining whether men were civilians, rebel fighters or rebel accomplices. A 1995 report from Human Rights Watch claimed that inmates were routinely tortured and that civilians were 'beaten with rifle butts, given electric shocks and subjected to attacks by dogs'.

Once the bombardment started, nobody was allowed to leave. The villagers sheltered in their basements in the hope of surviving the shelling, but it was relentless. After four days a small group of civilians managed to escape, reporting that up to 4000 people were still trapped in the village. They estimated that up to 600 others had been killed and told of women, children and old people being strapped to Russian tanks and armoured personnel carriers as human shields.

It had been impossible to confirm the accounts. Russian soldiers still surrounded the village and there were blockades to stop journalists entering. But we'd heard there was a dirt track into the village that was not always guarded. We left Grozny at dawn and managed to reach Samashki undetected.

There were now few people left in what had once been a village of 7000. After driving through nearly empty streets, we found a crowd of children playing in a schoolyard. One of the teachers, a young woman named Nura Khantayeva, agreed to show us what had happened. She took us down to the basement where she and 120 others had hidden for five days.

'Young men who went out to get water were shot at,' she said as we stood in the blackness of the cellar. 'At night the women crept out to bake bread so the babies wouldn't cry of hunger. We made tea right here in the entryway. We somehow survived.'

When the army stormed in after five days of shelling, she claimed, the *kontraktniki* went from basement to basement, massacring any survivors. 'They burned the cellars with grenades, they killed people. In a village over there they took the women, put them on tanks and used them as live shields. Then they robbed the whole neighbourhood.'

Her group survived only because a young conscript found them first. He saved them by shouting out to the *kontraktniki* that the basement was empty.

As we were filming in Nura's basement, a shell lobbed into a nearby field where two children were playing. A young boy was badly injured. His distraught family carried him to a car to try to rush him to a hospital. The villagers told us this happened almost every day.

We were all shaken by what we had seen. Slava was unusually quiet and seemed ashamed that Russians had done this.

'Are all wars like this?' he asked me.

'I don't know,' I said. 'They're not supposed to be.'

I'd read the Memorial report on war crimes in Chechnya before I left Moscow, but none of it seemed real until I came here. The Kremlin was literally getting away with murder.

Democracy Triumphs

The President of the United States, Bill Clinton, had a more charitable view about 25,000 or so dead Chechens.

A few weeks before I went to Grozny, he and several other world leaders popped into Moscow for a brief meeting of the G7, the group of seven most industrialised nations. It was an undisguised attempt to boost Yeltsin's election campaign, which was looking as sick as Yeltsin was. Clinton showered praise on his old pal Boris and made light of the carnage in Chechnya.

'There are some who say we should have been more openly critical,' Clinton told a press conference. 'I would remind you that we once had a civil war in our country over the proposition that Abraham Lincoln gave his life for: that no state had a right to withdraw from our union.'

Yeltsin as Lincoln seemed a stretch, even for Clinton, but not as much as his praise for Moscow waging war to maintain the 'union'. Five years earlier, the US had cheered Yeltsin as he dismembered the Soviet Union into fifteen different countries. The US was consistent in one area, though ... doing everything it could to keep the commies out of the Kremlin.

As unhappy as most Russians were with Yeltsin, Washington was not unsurprisingly delighted with him. He and Gorbachev had managed to turn their superpower adversary into a compliant developing nation reliant on US aid. American corporations had multibillion-dollar investments which would be jeopardised by a return to Communist rule. The Chechnya unpleasantness was never going to interrupt Washington's tradition of supporting democratic reformers, like Pinochet and Suharto.

Actually, most Russians would have preferred Clinton to be their president. He was hugely popular in Russia, despite being American. People saw him as young, virile and capable compared with the decrepit old boozer they were stuck with.

Clinton and his huge entourage stayed in our troubled hotel, the Radisson Slavyanskaya. US Secret Service agents in sharp suits and wrap-around sunglasses talking into their sleeves temporarily replaced the rival Russian militias wandering round the hotel.

We had to get special passes just to reach our office. The passes also allowed us into Clinton's press conference in the hotel cinema, not that we could do anything except watch. The front row was reserved for the travelling White House media corps. Behind them sat a specially selected group of Russian journalists. Only those two rows would be allowed to ask the president questions.

In the flesh, Clinton was an extraordinarily impressive and engaging figure. He charmed the room but paid special attention to the White House journalists, addressing them by their first names as he took their questions. I was surprised by how polite and sycophantic they were in return. Not one person bothered to press him about Chechnya. I sat at the back of the room holding up my arm in a pointless attempt to ask a question, like a schoolboy trying to get permission to go to the toilet.

Within weeks of the G7 meeting, Boris Yeltsin's campaign started picking up. Media coverage became much more positive, with journalists ignoring the issue of his ill health and presenting him as a strong, dependable leader. He seemed to have a new energy, doing daily meet-the-people walks and listening to their concerns. At the same time, Gennady Zyuganov's campaign seemed to run out of steam. He was barely visible on the evening news. Yeltsin's approval ratings rose steadily, putting him within reach of Zyuganov.

It wasn't until much later that the full details emerged of how it happened. Russia's richest men, the oligarchs who had made billions under Yeltsin's rule, were terrified of a Communist *revanche*, so they agreed to settle their differences and buy the ailing Yeltsin a victory.

Firstly, they used their own media holdings to promote his campaign while ignoring his opponents. Journalists were directed to praise Yeltsin while consigning Zyuganov's antics to short items at the end of news bulletins. It soon became embarrassingly one-sided. The airwaves were full of documentaries on gulags and food queues to remind everyone of what the Communists did the last time they controlled the Kremlin.

They also poured scores of millions of dollars into Yeltsin's campaign. While the plodding Zyuganov struggled to do more than address dull meetings of fellow Communists, Yeltsin's team was able to light up the country with election fever, through blitz advertising, mass rallies and rock concerts.

The International Monetary Fund (IMF) did its bit to help Yeltsin's campaign as well, announcing a new $10.2-billion loan to Russia in the middle of the campaign, despite the fact that the government was in clear violation of its existing loan conditions. This was, of course, sheer coincidence, the IMF being an independent lender immune from political pressure.

Yeltsin sailed through the first round of the election, making him the favourite to win the deciding second round two weeks later. But a week before the poll, he disappeared. Rumours began sweeping Moscow that he was seriously ill or even dead.

On voting day Yeltsin didn't even turn up to vote at the designated polling station, where Russian television crews and photographers had gathered. The Kremlin later released pictures of him looking deathly ill, casting his vote near a sanatorium where he had been treated the previous year for heart problems. That didn't stop the rest of the country re-electing him.

Five months earlier I would have found it alarming that Russia's first democratic election had turned into a farce, and that the winner was a candidate for life support. But I was starting to accept that Russia simply did things differently. Nobody even seemed particularly fazed that Yeltsin took the rest of the year off sick and underwent a quintuple bypass operation.

Yeltsin's absence left the government in chaos and the country rudderless. However, with the Communists once again safely marginalised, a sense of relative calm descended on Moscow, at least among the Novi Russki, who had feared an abrupt end to their newly accustomed excess. It also gave me a brief breathing space from work to try to get to know my new home. My attempts at settling into Moscow were not going well.

I had by now used up all the toilet paper, cough medicine and rice I had brought by the suitcase load from Australia, on the assumption that I would not be able to buy basics in Moscow. The reality was that Moscow's stores groaned with imported goods. They were just ridiculously expensive.

A jar of instant coffee cost $5; a can of soup could cost $10. (Curiously all the prices were listed in US dollars, although you had to pay in roubles at the shop's own exchange rate.) The ABC's first Moscow correspondent, John Lombard, had told me how he had felt like a millionaire in Russia. How times had changed. My local stores and supermarkets were all aimed at Novi Russki with money to burn, and at frightened expatriates without the wit to find cheaper places where ordinary Russians shopped. Still barely able to communicate in Russian and with little time outside work, I was stuck in the expat ghetto.

Apart from nervous foreigners, most of the apartments in my district belonged to the old elite — KGB colonels, army generals and senior bureaucrats. Privatisation had made them the owners of their state-assigned apartments, permanently entrenching the old Communist inequality. The new elite of bankers, politicians and *biznesmen* were also near neighbours. They lived a few kilometres down the road in newly built cloistered estates on the edge of the city, invisible behind high walls.

They would speed down the central lane of the nine-lane highway called Rublyovskoye Shosse, which fronted my building — cavalcades of luxury black cars with flashing blue lights signifying that they were exempt from road rules. The central lane of the highway was reserved for VIPs, so while the other lanes choked with traffic, the limousines and BMWs of the wealthy and influential could motor through at any time of day or night. The only flaw in this arrangement was that there was only one official lane for both directions. Every couple of months it was closed as police scraped up the remains of parliamentary deputies who collided mid-journey.

This was as close as I was getting to my rich and powerful neighbours. I had imagined being an Australian correspondent would open doors to the movers and shakers in the new Russia. Australia was, after all, an important player in international affairs, or so Australian politicians and media kept saying. But Australia was a long, long way away. Requests to interview anyone even remotely important were usually met with amusement, followed by a suggestion we fax a letter of request, which was invariably ignored.

To get around this, I started rehearsing my questions in Russian and ambushing important politicians. I would try to accost them coming out of meetings, getting into their cars outside the Duma (the lower house of parliament), or preparing to address rallies. I had mixed success in getting close enough to shout a question and usually had no idea what they were saying if they answered. Once, I got to within a metre of the Communist Party leader, Zyuganov, before two of his bodyguards lifted me in the air and dragged me off. Another time, I managed to get past them as Zyuganov was leading the May Day march, which he obligingly halted to talk to me. But after answering my two rehearsed questions, he started questioning me. I gestured mutely that we shouldn't chat as the 5000 marchers waiting behind him were getting impatient. On another occasion, I buttonholed the former Soviet president Mikhail Gorbachev and completely forgot my Russian. I managed to mumble, 'Yeltsin good, bad?', which was fortunately all he needed to launch into a three-minute answer.

Outside of work, I was in a miserable state. The few times I made the effort to go out to meet people I wound up in trouble — not from mafia, who never bothered targeting poor Westerners, but from the most dangerous men in Moscow, the traffic police.

Known as *Gaishniki*, after the acronym GAI (the Russian initials for State Automobile Inspectorate), they were the main hazard on Moscow roads. They stood on every major intersection waving rubber truncheons at passing motorists. There were so many rules that it was nearly impossible to drive anywhere without breaking at least one of them. U-turns were illegal, crossing lane markings was illegal (even if you couldn't see them under the snow), and speed limits could suddenly drop to 40 kilometres an hour for no reason and with no visible signs. That didn't mean people actually followed the rules; cars weaved about the roads like enemy missiles in a video game. In heavy traffic, drivers thought nothing of speeding along footpaths. But the rules gave Gaishniki an excuse to pull over anyone they thought was good for a shakedown.

As a Westerner, I was a prime target. I had a distinctive number plate (016K) from which a Gaishnik could tell that I was a journalist (the K was for *Korrespondent*) and from Australia (sixteenth on the country code). Sometimes I could barely get around the block without being pulled over. I started carrying $10 notes to cover the on-the-spot 'fines' (cash only, no receipt).

One of the oddest things about the road rules was a zero alcohol limit. It was odd given how many drivers (and police) were comprehensively drunk. Before I knew about the rule, I drove after one drink and stopped at a traffic checkpoint to ask a police officer for directions. He seemed surprised that anyone would actually approach him voluntarily. He inspected my documents and checked for defects. Unable to find anything wrong, he told me to blow into a tube. It turned blue. That meant I was over the limit. He smiled and called over two other police. They looked at me and laughed. Then they took me into a roadside booth.

After waving their fingers at me and laughing again, they started miming giving me an injection in the arm. I knew what they meant and I started to panic. One of the first horror stories expatriates would tell new arrivals was about police testing blood alcohol levels with used syringes. In a country with a raging AIDS epidemic, it evoked every foreigner's worst fears. I offered to give them money but they refused it. I pleaded again in my now 100 words of Russian. Eventually the fattest of the policemen asked me how much I had. I emptied my wallet of almost $200. They took the lot. Then they took out a map to give me the directions I'd first asked for. They laughed and waved as I drove off.

Police weren't the only problem on the roads. There was also the breathtakingly stupid Moscow road system, designed by central planners when there had been few cars. To minimise traffic lights they decided to limit the ability to turn into oncoming traffic. Most streets were one-way, left turns were illegal, and complicated loop roads were built in place of U-turns. Getting anywhere was like navigating a maze. Making things worse, most of the major arteries leading out of Moscow looked the same — multi-lane boulevards with signs in Russian, flanked by identical rows of apartment buildings. If you missed your turn it could take half an hour to weave your way back.

I have a bad sense of direction at the best of times and wound up driving in circles every time I went out. One night I was coming home from a movie and accidentally got on the wrong highway. I thought I was heading out to Rublyovskoye Shosse but, after driving what should have been the right amount of time, I was nowhere near it. In increasing despair, I drove for three hours looking for a landmark I recognised, watching the petrol gauge edge towards empty. I was shouting expletives and slamming the steering wheel in frustrated rage when the car shuddered to a halt somewhere on the edge of Moscow. I had no mobile phone. I checked my wallet and found I'd spent my last cash on a chocolate ice-cream at the cinema. It was two in the morning.

I looked up and saw a shining light in the distance. It said, 'CASINO'. Two bouncers stood outside, their thick necks bulging out of their Armani suits. Utterly despondent, I walked up to them and said in halting Russian, 'Hello, please you help. I lost. No petrol.'

Then something strange happened. Instead of hitting me, they asked me in, called a manager who spoke some English, then went off with me to fill the car with petrol. They drew me a simple map showing me how to get home. They never even asked for money.

This was the one act of kindness I would ever experience via a Russian casino. I felt like going back to thank them and losing lots of money to pay them back. But I couldn't find it again.

Russia, meanwhile, was even more lost than I was. Yeltsin's absence had immobilised the government. Rival factions in the Kremlin gave out contradictory orders and fought among themselves. Chaos ruled until the rare occasion when Yeltsin would step in to arbitrate. He would appear without warning after weeks unsighted, sack officials from one faction or another, growl something about 'reform' and disappear back to parts unknown. It made the warring factions dependent on his support, maintaining his authority despite his constant illness. But it was disastrous for Russia.

Occasionally, major problems were resolved despite the chaos. In August, the Chechen guerillas retook Grozny. Kremlin hawks gave orders to annihilate the city. But at the last moment Yeltsin re-appeared and agreed to a peace deal involving a complete Russian withdrawal. Against all odds, the war was finally over.

Then Yeltsin went back on 'holidays'. I kept updating his obituary, unsure if he was dying or perhaps already dead.

At the same time, people were starting to wonder about my own health. After the intensity of my first months in Russia, I hardly recognised myself. I had lost 10 kilograms, working constantly and skipping meals. I had to punch new holes in my belts to stop my pants slipping down. I had also become an insomniac, rarely sleeping more than four hours a night and finding I could manage on two or three. My parents in Sydney were worried I was ill, having seen me get thinner and thinner on nightly television reports. I told them I just didn't like Russian food.

Chapter 5
Baikonur and Belarus, August and November 1996

Back to the Future

Nothing was sacred in Russia's new capitalist culture. Even the greatest Soviet icon of all, the space program, was hired out to help sell soft drinks.

A few months after I arrived in Moscow, a public relations company invited me to witness a special event in the Radisson Slavyanskaya cinema. It was a live satellite cross to Mir, the space station that had been orbiting the earth for a decade. Three cosmonauts appeared on the giant movie screen, floating weightlessly around the capsule. The commander held up a can of Pepsi Blue and said, 'Pepsi, the drink of a new generation.'

It seemed a sad moment in humanity's quest to conquer space. For decades, many Russians had seen the space program as the Soviet Union's highest and noblest endeavour. It showed their system could compete with and even outdo the West. The Soviet military had always treated the program as a national security priority, making it off-limits to Western journalists. Intrigued by the Pepsi ad, I asked Slava to find out if there was any part of the space program we could film. The Russian Space Agency rang back offering us a package tour. For $1600 each, we could fly to the legendary Baikonur Cosmodrome in Central Asia, enjoy fine wine and dining in a nearby hotel, and film every stage of a rocket launch. Interviews with cosmonauts would be subject to further cash negotiation.

This was a boyhood fantasy come true. Baikonur had been the Soviet Union's Cape Kennedy, but with mystery and intrigue thrown in.

It had even launched the first man into space. In 1961 Yuri Gagarin blasted off in what another cosmonaut, David Polfeldt, later described as 'a tin can strapped to a bomb'.

Gagarin's successful orbit and landing became the Soviet Union's biggest source of pride since defeating Hitler. Every city, town and village had a Gagarin Street. Many had Gagarin Squares with Gagarin statues. Primary school children knew the date of his feat by heart. Rumours about Gagarin's premature death seven years later, that he'd been flying a MiG fighter while drunk and had hit the eject button before releasing the cockpit canopy, had done nothing to diminish his status as a national hero.

Tim, Slava and I flew on a chartered jet from a military airbase outside Moscow directly to the town of Baikonur, next to the cosmodrome. There was not even a Customs check. The odd thing about the Russian space program was that its main cosmodrome was not in Russia. It was in Kazakhstan, a former republic of the USSR that had suddenly become independent when the Societ Union collapsed around it. The Russian Federation was leasing back the space base from the Kazakhs for a rumoured $115 million a year.

The plane was full of Russian space officials and chain-smoking French journalists. They were coming to watch France's first female astronaut, Claudie Andre-Deshays, fly up to Mir. The French Government was contributing $20 million to the rocket launch for the honour of putting a woman in space. There was no other way Soyuz flight TM24 could get off the ground.

The plane landed on the barren Kazakh steppe in the early afternoon. Only the occasional camel herd had wandered through this area before the space race. It was a vast sandy plain, but the Soviets, being Soviets, had built a city of five-storey concrete apartment blocks.

Baikonur had obviously seen better days. Most of the scientists and engineers had returned to Russia, their abandoned apartments now trashed by drunken, unemployed Kazakh youths. Only the most dedicated space workers had stayed, hoping that one day they could relive the glorious past.

Some of the French journalists objected to our being part of their official group, so we were given our own van and guide to explore the cosmodrome. Formerly top-secret spacecraft lay rusting on the sand. We found a prototype of the Soviet space shuttle, the Buran, meaning Blizzard. We climbed up on its wings for happy snaps, being careful not to knock off any heat tiles. Some were already lifting off the surface.

Our guide explained that the whole program had been a dud. The Buran flew only once before budget cuts grounded it. Another prototype had been shipped off to Moscow to be an amusement ride in Gorky Park.

We got up before dawn to watch the ground crew transport the giant rocket by train to the launching pad. It glided along the sandy track, brilliantly reflecting the early morning desert sunlight. The assembly crew took just three hours to position it for takeoff — a process that would take three days in the West.

With the launch imminent, the two cosmonauts and their French *sputnik* (travelling companion) were in isolation. They gave a press conference from behind glass to prevent infection from diseased journalists. About 50 people crammed into a small room in front of the glass, fighting for a glimpse of the cosmonauts. The French media crews shoved us then each other. Russian crews, who appeared from nowhere, shoved the French, and a giant IMAX camera carried by three people shoved everyone aside for the prime position. It didn't make much difference because another Russian had brought a wind-up film camera which made such an intrusive whirring noise it drowned out most of the answers.

We'd asked earlier if we could do our own interview with the cosmonauts, mentioning that we 'might be able to assist the space program'. A shifty-looking official told us to come back in half an hour and to bring $200 for each cosmonaut we would interview. I doubted much of that would get past the go-betweens. After the room cleared, we came back and waited for the rocket crew to return.

The cosmonauts, Commander Valeriy Korzun and Port Engineer Aleksandr Kaleri, filed in, still behind the glass. I greeted them in my fractured Russian. They were happy to talk openly about the Russian space program's plight. 'I am sure that Russia is and will be a great space power despite certain difficulties in financing the space program,' Commander Korzun said. 'I think that such a great country as Russia must be present in space and it will be.'

His chance to prove it came the next day. We filmed the trio leaving the base in their tight-fitting spacesuits, marching like awkward penguins to the bus that would take them to the launch site. They smiled and chatted, looking relaxed despite being about to strap themselves into the world's largest firecracker. The Frenchwoman, Claudie Andre-Deshays, was immaculately made-up and coiffured. When their bus departed, we were taken to the observation post, a few kilometres from the launch site.

The base commander, General Alexei Shamulin, was visibly nervous, even though he had taken part in every rocket launch since Yuri Gagarin's flight. 'Some people think that you get used to it, but you can't get used to it,' he told us. 'Every launch is different, there may be different complications.'

One of the Russian officials explained to us why they were particularly nervous. The last two launches of this rocket model had gone disastrously wrong, blowing up within minutes of takeoff due to a faulty sealant in the nose. Fortunately they had only been carrying cargo. This one was carrying two Russians and a $20-million woman.

As the countdown approached, I had an extraordinarily bright idea. I would do a piece to camera with the rocket in the background seconds before it took off. As ignition began, I would walk out of frame to allow Tim to film what could be his finest shot.

'You've got to be joking,' Tim said.

'No, I can do it.'

'You'll stuff it up and you'll ruin my shot.'

'Trust me, it'll work.'

I stood in front of the camera while Tim fumed, listening to the countdown. As I began my perfectly timed piece to camera, the rocket appeared to ignite ten seconds early. The blast ruined what I was saying. I stood stunned and half deafened as I completely blocked Tim's shot. The rocket had orbited the earth three times before he spoke to me again.

His words were: 'You're a dickhead.'

We flew back to Moscow that night. Tim sat twenty rows away from me. Two nights later, the media pack converged on the Mission Control Centre at Korolyov, an hour's drive from Moscow, to watch the Soyuz dock with the Mir space station.

Like much of Russia's space program, Mission Control was surprisingly low-tech. Brilliant but poorly paid scientists sat at black-and-white computer screens, watching a weak satellite signal projected onto a giant screen above them. But it all worked perfectly. On cue, the vessels docked and the cosmonauts floated grinning into Mir.

As easy as it was to laugh at Russian-made cars, clothes and toilet paper, you couldn't help but share the pride that Russians felt in their space program — excelling against the odds and prevailing against difficulties that would have grounded any other country's spacecraft. Or so it seemed. The next time I was at Korolyov I watched them struggle to stop Mir crashing back to Earth.

Alexander Grigorievich Lukashenko was having a bad hair year. He was just 43 but it had receded alarmingly, exposing a shiny and unappealing pate. He'd grown his hair long on one side and wore it combed over the top. He also had a weak upper lip that he'd tried to improve on by growing a large Stalin-style moustache, but it just made him look sillier. Some people thought he was a fool, many thought he was mad. He had once even compared himself to Hitler and fantasised about being a new tsar.

It would have all been quite pathetic for a man whose greatest achievement by middle age had been managing a run-down collective farm. But Lukashenko was having the last laugh. Quite unexpectedly, he'd become the president of Belarus. And he now had a police force that he could use to beat the crap out of anyone who mocked him.

I hadn't heard much about Belarus before I came to Moscow. I knew it was one of the Soviet republics that supposedly became democratic after it won independence in 1991, and I had a vague idea of where it was: sandwiched between Russia and Poland. But it was one of those sleepy places that never really made the news. Until now.

For the past few months there had been extraordinary stories coming out of the capital, Minsk, about the battles between its strange president, Alexander Lukashenko, and his battered and dwindling opposition. Lukashenko had called a referendum that would give him dictatorial powers, allowing him to crush the new democracy. He was also trying to reunite Belarus with Russia, which would end the country's newfound independence. The stunned opposition parties had been taking to the streets to protest, and the police had been duly beating the hell out of them. I decided to head down with Tim and Robert to catch the next bout.

Enough weeks had passed since the rocket incident for Tim and me to have seats next to each other on the flight.

From the moment we arrived, it was as if we'd flown to a different era rather than just a different country. The airport didn't have a single trapping of capitalism. There were no shops, advertisements or vending machines. More disturbingly, there were no people, not even a Customs or Immigration check. We walked straight out into a huge, deserted terminal. There must have been other life forms somewhere, because eventually our luggage came out on the carousel. Robert found a lone taxi outside to take us on the 50-kilometre drive down a forest highway to the city. In 25 minutes we saw just two cars.

Lukashenko had only been in power two years, after a surprise victory as a minor anti-corruption candidate. But he had already made significant strides in taking the country backwards. True to his pledge to restore 'stability', he scrapped the post-Soviet economic reforms and reinstituted a command economy. As a result, Belarus was like a living museum of the Soviet Union.

The shops still stocked Soviet-era produce. Tins of shredded beetroot, plastic bags of milk, and toilet paper that could strike sparks sat sadly on shop shelves behind glass counters. As in Soviet times, you couldn't actually put them into a basket yourself, but had to pay for them at a separate counter and get a receipt before the grumbling salesperson would hand them over.

Unlike Moscow's, the streets were clean and uncongested, probably because few people could afford cars. Those who could bought Soviet cars; the kind built for short people, which lasted 100 kilometres before parts started falling off. There were no glitzy billboards, as there was little private industry and therefore little consumer choice. Dissidents were persecuted. People wore daggy Soviet clothes. Industry was heavy. The main export was tractors. And almost everybody was equally, dependably and grindingly poor.

For the first time since arriving in the former USSR, I felt like a millionaire. The value of the Belarus rouble, once officially higher than the US dollar, was now officially 12,900 to the dollar and plummeting fast. This made everything astonishingly cheap, provided you had hard currency. I could have bought a truckload of the scratchy grey toilet paper with my daily travel allowance and still had change for a set of tractor tyres.

We filmed a predictable interview with one of Lukashenko's senior advisers, who assured us that Belarus had the highest economic growth rate in Europe and recommended that we film the tractor factory. Tim and Robert wanted to have a quick lunch before the next appointment. However, I'd been warned that food in Belarus could give you a special kind of warm inner glow. Belarus had taken the brunt of the radioactive fallout from the explosion at the Chernobyl nuclear reactor in 1986, most of it landing in the main agricultural region in the south. All dairy products were suspect, as were the vegetable staples of cabbage, potatoes, beetroot, cucumbers and tomatoes. Beef was also questionable and calves were sometimes born with deformities. Even the bread, made from locally grown wheat, was feared to be contaminated.

The authorities insisted they had taken steps to ensure that the food reaching the market was safe. You just had to put your trust in the government's honesty and expertise. As Lukashenko discouraged food imports in order to protect state producers (police often searched trains returning from Moscow for illicit sausage), there was no choice. We were hungry, we hadn't brought our own food, things were cheap and we'd just flown Aeroflot (which only served inedible food we hadn't eaten), so we went to a restaurant and ate.

A few months earlier, I'd been to the Leningrad nuclear plant in the town of Sosnovy Bor, outside St Petersburg. Like Chernobyl, it had outdated and inherently unstable carbon-graphite reactors. The plant director had given us his expert advice on how to minimise the risk of radiation poisoning, as he handed us flimsy cotton masks. 'Drink lots of red wine,' he said with conviction. 'It's good for everything, except AIDS.' The Minsk restaurant we were in now didn't serve red wine with its cabbage soup and beef stroganoff, but we downed some cheap Belarus cognac, just in case.

The Chernobyl disaster had fuelled intense resentment against Soviet domination, but the horror was compounded by the discovery two years later of a mass grave outside Minsk containing the remains of some 250,000 victims of Stalin's purges. Belarus had known tragedy on an epic scale.

That evening, Tim and Robert decided to have an early night but I was feeling restless. I was also curious to see if nightlife in Minsk was as 'Back in the USSR' as the rest of the city, imagining students with permed hair listening to bootleg tapes of Wham and Boney M.

The hotel receptionist recommended I go to the Palace of Youth in the city centre. These so-called palaces had been the home base of Young Pioneers, the Communist version of scouts, in which children and teenagers organised trips to the countryside to dig for potatoes, and painted banners for upcoming celebrations of Revolution Days, International Labour Days and End of Great Patriotic War Days.

A hotel taxi took me to the Palace. Judging me a gullible foreigner, he demanded an outrageously inflated fare ... about 13 cents. I walked inside and heard the muffled thump of music from behind a door at the top of the stairs. It didn't sound like a Young Pioneer rally. I opened the door. And gulped.

About a month earlier, I'd been at a party in Moscow where I met Artyom Troitsky, the founding editor of *Russian Playboy*. He'd been holding forth on how the women of Minsk were the most beautiful in the former USSR. He was right. On top of that, the décor, music and clothes could have been transplanted from anywhere in New York or London. The only difference was that it was unbelievably cheap. Everybody even spoke English. Best of all, they wanted to practise it on the only Westerner there ... me.

I soon struck up a conversation with two students whom I thought introduced themselves as 'I'm nasty' and 'I'm nastier'. I eventually worked out that they were both called Nastya, which is short for Anastasia. Both Nastya, who was blonde, and Nastya, who was brunette, were studying accounting. They looked quite unlike any accountants I had ever seen. The few times I'd gone out in Moscow, I'd been taken to sleazy, overpriced clubs where I stood shyly at the bar. The only women who approached me couldn't speak English and turned out to be hookers. Now, after months of feeling sorry for myself for being alone, I suddenly found I could talk to women again without feeling like a large dollar sign.

I also struck a peculiar phenomenon, which was to recur throughout my four-year stay in the Slavic East. Both Nastya and Nastya thought I looked just like Quentin Tarantino. I had no idea why, given that I looked nothing like Quentin Tarantino, as I was able to verify personally when, years later at a club in Beijing, Quentin Tarantino himself walked in from the set of his splatter movie *Kill Bill*. Within minutes of Nastya and Nastya telling me how much I looked like the cult director, a woman came up and asked me if I was Quentin Tarantino. Many drinks later, I still hadn't spent ten dollars. Perhaps they were giving me a discount for being a Hollywood celebrity.

At two in the morning, remembering I had to be at a collective dairy farm in four hours, I took the Nastyas home by taxi. One of them suggested we meet again that night. For the first time in many months, I realised there was life after divorce. I drove back to the hotel thinking: My God, I am really happy.

Three hours later, I was standing outside a collective farm with a giant hangover, sinking down to my knees in cow shit. We had come for the early shift to meet Lukashenko supporters before filming the opposition march. Feeling unwell, I took a short cut to the entrance, wanting to get in and out as soon as possible. I had taken three steps before the mud and dung swallowed up my gumboots. 'You should walk down the path,' a worker shouted helpfully.

I managed to extract myself and shake out the moist dirt. Working on a bovine collective farm was not at the glamorous end of career choices, but it was all the mainly older workers had ever known. When the reforms began in the early '90s they watched many get rich while prices soared, and feared their cradle-to-grave jobs were under threat. Lukashenko had brought back the dull, dependable poverty in which they had grown up. Their wages were now worth less than in Soviet times, but at least they could be guaranteed to receive them, unlike in Russia. It was as though they were happy to stay on a sinking ship rather than try to swim somewhere better. In reality, they had little choice. While a new economy might mean opportunities for young people — like Nastya and Nastya, who despised Lukashenko and resented his efforts to drag the country back to the past — the only thing it could bring a 50-year-old collective farm worker who had shovelled cow dung all his life was unemployment.

A group of workers came out for a cigarette break, somehow keeping them alight in the sleet. I asked them what they thought of Lukashenko. 'He wants to help farmers, people who work in the country,' one woman said, her gold-capped teeth glinting in the camera light. 'The parliament just puts obstacles in his way.'

Back in town, we found protesters gathering in their thousands in the square opposite the parliament. But I couldn't see Lukashenko needing much more than truncheons to crush this opposition. They looked too mild-mannered. They were intellectuals, schoolteachers, artists, dissident journalists, small entrepreneurs and students. I asked a young woman what she thought would happen with Lukashenko's referendum. 'I think he will win, and Europe will have a new Stalin,' she said.

The march headed off peacefully, protesters waving the banned Belarusian flags and chanting '*Zhi-ve Belarus*' (Long Live Belarus). We were the only foreign crew who'd come to cover the protest but there were several dozen local cameramen filming the crowd. 'They are all KGB,' a marcher told me.

We had gone about 700 metres towards the presidential palace when the road was blocked by a phalanx of riot police holding shields and truncheons. The protest leaders went to talk to the police and came back looking disheartened. They would not be allowed through. Rather than confront the police, the protesters changed course and tried to march down a parallel street. This was also blocked by riot police. The organisers urged people to move quickly to the next street and within seconds everyone was running.

This was no longer a protest. It felt like a trap. As we rounded the corner, a line of riot police came running up beside us, pounding their shields in unison to intimidate the marchers. People screamed in terror but kept running. Then another line of riot police appeared in front of us, blocking the road. There was no escape. Everyone stopped and looked around at the baton-wielding police surrounding them. We waited for them to attack. Some women and children began crying. But after a few frightening minutes, it became clear the police had orders to wait.

For half an hour the demonstrators stood around uncertainly, walled in by riot police. Robert had fallen behind when we ran, and found himself on the other side of the police line, just a couple of metres from the commander. He heard him say, 'If I had my way, I'd shoot them all.'

Eventually the police opened a gap, allowing the now despondent protesters to go home defeated. Oddly enough, the demonstration didn't rate a mention on the government-controlled television news. But Lukashenko spoke of the importance of the upcoming referendum.

'It is not a choice between president and parliament. It is a choice between chaos and anarchy on one side, and discipline, order and a change for the better on the other,' he told viewers gravely.

That evening, the dark Nastya met me on the steps of the Palace of Youth and said she was going to take me to a restaurant she knew I would enjoy. It was a drab room with the usual stodgy and possibly radioactive dishes, and a couple of noisy families with small children. But I sat transfixed by Nastya. She talked about her dream of getting a job in a small business here and succeeding despite all the problems. She drank little, telling me her father had been an alcoholic who beat her mother. She was proud that her mother had found the strength to leave him and make her own life.

Suddenly, for no apparent reason, a woman came out to the dance floor and began taking her clothes off. Grinding music started thumping from a tinny sound system. The children at the next table giggled. During the next half hour, four different women came out and gyrated naked in front of me.

I wasn't sure what the polite thing to do was. I smiled awkwardly and looked away from the women to show Nastya I wasn't interested in such sexism. She looked disappointed. Perhaps striptease was a fashionable new phenomenon and it was unsophisticated to be embarrassed. I tried to compromise by looking appreciative and commenting on the dancing.

I had to return to Moscow the next day, but the ABC agreed I could come back to cover the referendum result. I found myself wanting to stay in this retro-Soviet world. It was a small, bizarre place with distinct heroes and villains. Moscow, on the other hand, was a huge, bizarre place where everyone seemed a villain.

As we drove to the airport, we passed a sporting goods and self-defence store. It was advertising a special on Mace, a portable spray for immobilising attackers. Most countries had outlawed it for anyone except SWAT teams. Tim thought it would be a nice gift for his wife, Lise, who was nervous about being on her own in Moscow. Robert decided it was too cheap to pass up. I decided to get some too. How often do you get a chance to buy discount Mace?

We arrived at the airport and found there were Customs checks on the way out. Fat, mean-looking guards were pawing through everyone's hand luggage. Tim and I hurriedly dropped our Mace in a rubbish bin but Robert thought he'd be able to walk straight onto the plane. He was wrong. X-raying his luggage, the Customs police spotted his Mace instantly. They arrested him for attempting to smuggle weapons onto a plane and led him away.

Tim and I suddenly realised how serious this was. We were in a police state where the accused had no rights, sentences were draconian and Robert had arguably just committed a major crime. They could imprison him for years. We knew we couldn't leave without him but we had no idea how to help him.

Five minutes before takeoff Robert returned looking unconcerned. 'Let's go,' he said. We looked at him quizzically. 'I had to pay a fine. Fifty roubles.' It was less than one cent. This might have been a police state but it was damn cheap!

A week later we were back in Minsk to see Lukashenko win the referendum with a suspiciously high 70 per cent of the vote. European Union observers condemned the referendum as a farce. The opposition deputies vowed to occupy the parliament forever rather than let Lukashenko dismiss them. Police surrounded the building. The country braced for a violent showdown. But after a few days without food and water, the deputies gave up and went home. Lukashenko shut down the Constitutional Court 'for redecoration', later reopening both the court and the parliament with his own appointees. The country's brief flirtation with democracy was over.

On my last night in Minsk, Nastya took me to a nightclub called Reaktor. It had a neon model of Chernobyl in the corner, spouting neon radiation. It was the kind of black irony you could find only in the former Soviet Union, where people confronted the misery of their situation but decided to enjoy life anyway. They'd need this quality for many more years under the new, expanded rule of Comrade Lukashenko.

Chapter 6
Belgrade, December 1996

Talking about a Revolution

Just days after Lukashenko began his dictatorship, Europe's other dictator was suddenly facing a revolution. The Serbian president, Slobodan Milosevic, had ruled his blighted nation with near absolute power for more than six years. Now, completely unexpectedly, hundreds of thousands of his ungrateful subjects were marching through the streets of his capital, Belgrade, denouncing him and his corrupt regime. For a few weeks, Milosevic seemed to have no idea how to react. His police and soldiers stood by as the people staged protest after protest. Finally, with Christmas approaching, he decided it was time to spill some blood.

On 24 December, Milosevic bussed in thousands of blue-collar supporters from the countryside to take on the anti-government protesters. Within moments of the two groups colliding, they were fighting pitched street battles with clubs and sticks. Within minutes, one of the protesters was shot in the head. Within hours, the ABC's Foreign Desk rang to scramble Tim and me to Belgrade.

There is possibly a worse place to spend Christmas than on an Aeroflot flight but as I queued at Moscow airport at dawn the next day I couldn't think of one. Not that Aeroflot was even marking the occasion — the Russian Christmas falls on 7 January. The Aeroflot meal was the usual cabbage salad and questionable meat in impenetrable plastic packaging, served with a sneer. Tim and I sawed through the plastic with our Swiss army knives anyway, assuming we were flying into a country where the food could only get worse.

Milosevic's misrule had left Serbs with much to protest about. He had led them into two disastrous wars with their former compatriots in Croatia and Bosnia, promising to carve a Greater Serbia out of the breakup of Yugoslavia. Hundreds of thousands of deaths later, Serbia was a rump state, the economy was in ruins, the reputation of Serbs had been blackened around the world, and everyone lived in hopeless poverty except for Milosevic's family and corrupt cronies.

The actual spark for mass revolt was something minor in comparison. Milosevic rigged some relatively unimportant local council elections. In November, his government tried to invalidate opposition wins in several towns and cities. Angry voters poured out onto the streets in protest and had been marching every day since.

It was a bleak, grey day when we landed in Belgrade. The temperature was well below zero but the snow fell like rain and turned to slush as soon as it hit the ground. We drove to Republic Square in the town centre where the demonstrators usually assembled. I doubted that many would turn up after the beating they'd been given the previous day. The police had waded in to 'restore order', clubbing all the anti-Milosevic demonstrators while ignoring the pro-Milosevic gangs attacking them. But Republic Square was already filling with thousands of people as we arrived.

Despite the dark sky and sleetish snow, there was a buzz of excitement. Serbs of all ages were getting ready to march again. Mothers had brought their young children; old couples had brought their walking sticks. Musicians on the back of a truck were playing stirring Serb folk music, and young demonstrators carried in giant puppet and poster caricatures of Milosevic.

The crowd went silent as a charismatic opposition leader, Vuk Draskovic, climbed onto a podium in front of the huge statue of a horse and rider which dominated the square. Draskovic was a famous poet, with wild eyes, an unruly mane of greying hair and an unkempt beard. He was also an ambitious politician determined to milk the growing discontent.

'Mr Milosevic brought drunk and armed people here with the aim of provoking bloodshed,' he told the crowd. 'But we are not afraid!'

The crowd surged down the main street, as office workers stood at their windows or stepped out onto the pavement to cheer them on. A wave of applause followed their progress around the city centre. It was obvious that the protests had overwhelming public support. As the demonstrators passed the state television station — a mouthpiece for Milosevic's regime — the crowd hurled eggs and flour bombs at the windows. This time there were no police to be seen.

Draskovic walked at the front of the crowd alongside two other opposition leaders: a smooth and handsome philosophy lecturer, Zoran Djindjic, and a diminutive middle-aged civil rights activist, Vesna Pesic.

According to everything I had read about the protests, Djindjic and Draskovic were longstanding rivals. Both headed separate political parties and both dreamed of replacing Milosevic as Serbia's leader. For now, though, they had formed an alliance of convenience to lead the protests. I watched Draskovic hand Djindjic a piece of chewing gum as they chatted amiably in the snow. They almost looked like friends.

Draskovic spoke English, so I negotiated my way past his bodyguards to interview him as he marched along. 'Look, today, there are not Milosevic supporters, no police, everything is again fantastic, beautiful, like before,' he told me. 'But nobody knows as far as Milosevic is concerned what he is ready to do.'

After walking a few uneventful kilometres with the opposition, Tim and I wandered down the cobblestone streets of the old town to the university's philosophy faculty, an architectural monstrosity that had become the centre of student protests. Every afternoon, students were holding their own marches, separate from the politicians, to condemn Milosevic and demand reform of their university.

The faculty had been transformed into a college of advanced protest. Young intellectuals with goatee beards sat in one room discussing tactics, while their girlfriends looked on adoringly. In another room, students were painting placards with slogans like 'Hasta la vista,

Communista' and drawing grotesque caricatures of Milosevic. Medical students were giving other students first-aid advice on what to do if they were beaten. Sympathetic lecturers wandered around offering support. Upstairs the best English speakers were running a foreign press office. They were all chain-smoking as if they'd never heard of lung cancer.

The first person we met at the press office was Miroslav Maric, an intense, stocky archaeology student with long hair, an earring and an attempted beard. 'A lot of society has united around these protests, a lot of people, a lot of students united,' he said in self-taught English with a slight American accent. 'We become a very connected generation now, we are in contact with a lot of students from the other faculties, so we become connected or united. I think that's the best thing about the protests.'

The atmosphere was more like a party than a desperate fight for democracy. The students had grown up in a dark world of civil war, hyperinflation, political extremism and national disintegration. Suddenly there was a clear-cut issue of ballot-rigging that everyone could agree on and do something about. There was a feeling of both unity and catharsis.

The one thing that distinguished the students from the opposition parties was their complete distrust of politicians. They weren't campaigning for Draskovic or Djindjic, but simply for the right to make politicians accountable.

'That's why we don't march with them,' Miroslav said. 'Who knows, in a year's time we may want to get rid of them too.'

Milosevic was clearly in trouble but he had two weapons that still gave him the edge over the protesters. The first was state television, which praised everything he did and vilified the opposition. (Surprisingly, it was also open to cash offers. In return for an exorbitant fee, we were able to satellite our unflattering stories from the control room of TV Belgrade.)

The other weapon was the police. They received relatively generous salaries and conditions, and had become a dependable attack dog for

Milosevic. Even so, Miroslav said many were being bussed in from outside Belgrade in case the local cops became squeamish about beating up friends and relatives.

The next day a thick, grey line of riot police appeared from nowhere, stopping the march before it had gone 100 metres. A senior officer declared by megaphone that new traffic regulations required the streets to be kept clear of pedestrian traffic. The crowd retreated to Republic Square to plan the next day's move.

We had just left for the hotel when police started picking off stragglers. A German crew we had been filming with for most of the day were attacked by plainclothes thugs with iron pipes. Riot police formed a circle around them to stop anyone seeing what was happening. But they were as stupid as they were vicious. The attack took place directly below the balcony of the news agency WTN. Half a dozen camera crews shot the whole attack from above. The cameraman on the square suffered several broken bones and pictures of the assault were shown all over the world.

TV Belgrade, meanwhile, was giving a very different picture, known derisively as 'Milosevic and the weather'. As always, the daily news began with at least three stories about the president. He never ventured outside to meet his people but every meeting he had with officials was headline news. After several minutes of Milosevic shaking hands and signing documents, the news would move on to good news stories about the improving economy or distressing tales of victimisation of Serbs. Then a short and usually derogatory piece on the protests, pointing to the traffic chaos the marches had caused or 'new evidence' that they were funded by the CIA. Then came the most reliable and objective part of the program: the weather report.

That news was consistently bad. Heavy snow was predicted for several more days and the evening temperature was expected to drop below minus ten. But the protests went on. Unable to march on the streets, the masses moved to an old pedestrian mall behind Republic Square called Knez Mihailovo. Even Miroslav's mother, Golubica, a delightful cake-baking housewife, joined the student protests every day. She said she wasn't interested in politics but, like all her neighbours, had decided it was time to get rid of Milosevic. 'Even after the war has ended we still live in poverty,' she said. 'You'd expect things to improve but they're getting worse.'

While Milosevic seemed to have lost the capital, he still had a groundswell of support in the countryside. On 31 December, Miroslav took us to meet his relatives in the village of Nemenikuce, about two hours' drive from Belgrade.

The Jekic family lived in a small house on a small plot of land they had owned for generations. They were also poor, but it was a different kind of poverty from that in Belgrade. The family lived simply and was almost self-sufficient. They grew much of their food and made their own plum brandy. A pathetic wage from a nearby state factory, followed by a miserable state pension, was enough to cover the other basics. Miroslav's relatives had never lived any better and never expected to. They saw Milosevic as providing stability and defending the rights of Serbs.

'I don't approve of everything Milosevic does,' Miroslav's second cousin Jovan said. 'He didn't keep his promise that all Serbs could live in one country. But right now I don't see anybody else who could do that job. What good is democracy for us if we can't sell our crop?'

Jovan was in his sixties and in poor health. He clearly disapproved of Miroslav's involvement in the protests. State media had done their job in portraying the protesters as troublemakers.

'I can see nothing good in them,' he complained. 'They're protesting for four or five hours a day now for 40 days. A couple of days ago I couldn't even get to the hospital because the traffic was paralysed.'

Miroslav didn't bother to argue with them. He listened politely then switched topics to family matters: of who had what ailment and how each small child was. As we walked back to the car through the snow, he said, 'They don't know anything else. They've got used to thinking in only one way. My point is I want changes. I had the same government for eight years, now I want them to go because they are no good any more.'

Like most of the students, Miroslav saw a world greater than Serbia and feared it could be beyond his reach. He read widely, he trawled the internet, he was studying for a career and he wanted desperately to travel. He knew that if nothing changed he could be trapped in a failed nation. Perhaps it would have been easier to be as unworldly as his cousins.

We drove back towards Belgrade. After about an hour, we stopped at a scenic stretch of forest to get a shot of the car driving through for a news feature on visiting Miroslav's family. As it drove past on the second take, a police car screamed up beside us. Two policemen got out and started shouting at us in Serbian. Miroslav ran up and tried in vain to calm them. They bundled us into the back of their car and drove off. I protested but they gestured at me not to speak. We were under arrest and had no idea why.

At the police station they took our documents and made us sit on chairs facing away from each other. I turned round to face Tim and a police officer ordered me to look the other way. It seemed they were worried Tim and I could be signalling each other in code.

Finally a police officer who spoke English and appeared to have an IQ above room temperature arrived. I was taken into his office to be interrogated first.

'What were you filming?' he asked.

'I was filming our car.'

'Why were you filming your car?'

'I'm a journalist. I'm doing a news story about visiting people in the countryside.'

'So why were you filming at a military installation?'

'Huh?'

He explained that there was a fuel tank 300 metres behind where we were filming. It belonged to the military. It was illegal to film military installations.

'Ah-huh,' I said, and explained that we didn't know the tank was there, couldn't see it from where we were standing, had no interest in a fuel tank and hadn't filmed it anyway.

He nodded and sent me back to sit on my chair, facing away from Tim. I heard him make several phone calls. Then Tim and I were brought into his office together. He was holding our passports.

'Do you have any complaints about your treatment?' he asked.

'Absolutely none,' I said.

'So you have been treated well?'

'Very professionally.'

'Good. You may go.' He handed us our passports.

Miroslav met us outside. 'Lucky for you that guy knows my cousin,' he said.

We arrived back in Belgrade to find a flurry of preparations for New Year's Eve in progress. Rather than marching around Knez Mihailovo, the cobblestoned walkway in the old city, the protest groups had decided to hold a giant party. Opposition parties were decorating the adjacent Republic Square with lights and banners. Two hundred metres away, the students were setting up for a rock concert in the forecourt of the philosophy faculty.

Four hundred thousand people came along for the party. There was not a single riot policeman in sight. TV Belgrade broadcast live crosses to New Year's Eve festivities in New York, London and Moscow but didn't show any pictures of the huge rally just four streets away from its building. Milosevic appeared on television to give his traditional New Year's greeting and didn't mention the protests.

In Republic Square, Vuk Draskovic climbed onto the podium and offered a toast to a new year without the dictator. 'We are going to finish what we started in '96,' he said as the crowd cheered. 'Onward to a democratic Serbia!'

When the main rally died down at about one in the morning, a group of students invited me to a party across town. We wandered off down the streets, drinking cheap beer and laughing and singing stupid songs. Everybody spoke English for my benefit. Most of them were fluent in three languages. They were smart and educated and just wanted their country to be a normal part of Europe. Instead they lived with corruption and psychopathic leaders. But that night — that whole winter — there was a euphoric feeling of hope and possibility.

The party was in a run-down block, in a small two-room apartment which was heaving with students. One room was packed with people dancing to music that flipped from Iggy Pop to Serb folk. Even more were crowded into the kitchen, chain-smoking, drinking and talking. Marijuana joints kept circulating round the room, courtesy of a thriving black market nurtured by Western sanctions. Being Serbia, it wasn't long before talk shifted to politics. A circle of students wanted to know what the West thought of Serbs. I told them most people had only heard of the civil war and the terrible crimes that all sides had committed.

'Does the West think Serbs are guilty?' an attractive girl with a rasping smoker's voice asked.

'Well, you can't blame a whole community for crimes of individuals,' I said.

'But do you think Serbs are more guilty than Croats or Muslims?'

I felt uncomfortable having to answer for the West, so I asked them what they thought.

Everybody blamed the politicians. The Croat leader, Franjo Tudjman, and the Bosnian leader, Alija Izetbegovic, were as bad as Milosevic, they said. They had all stirred up hatred and were equally responsible. I asked what they thought of nationalists and they said nationalism was bad but patriotism was good. I asked what the difference was and they said patriots loved their country but nationalists thought others were inferior. They said they didn't care if someone was a Serb or a Croat or a Muslim. Things had been better when they were all Yugoslavs.

The images of heroic protest in those weeks led many in the West to assume the unrest was a reaction to Milosevic's crimes in Bosnia. But it was all about what Milosevic had done to the Serbs. He had made them fight two wars for nothing. He had ruined their economy for nothing. They were impoverished for nothing. Few had any idea of the extent of the crimes against others that had been carried out in their name.

I wanted the students to be as appalled by Serbia's war crimes as I was. But they hadn't seen the same images that the West had been seeing for years and they knew more about the crimes carried out against Serbs than the West could ever understand.

Vuk Draskovic, on the other hand, knew how to say exactly what the West wanted to hear. I interviewed him in his party headquarters on Knez Mihailovo, over the din of a student protest below.

'People are angry about what Milosevic has done in the war, what he has done in their name,' he said. 'That is the major reason for their energy. People are disgusted by the ethnic cleansing, the murder, the violence.'

Draskovic had once had a very different message for domestic consumption. When Yugoslavia began to break up in the early 1990s, he was a radical Serb nationalist and an advocate of Greater Serbia. He derided Bosnian Muslims as 'Turks', a reference to Serbia's long occupation by the Ottomans. And there were persistent rumours he had formed a paramilitary group called the Serbian Guard that had terrorised Croat civilians. I asked him if the rumours were true.

'The government launched that stupid lie about me according to my nationalist views,' he said.

'But you did form the Serbian Guard which was a paramilitary group to fight in Croatia,' I said.

'No, that's a lie.'

Miroslav had come with me to meet Draskovic and listened to him in silence. Later he told me it was Draskovic who was the liar. The Serbian Guard had been run by his political party. 'Maybe he didn't form it directly but he was one of the leaders of the Serbian Guard,' he said.

'How do you know for sure?'

'Because my stepbrother fought for it. He was in eastern Slavonia in 1991 and he fought there, and in one of the actions of that Serbian Guard he lost three fingers and an eye. So Mr Draskovic can say whatever he likes. I know the truth and you now know the truth.'

It wasn't Draskovic's past that upset Miroslav, but his denial of it. 'You know he can tomorrow turn his back on us in same way as he turned his back on Serbs who fought for him.'

Milosevic appeared to be fighting a losing battle to stop the protests. When he tried to ban marching in Knez Mihailovo, the opposition organised a car protest. Thousands of vehicles arrived in the city centre and pretended to break down. The drivers opened their bonnets and scratched their heads while the city centre came to a standstill. Police stood around, not knowing what to do.

The biggest rally was held on the night of 6 January, the Orthodox Christmas Eve. Half a million people marched to the main Orthodox church near the city centre. As the rally occurred in the guise of a religious festival, the authorities didn't dare to stop it. Patriarch Pavle, the octogenarian leader of Orthodox Serbs, who had been seen as a key supporter of Milosevic and his wars in Yugoslavia, shared a platform in front of the church with Draskovic and Djindjic. It seemed as though the entire city had come to watch them, and I was starting to wish they'd stayed at home. I was caught in the middle of a crush, as tens of thousands tried to push their way towards the front. I'd always had a problem with claustrophobia and this was worse than anything I'd experienced. I wasn't just suffocating. I felt as if my clothes were strangling me. I clawed my way through the crowd to the front door of an apartment building and started pressing buzzers as I felt the crowd squashing me against the door. Other people around me were also starting to panic. Finally, one of the residents buzzed the door open and I fell into the entrance lobby as half a dozen people fell on top of me. I crawled forward and ran up the stairs. Hundreds ran up behind me. At last we could breathe again. And, being Serbia, everyone lit a cigarette. Within seconds, the stairwell was filled with choking smoke.

Tim and I left Belgrade the next day, not because we wanted to but because our visas had expired. The authorities had had enough of foreign reporters and refused to extend our stay. But I wanted desperately to stay. It felt as if we were leaving a piece of history, an extraordinary turning point for the nation that could lead to popular triumph or terrible defeat.

It was Orthodox Christmas. For the second time in two weeks, I spent Christmas on an Aeroflot flight, with a lunch of cabbage salad and questionable meat in impenetrable plastic packaging, served with a sneer.

Chapter 7
Grozny, January 1997

Bandits Rule, OK

Sometimes war-torn lands have to choose between the ballot and the bullet. Lucky old Chechnya was going to have both. Four months after the Russian military began its ignominious withdrawal, internationally monitored free and fair elections were scheduled to take place amid Chechnya's heavily armed ruins. It was an ambitious undertaking given that nobody was even sure how many voters were still alive. Estimates of the number of people killed in the war ranged from 18,000 to 100,000, most of them civilians ... this from a population of just one million.

Technically, they were to be elections for a Russian republic. But everyone knew they would decide the leader of what was effectively an independent state. All of the candidates were men the Kremlin had denounced as bandits: the Chechen guerilla commanders.

Having spent more than two years trying to kill them, the Kremlin was putting on a brave face, official spokesmen expressing President Yeltsin's confidence that the elections would lead to a new beginning for this Russian republic. What Boris actually thought could only be guessed at, as he was rarely seen and never heard. On the few occasions when state television showed Yeltsin meeting officials, there was no longer any audio of what was being said.

It promised to be an interesting election campaign. Each of the commanders still had his own militia. Every campaign worker would be carrying an AK-47 assault rifle.

A new friend, Eve Conant, decided to come with us to get some experience in the field. She was a 26-year-old Russian-speaking

Californian of Ukrainian descent working as a researcher for NBC in Moscow. She had never been to a conflict zone before and was looking forward to getting out in the field. I was looking forward to seeing Grozny without Russians and Chechens shooting each other.

As we drove into the city from Ingushetia (the airport was still closed), it was extraordinary to see how much things had changed. Chechens controlled all the checkpoints and waved us through with barely a glance at our documents. Grozny was even more ruined than I remembered it. The last weeks of fighting had destroyed what was left of any public buildings. But the mood on the streets was celebratory.

We saw a wedding party in a ground-floor apartment. A man on the doorstep flashed a gold-toothed smile and gestured for us to come in. The guests were doing the exuberant Chechen traditional dance, in which a man struts like an eagle and a woman glides like a swan as the onlookers clap and stamp their feet. The dancers are forbidden to touch, making it both chaste and strangely erotic. Suddenly one of the men picked up a machine gun and fired wildly out the window. For an instant I thought we were under attack, but the wedding guests clapped and cheered even louder. The Chechens had simply revived a traditional custom — shooting during celebrations — which the Soviets had tried to ban; in part because they built twelve-storey apartment blocks around the city and residents in the top floors were being accidentally hit.

There was another change in Grozny that was more alarming. The interim Chechen administration insisted we have round-the-clock bodyguards. Ever since the Russians left, there had been increasing instances of kidnapping for ransom. The Chechen administration blamed bandits (by which it meant criminals rather than fellow rebels) and feared that Westerners could become targets.

Our previous hostess, Tamara, had left Grozny months earlier so we found a different apartment to rent in one of the less damaged buildings. It belonged to a well-known Chechen actor with the Grozny Theatre Company. In a mark of the strange optimism of the time, Ahmed had just finished renovating his apartment. While most of the neighbourhood had been flattened, he'd installed new parquetry floors and a shiny white toilet. There was no running water in the apartment, so we carried buckets up the stairs to fill the cistern for flushing. For Grozny, it was five-star luxury. Ahmed and his wife and daughter moved into his sister's apartment downstairs.

Each morning at nine, Ahmed went out in his best suit to spend the day in the theatre, planning the first production since the war had begun. His wife bustled around our apartment cleaning, while their thirteen-year-old daughter, Zaina, read her school books, preparing to go back to classes. The schools had been closed for months, first because of the bombing, now because the buildings were flattened and the teachers had fled. But the family was feeling confident. 'All we need is peace,' Ahmed said.

Relative normality was creeping back into Grozny, but there was also a feeling of increasing lawlessness. The city was awash with guns. It was like the Wild West except that people carried machine guns and rocket-propelled grenades (RPGs) rather than pistols. There was even a thriving open-air gun market in the centre of town. Nobody had managed to film it so Eve decided to try on her own. Short, pretty and unthreatening, she thought she'd arouse less suspicion than Tim and I would. A few minutes later, she came back looking flushed and frightened. 'I tried to take a picture of it and they grabbed me and held a gun to my leg,' she said. 'I don't think you should go there.'

The main problem for the local economy — apart from the fact that almost every town and village had been shot up and bombed — was that there was no work for the gunmen. Tens of thousands of heavily armed fighters, whose main job skill was killing Russians, milled around the streets with their weapons, looking for something to do.

A group of fighters came up to us to ask about opportunities in the West. The commander wanted to know if there was any work for fighters in Hawaii.

'I'm afraid not,' Eve said. 'There's no war in Hawaii.'

'Really?' he asked. 'We heard they were having lots of problems with America and needed fighters.'

'No, I'm sorry,' Eve said. 'It's very peaceful.'

The commander sighed. 'That's a pity. We saw some pictures of Hawaii and it looked beautiful.'

The would-be Polynesian freedom fighters served Aslan Maskhadov, one of the main contenders for the Chechen presidency. He had been a career officer in the Red Army, and was widely viewed in both Chechnya and Russia as a respectable moderate. The Kremlin made little secret of its preference for Maskhadov, if only compared with the alternatives. His main rival, Shamil Basayev, was Russia's most wanted man.

The 32-year-old Basayev was a former computer salesman, a brilliant guerilla fighter and a radical Islamist. He had led a daring hostage raid inside Russia during the war to force the Kremlin to halt the bombing, after Russian soldiers killed eleven members of his family in their village of Vedeno. On 14 June 1995, 150 of his militia drove into the southern city of Budyonovsk and took over a hospital with 1600 patients. During a three-day standoff he executed at least seven hostages before Russian tanks opened fire. The official toll was 129 dead, 415 wounded, mostly from Russian gunfire. He finally forced the Russians to allow him to leave in a bus with the remaining hostages and drive back into Chechnya. It made him an instant hero to the Chechens and Public Enemy Number One to Russia. Relations were going to get very frisky if he were elected president.

The next day we went to a village outside Grozny where Basayev was holding an election rally. Most of the village had turned out to see the legendary fighter. A dozen of his soldiers stood on the roof of the concrete hall where he was due to speak, scanning the crowd for potential assailants. Basayev arrived in a high-speed convoy, flanked by bodyguards. Instead of his trademark military fatigues, he was dressed in an overcoat and had trimmed his unruly beard. Shaking hands like a seasoned politician he moved into the hall, followed by six fearsome-looking bodyguards. Only two other journalists had come to cover the rally, so we had complete freedom to roam around the hall and even wander on stage to film Basayev. It was clear he was making a serious bid for the leadership, telling the crowd his first act as president would be to declare Chechnya forever independent of Russia. The crowd of Chechen men stood and cheered.

At that moment, another group of armed men swept into the hall. It was the personal militia of another contender, the acting president, Zelimkhan Yandarbiyev. He had been the overall military leader of the rebels during the war, so Basayev was technically still under his command. He could do little but scowl as Yandarbiyev entered and took over his election rally. Yandarbiyev congratulated him on his efforts in the war and started giving his own speech about what he would do as president. The two militias clearly didn't like each other and each was as heavily armed as the other. It seemed a recipe for a bloodbath and Tim and I were standing on the stage less than two metres from their leaders. But the audience was enjoying the show. Basayev eventually said his goodbyes to the crowd and skulked off with his men.

Yandarbiyev had already been putting his special touches on the interim administration. One of his first acts had been to introduce Sharia law, making it an offence to drink, smoke or gamble — three of the leading pastimes of Chechen men. At this stage, it was more show than substance. A Sharia court had lightly whipped a suspiciously compliant-looking offender on Grozny's new TV channel, but the popular vices were still widely available, even now, during the holy month of Ramadan. Every night our bodyguards ducked out to a sly-grog shop to bring back beer.

Many people were alarmed, though, by what the new government might bring, including our hosts' daughter, Zaina. 'Young people won't accept strict Islamic law,' she said. 'We just want to have a normal life. We don't want to have to cover up. Maybe in the countryside they do, but in the city we're not interested.' She was also scared that another Chechen tradition banned by the Soviets might return — bridenapping. If a young man saw a girl he wanted for a wife, he could turn up with his friends at her house, kidnap her and marry her with the automatic consent of her family. The girl could refuse, but would be stigmatised by the whole community.

The family was already nervous about the behaviour of our bodyguards. On the first night the men had slept in a car outside, taking turns to keep watch over the entrance. Then they began to come in to pray five times a day and demanded that the family feed them. Now they were insisting that they be allowed to sleep in the family's apartment. We were paying the guards a fortune by Chechen standards, so I told our interpreter, a huge, one-eyed Chechen named Ruslan, to sort them out — they weren't to come into the house and they weren't to bother our hosts. Ruslan was a former guerilla fighter himself and said it would be best not to say anything. 'You don't want to make these men angry,' he warned, smiling.

Like many of the rebels, Ruslan had been working in Moscow when Yeltsin ordered the invasion. He had never intended to be a soldier, but after watching Grozny's daily annihilation on the TV news, he decided to go back and fight. 'The first few nights I was here I was thinking what the hell have I done?' he said. 'I was in a basement being bombed, wondering how I would survive, wishing I was back in a warm place in Moscow. But eventually you start to love it, it becomes a drug. You have the most intense experiences of your life. You form closer friendships than you ever imagined possible. Nothing is the same after.'

Ruslan's days as a guerilla ended when he was shot in the eye. He began working for a foreign news agency, carrying videotape of the fighting out through the frontline so that the world could see what was happening. He was now making a living as a freelance television producer. He wanted peace, but war was better for business.

The Chechens were still nervous that Russia could re-invade. We went to a former Russian military base that Chechen fighters now occupied. They were training new recruits. One of them looked to be about twelve years old. The commander insisted he was sixteen but admitted that Chechens were learning to fight young. Holding up a machine gun and, loading it as he spoke, he said, 'A Chechen is a born soldier. Give him a gun, he'll take it and fire it two or three times and that's all he has to be taught.'

As if the air wasn't already thick enough with testosterone, they started playing pass-the-hand-grenade. One of the older fighters pulled out the pin and passed the grenade around the circle. Each had to hold it for a few seconds before passing it to the next soldier. The young boy took particular delight in holding the grenade up to my face and smiling. I decided we had enough pictures and thanked them for their time.

'Don't you want to see our prisoners?' the commander asked. He led us round to the back of the building and downstairs into a cellar. Two young Russian conscripts were sitting quietly on double bunks that took up almost the whole cellar. 'We are keeping them to exchange for Chechen prisoners,' he explained.

The Russians smiled sheepishly. They looked like nervous schoolboys trying to be brave. Alexei was nineteen, Dmitri twenty. Both were painfully thin. They had been held in the cellar for seven months. They told us they were fine but wanted to go home. Eve asked if their families knew where they were. They shrugged. She took down their details, promising to contact their mothers when we were back in Moscow.

The commander invited us to eat lunch and ordered his men to bring up the prisoners to join us. The young Russians greeted their captors meekly and sat at their own table looking glum.

None of the fighters received a wage but the community provided them with food. A Chechen *babushka* cooked for them three times a day. As we waited for the stew to be ready, the commander talked of his time in the Red Army. Like most of the Chechen officers, he was Soviet-trained. He had even fought against the mujahideen in Afghanistan. But he was derisive about the Russian military today. 'They did not fight like soldiers,' he said. 'They killed women and children.'

While he talked, two of the younger fighters started playing with a pistol. One of them kept pointing it at Tim and pretending to fire. The commander noticed and roared him out like a mess sergeant. The young fighter, suddenly on the verge of tears, put down the gun and started eating his slop.

On 30 January, Maskhadov was elected president. The Russian Government breathed a sigh of relief. Yeltsin offered his congratulations. Shamil Basayev and the other commanders vowed to work with Maskhadov to rebuild. But it wasn't to be. An even worse nightmare was to come for the Chechens and an even more brutal war. For this brief time, though, perhaps for the only time, it seemed as though Chechnya had a chance to be normal and free.

I flew back to Sydney for my first real break since coming to Russia. I found myself marvelling at how clean the streets were, how nice the shops were, how prosperous ordinary people were and how much they complained about how hard their lives were. I read newspaper articles about the wrenching social changes Australia was going through. I looked at a society that most people in the world could only dream of having and wondered why I felt such a stranger after just one year away.

After Hours

Moscow didn't exactly feel like home but the sheer abnormality of it had started to feel normal. I was growing used to roads that took you where you didn't want to go, police who were a threat to public safety, shop assistants who refused to serve customers, food that was inedible, prices that nobody could afford, a president too sick to preside and planes so dubious that passengers broke into applause every time they landed safely. The raw intensity of it all made the West seem soft and bland.

One of my first real friends in Moscow was a 30-year-old Kazakh artist named Aelita. She had come here on the Russian equivalent of a green-card marriage. Her 'husband' was the 55-year-old father of a friend. The marriage was a sham, but the marriage licence gave Aelita the magical *propiska* to live in Moscow. This was a residency permit which had to be carried at all times for inspection. Without it, police could arrest or expel you.

Aelita was making a living as a graphic designer at a television station. The pay was awful but it was far more than she could make selling paintings in her native Kazakhstan. Being in Moscow gave her hope. 'There are opportunities here,' she told me. 'But you have to be strong. You cannot let people beat you.'

Aelita lived with a Russian boyfriend she didn't like, but felt she needed the protection of a man. The relationship seemed a matter of convenience on both sides. He didn't mind her going out with other men. I rarely saw the two of them together.

In some ways Aelita was an outsider like me. Her Russian was better than the Russians' — or so she claimed — but her Asiatic features marked her as being from the edge of the old empire. In Soviet times all the minority groups in all the republics were told they were equal, although they always knew better. There was now little pretence. Most of her friends were fellow Kazakhs and they had to work harder and better than Russians if they were to keep their jobs.

Aelita spoke no English but we both had German, which she'd picked up studying design in Hamburg. She introduced me to a side of Moscow obscured by the city's tacky new consumerism. On weekends we'd go to art galleries, walking in off the grey, gloomy streets to halls full of French impressionist paintings and Russian avant-garde. We went to jazz concerts in cellars, rock concerts in basements and performance 'events' too obscure to understand.

I even went to see some ballet. It was quite an experience to sit in the Bolshoi Theatre with its ornate interior and red velvet curtains embroidered with hammer-and-sickles. One night a friend of Aelita's who worked for the orchestra let me sit in the gilded Royal Box where Stalin used to relax between homicides.

Going to concerts took you back to an older Moscow but the new Moscow was always just outside. In the case of the Bolshoi Theatre, it was the ballet mafia. Corrupt management sold tickets directly to scalpers who paid off police so they could block the theatre steps each night to sell seats at inflated prices. A 10-rouble ($1.40) ticket could sell for the equivalent of $50. None of it went to the artists, of course. This was the age of Western-inspired economic reform.

One night I was invited to a place called Club Fellini, where an American jazz singer I knew, Tim Strong, was performing. The event was sponsored by Hennessy cognac, which was trying to market itself as a premium drink to rich Russians who didn't know any better. There were twelve of us at a table of invited guests. The only other people in the club were a handful of members who'd paid several thousand dollars for the privilege of joining. They were old, evil-looking *biznesmen*, surrounded by young, glossed-up hookers. Our table of non-paying guests had a glass of

Hennessy cognac laid out in front of each of us. By now, I was a little more used to the ways of Moscow and asked the waiter how much it cost.

'*Podarok,*' he said, which is Russian for a gift.

'*Otlichna, yeshcho pozhalsta,*' I replied (Great, more please).

We had two more rounds while Tim performed. As we were leaving, the waiter presented us with a bill for $960. It seemed only the first round of cognac was free, the rest was $40 a shot. I thought I'd misunderstood him, but the others at the table spoke fluent Russian and it was true. On a promotional night for cognac, the cost was $40 a shot and our bill was almost $1000. We argued and several large men with no necks appeared. We argued more and they made it clear that we would not be leaving until they had the money. We paid.

Being a place of extremes, Moscow also had bars that gave alcohol for free, but only to women. The notorious Hungry Duck — almost hidden in a basement beside Kutuzovski Most metro station near Red Square — was dirty and dark with a giant U-shaped bar surrounded by booths. Three nights a week, from six to nine, it gave an all-female crowd unlimited drinks while they watched male strip shows. They went wild when the men took their clothes off, some stripping themselves, throwing bras and underwear at the naked men to the hoots of the crowd. I filmed it one night, interviewing a nineteen-year-old university student named Masha who had come with her mum. 'I like it a lot,' Masha said giggling. 'They're very nice boys.' Her mother agreed. 'My husband let me come here and look. He said maybe he could strip for me. But I said no need, I want to look at the young boys.'

At nine o'clock the club opened its doors to men, who had been queuing for hours outside. The women leapt on them as they came in. Masha was soon crawling down the throat of a man she'd met five minutes before. I hate to think what happened to her mum.

Some colleagues once took a visiting sound-recordist to the Hungry Duck and he stood by a booth, cigarette dangling from his lower lip, stunned at the sight of a couple having sex under the table. A bouncer came up shaking his head. The sound-recordist thought he was going to stop the couple, but the bouncer waved his finger at him and said, 'No smoking here.'

Some clubs had more emphasis on art than on rutting, but were no less strange. Young bohemian types frequented *Krai*, meaning The Edge. The entertainment program ranged from belly dancers to avant-garde performance art. One night I saw an interpretation of Faust in which a man slowly drew blood from his arm with a syringe. He then squirted it into a beaker and drank it to murmurs of approval from the crowd.

Then there were the gay clubs. Homosexuality had been illegal in Communist days but the gay scene was now thriving. Women tended to flock to there, if only to have a break from drunken men trying to molest them. The most popular venue was Chance, which featured an underwater male ballet in giant fish tanks.

The Soviets had also banned striptease but, as I discovered with Nastya in Minsk, it was now almost *de rigueur*. Just about every club I went to had at least one woman undressing. Often they were just customers who had had too much to drink.

Young women were especially friendly to foreigners but it was sobering to remember that much of the attraction of foreign men was their passports. The second appeal was their income. Finding a Western husband and getting out of Russia was a prime motivation of many women, even in Moscow. Some had long checklists of what they wanted. I once watched a woman I knew in action at a mainly expatriate party. An American friend was keenly interested in her and thought he was doing well. When she asked what kind of business he did and he answered 'I'm a student', she stood up without a word and walked away.

Women tended to marry young and divorce early. I was surprised by the number of women I met in their mid-twenties who were already single mothers with a child at school. One friend, Vika, was typical. She had married when she was nineteen and had a daughter at twenty-two. Her husband left her three years later.

'It is so hard sometimes but I have to go on, I have to look after my daughter. What choice I have?' she said.

Vika was strikingly attractive and had worked in some of the most glamorous new jobs on offer, from television presenter to fashion reporter. But even those jobs didn't pay enough to support her daughter. She often hinted she would be a good wife, stressing that she was still young enough to have another child. I suspected her preference would be to marry a rich Russian, but Novi Russki would only consider a childless and exceptionally glamorous model-type in her early twenties.

Some women told me they wanted nothing more to do with Russian men, who could be brutal, drank too much, and saw nothing wrong with having affairs. This was usually designed to stroke my foreign ego, but I also heard horror stories about rape and domestic violence. There was even a Russian saying, '*Byot znachet loobit*', meaning 'If he beats you, it means he loves you'.

I saw it one night in a restaurant outside Moscow. A man at the table next to us started punching his wife. Nobody lifted a finger to stop him. I lamely shouted, '*Ne nada*' (not necessary), and he stopped, looking embarrassed. The manager came out to see what was happening and abused the woman for causing trouble. When we left, the man was drunkenly kissing his wife to make up.

Feminism had gone backwards since Soviet times, when propaganda stressed that women could do anything men could. It had now gone to the other extreme. Women on billboards and in television commercials were always slender, beautiful, sexily dressed and pouting at males.

The Western concept of a SNAG (Sensitive New Age Guy) was incomprehensible. A man had to be a *Nastoyashi Muzhik* (Real Man). An Australian friend, Michael, who had Russian relatives, came out to Moscow to investigate his roots. Speaking no Russian, he could barely communicate with his eighteen-year-old cousin, Vera, or her best friend, Katja, but he managed to fall for Katja anyway and asked a friend and me to meet them.

We started talking about the qualities they admired in a man. Both Vera and Katja believed the most important thing was for a man to be strong.

'Can he ever cry?' I asked.

'No, a man should not cry,' Vera said. 'Maybe he can once, when his mother dies, but not more.'

'He may have feelings but he must not express them in public,' Katja said.

'What about being faithful?' I asked.

That was a tough one. 'Men shouldn't have affairs,' Vera began. 'But if a woman tempts him a man can't resist.'

Katja agreed. 'It is wrong for a woman to seduce a married man.'

Real men should also be able to hold their drink, they said. But if he drank too much, it was the woman's fault.

'What about housework?' I asked.

'No, no,' Katja said. 'He must never touch a mop or cook. That is woman's work.'

Michael could have cried with joy. But from now on he wasn't going to do it in public.

Despite Moscow's reputation as a mafia town, it was rare to be threatened. I felt safer walking the streets of Moscow late at night than I would have in parts of New York or London. Our American landlord, Paul Tatum, was not so lucky. He continued to claim a large stake in the hotel business centre from which the ABC rented our office. The Chechen businessman Umar Dzhabrailov, who managed the Moscow City government's share of the hotel, continued to dispute it. Large numbers of armed men continued to roam the hotel. It was clear that things were going to get nasty. Dzhabrailov was heard to tell him, 'It is time you leave, Mr Tatum.'

A few months later Paul Tatum did leave. He walked from the hotel entrance towards the nearby Kievskaya metro station with two bodyguards. As they descended the stairs at the metro entrance, a gunman fired eleven bullets into him. The bodyguards mysteriously escaped injury and even more mysteriously failed to stop the assassin driving away.

We decided it was time to move the office.

Chapter 9
Kabul, May 1997

God's Drug Smugglers

At first glance, the Taliban might have appeared intolerant. They had, after all, banned music, radio, television, films, alcohol, cigarettes, gambling, Western dress, sport, shaving, and sex outside marriage, not to mention women leaving the house unaccompanied or showing even a centimetre of flesh. In the five years since the Taliban had emerged from religious schools, they had conquered most of Afghanistan and were routinely amputating body parts from anyone offending their strict religious codes.

But even the Taliban stopped short of banning *everything* sinful. In the interests of money and politics, they had decided to continue selling drugs.

Ninety per cent of Afghanistan's opium crop was being grown on Taliban-controlled territory. It was technically illegal but the religious police allowed its cultivation and sale for processing into heroin. The Taliban were even levying a 10 per cent tax on all opium sales to the drug cartels.

Much of the opium was ending up in the veins of fellow Muslims in neighbouring Pakistan, where addiction is endemic. The UN Drug Control Program had a plush office in the capital, Islamabad, with a chart showing the location of Afghanistan's opium fields. But the director, Gary Lewis, admitted they were failing utterly to stop the opium coming into Pakistan or to persuade the Taliban to stop producing it. 'They are focused on winning the war,' he explained. 'They believe they have a duty to do so and everything else will come afterwards.'

In the meantime, they were making a killing out of selling dope. Tim and I were on our way to Afghanistan to film the final days of a record poppy harvest. The last fields were now being cleared for sale to the heroin middlemen.

The border between Pakistan and Afghanistan lies at the end of the Khyber Agency, a lawless territory of Pashtun tribes where Islamabad has little if any authority. Pakistani police rarely venture into it for fear of upsetting tribal leaders, but drug syndicates operate freely. We drove through without stopping, passing markets selling drugs and weapons. We risked a quick photo-stop at the Khyber Pass, one of the world's greatest views, watched by a motorcyclist who was now tailing us. Then we arrived at the chaos of the border.

Hundreds of people were carrying luggage and goods between the border posts where Pakistani and Taliban officials vied for the status of Most Obnoxious Border Guards. By the time we reached the Afghan side, it was clear the Pakistanis had the edge. The Taliban guards were meaner but they were obviously illiterate, so they could do little but look at our visas and assume they were valid. They searched every item of gear to make sure we had no cigarettes or alcohol and grudgingly waved us through.

An Afghan aid worker in Peshawar, Shams-ul-Rahman, had agreed to come with us to translate. He helped us heave our cases through the no-man's-land and hired an old van from two touts on the other side.

The opium wasn't hard to find. We stopped at a field outside the Taliban stronghold of Jalalabad where villagers were still harvesting. Some were praying, bowing down behind the poppies that would soon be turned into high-grade heroin. A tall, thin farmer named Abdul Wahid proudly showed us his field. His sons and nephews were working frantically, getting everything ready for the drug buyers they expected in the next few days. 'It's got high value,' Abdul said, as he inspected the crop. 'We can buy food from it.'

I asked him if he grew anything except poppies and he shook his head. 'There is not enough water here. This crop needs less. Other crops would die from dryness.' He added that he was grateful to the Taliban for their help. A former governor of Jalalabad had once tried to stop them growing opium so the farmers revolted. 'If the Taliban do the same thing the people will rise up against them and there will once again be anarchy,' Abdul said.

As we were leaving, one of the farmers handed me a pile of opium buds and made a short speech. I thought I was being honoured so I smiled and thanked him. Afterwards, I asked Shams what the man had said.

'He said, "Take all this. It's enough to kill you."'

It was getting dark and the driver was impatient to get to Jalalabad. We sped off into the night along unlit, potholed dirt roads. As we raced through a darkened village, two boys suddenly appeared in the beam of the headlights, pushing a wooden cart across the road. The van driver hit the brakes and veered left, smashing into the cart and skidding off the road. We slammed into a house wall and scraped along for another ten metres before hitting a tree.

For about ten seconds, nobody moved or made a sound.

The driver stirred first. He had had a bad knock, like all of us, but was otherwise OK. He was just highly pissed off. He jumped out of the van and started shouting for the boys. I was regaining my senses and jumped out too. I wanted to see if they were all right. The driver wanted to kill them for damaging his van. Finally they emerged from the darkness. They were fine — we must have missed them by centimetres — but their wooden cart was a wreck. So they wanted to kill the driver.

Moments later, the villagers came spilling out of their homes and began shouting threats at the driver. His assistant jumped out and started shouting back. Soon they were shoving and hitting each other, illuminated by our one functioning headlight.

This was ridiculous even by Afghan standards. It was clear there was about to be blood shed over an accident in which nobody was hurt, a cart that was virtually worthless even before it was wrecked and van repairs the village couldn't possibly pay for anyway. It was a pitch black night in the middle of nowhere and we would have no chance of getting away if it turned violent. Tim suggested we offer to pay for everything and get the hell out of there.

I called Shams over to make the announcement. We would pay for a new cart and cover the van repairs, but we would have to leave immediately.

The villagers considered this and demanded we give them $100 for the cart.

'Shams, it's a toy cart, it's not worth a dollar,' I said. But at his nervous urging, I agreed to give them $50.

The van owner sullenly agreed to leave after hurling more insults and punching an old man, which nearly brought on a lynching. We managed to drag our companions into the vehicle and persuade them to drive off, as the villagers slapped and kicked the van.

Arriving in Jalalabad twenty minutes later, I felt shaken and utterly drained. There was one dirty guesthouse to stay in. We unloaded our gear and I sat down with the driver and his offsider to work out the cost of repairs.

'You are a guest in our country and it is our honour to serve you,' the driver said. 'You may pay whatever you wish. It is up to you.'

The left-hand corner of the van was smashed. It would need extensive panel beating, a new headlight and a new bumper bar. It was a big job and we weren't going to be able to hang round to get a quote. But I knew that in a city as poor as Jalalabad it was going to be relatively cheap.

'OK, I said I'll pay for it and I will,' I told them. 'I think $500 will be more than enough.'

'No, you must give us $5000.'

I was gobsmacked. The whole van wasn't worth half that. 'Shams, tell them no way. It's $500.'

He did and looked worried by their reply. 'They say they will tell the Taliban what you were filming unless you pay.'

'I thought we were guests in their country and they were honoured to serve us,' I said.

'These are very bad men,' said Shams.

We haggled but they knew they had me. If the Taliban knew what we'd been shooting, we'd not only lose the tapes, we'd probably wind up in prison.

'OK, Shams, tell these thieves I'm going to give them 1000. They can take it or they can report us, but I'm not paying a cent more.'

They were surly but agreed. I paid the money and took out my expenses notebook: *Jalalabad — $1000 — bribe — driver — no receipt.*

At dawn we found a new van and driver and began the long journey to Kabul. It should have been a short drive but the road was one of the worst in the world. What was once a proper bitumen highway had degenerated into a rocky track, thanks to decades of war and government neglect. Bombed-out bridges and the burnt remains of Soviet tanks littering the roadside slowed us down further. It took us eight hours to cover just 140 kilometres.

Kabul was in almost as bad a state as the road. Parts of the city were more shattered than Grozny; but the Afghans had done this to themselves. No fighting had taken place here until the Soviets had left and rival mujahideen factions started shelling each other.

Cars and trucks were the only immediate sign of modernity. Nobody was wearing Western dress, as the Taliban had outlawed any tight-fitting clothes. Women were invisible under the all-enveloping burqas the Taliban forced them to wear — they looked like blue tents walking down the street. As we drove further into town, we passed Taliban checkpoints manned by young men with assault rifles, turbans and long beards (fist-length beards were now compulsory). Audio cassette tapes they had seized from cars were wound around posts as a warning. The Taliban had banned videotape and audiotape, believing it was sinful to record a person's voice or image.

We checked into the world's most inappropriately named hotel, the Kabul Inter-Continental, the one hotel where the Taliban permitted foreigners to stay. Many years earlier it had been part of the luxury Inter-Continental chain. The rooms still had Inter-Continental coathangers and there was even a faded Inter-Continental ballroom. But ever since the Soviet Union invaded, it had been claimed and fought over by warring parties. The Soviet military seized it for its officers, the mujahideen shelled and mortared it, rival factions riddled it with bullets, and now the Taliban had taken out the mini-bars.

Our next stop was the group Shams worked for — ACBAR, the Agency Coordinating Body for Afghan Relief. This was the umbrella group for some 70 non-government organisations which were effectively keeping Afghanistan's social services running. The boss was Ross Everson, a gruff young Queenslander with a token ginger beard.

'What the bloody hell are *you* doing here Shams?' he said in greeting.

'I am working for ABC Australia,' Shams replied.

Ross looked at us and scowled. 'Did you bring any beer?'

'No, sorry,' I said.

'Bugger.'

Ross had been here six months and was fighting a one-man war against the Taliban. He was the chief negotiator on behalf of the aid groups, but felt there was no point in trying to appease them.

'They came round one day and told me they'd decide who we could hire from now on,' Ross said. 'I told them to piss off.'

It was politically incorrect but it seemed to be working. The Taliban had temporarily given up trying to interfere in the aid groups' operations. They seemed to respect a man who was as obstinate as they were.

'Don't tell the bastards you're here or they'll give you hell,' Ross advised us. But I knew we'd be spotted eventually and be in worse trouble if we hadn't registered. The next morning we went to the Taliban Foreign Ministry, housed in a beautiful old Victorian-style building — one of the few public offices the warring factions had never shelled. The officials, with their long, bushy beards and black turbans, were rude and unwelcoming, ordering us to wait and refusing to answer any questions.

Eventually a man with a longer beard, which I assumed indicated he was very, very important, came out to tell us the rules for our stay. Chief among them was that we not to film any human beings or animals. 'You must only take pictures of buildings and mountains, nothing else,' he warned. Then he assigned us one of their official translators. I thanked him and declined the offer, explaining that we had brought our own.

'He is not permitted,' the senior beard snapped.

Shams seemed quietly relieved that he wouldn't have to navigate his way through the Taliban's insane restrictions and went back to the ACBAR office. Our new Taliban interpreter, Abdul Sabooz Salehzai, was about 40, well educated and pleasant. He displayed none of the Taliban's fanaticism and I suspected he was working in the only job he could get.

We tested the water by asking permission to film the area most damaged by the civil war. Tim began filming buildings with a small digicam he had brought with him in order to film discreetly. He slowly panned towards a group of people — Salehzai did not object. Tim moved in to get closer shots and Salehzai discreetly looked away. It was reassuring that even the people who worked for the Taliban thought their rules were ridiculous.

We drove up to the frontline village of Charikar, about 50 kilometres north of Kabul. There was no vegetation in sight, only a dusty beige wasteland. The plains are called Shamali, meaning windy in Dari, the Afghan dialect of Persian. It had once been one of the most heavily populated areas in Afghanistan, a lush region of orchards and vineyards. The Russians destroyed part of it; warring Afghans finished off the rest.

The Northern Alliance forces were in the nearby village of Jabal-e-Saraj, where their latest push to retake Kabul had been halted a few days earlier. The Taliban fighters were mainly in their teens and early twenties. They were simple country boys who had seen little of the world outside their remote villages where they signed up to fight. Few understood what they were fighting for, but the Taliban, financed by Pakistan and Saudi Arabia, offered higher wages than any other job on offer.

We asked the soldiers if we could film them preparing to fight their enemy. None objected. As Tim got his camera out, I asked Salehzai to find out if they were worried about further attacks. They told him that it happened all the time. Defensive frontlines are usually spaced far enough apart that the two sides can't easily hit each other but, given that nothing about the Taliban made any sense, I thought I'd check.

'They can't hit us here, though, can they?' I asked. Salehzai seemed to think it was an odd question. 'Yes, of course their shells can hit here.' That was our cue to leave.

I was about to tell Tim to get in the car when a red Toyota Landcruiser roared up beside the soldiers, its lights flashing and horn blaring. A crazed-looking man with an AK-47 slung over his shoulder jumped out and ran around to the passenger side. He picked up a rock from a pile on the front seat and threw it at us. For a moment I stood stunned, then I turned and ran. Tim was ahead of me but struggling to haul the camera. We raced back towards our car as more rocks whizzed past our heads. Salehzai overtook us but our driver decided to flee and screeched off before we reached the car. Salehzai screamed out to him and he stopped about 50 metres down the road. We piled in and drove off as rocks continued to thump onto the ground behind us. I was panting and could feel my heart thumping.

'He is a crazy man,' Salehzai gasped.

He was also a policeman. Salehzai explained that he was from the Taliban Ministry for the Prevention of Vice and Protection of Virtue, known as the Vice and Virtue Police. They were the armed enforcers of Taliban law.

'But you are with the Taliban too. Why couldn't you stop him?' I asked.

'I cannot talk to such a man,' he said. 'He will say, "It is my religion." You cannot argue with that.'

It was our second close shave in three days. We were badly shaken but thankful to have escaped unscathed. As we rounded a corner, three heavily armed Taliban fighters waved at us to stop. The driver immediately pulled over. One of them spoke briefly to Salehzai and he smiled and nodded. The three men climbed into the back with Tim and me, two of them sitting on our laps as they nursed their Kalashnikovs.

'Um, Salehzai, who are these men?' I asked.

'We must give these men a lift,' Salehzai said. 'We are from the same province.'

I was in no position to argue. We dropped them in a small village just outside Kabul. They invited us in to share tea with them but we thanked them and declined. We just wanted to get back to the hotel before the day got any worse.

That afternoon Tim decided to go for a walk around town and sneak some shots. As well as his digicam, he had brought a tiny camera the size of his hand, which he concealed inside a brown carry bag with a small hole cut for the lens. He wandered over to a suburb on a hillside opposite the hotel. Unfortunately, a Western man roaming the back streets of Kabul carrying a brown leather bag in front of his face looked about as inconspicuous as a lap dancer in red lingerie. Within minutes, scores of children surrounded him, demanding money and asking to be photographed.

After hearing of Tim's experience, I decided to take a walk in the hotel grounds. At least I wouldn't be bothered there, or so I thought. As I left the building, three young Taliban fighters joined me. Unable to understand a word of what they were saying, I wasn't sure if they were being friendly or trying to check up on me. As we walked, more Taliban appeared in front of us. It seemed to be a popular walking route.

I was starting to feel like a Pied Piper for lost Taliban when a group of students joined me. One of them, Najib, spoke some English. He was about nineteen and making a brave, if so far unsuccessful, attempt to grow a regulation Taliban beard. He asked the usual questions: 'Which country you from?'; 'What you do here?'; 'How old you are?'; 'How many children you have?'

I explained I had no children. Najib seemed puzzled and concerned. He couldn't believe that someone as ancient as me (I was now 37) and with no overly apparent physical defect, had not yet managed to reproduce. By Afghan standards, I should have been a grandfather. I explained that I was divorced, which upset Najib even more.

'What is your religion?' he asked.

'Don't tell your friends, but I'm an atheist,' I replied.

'What is that?'

'It means I don't believe there is a God.'

By now Najib was extremely worried for me. 'No, but you must believe in God, he is everywhere, even if you cannot see him.' He went on to explain the many great things about Allah. I thanked him for what he had told me and said I would think about it. He smiled in relief.

I asked him if he was married.

'No,' he said. 'We cannot marry until we are 25.'

I thought I must have misheard him. Afghan youths wed as young as sixteen. But Najib assured me it was one of the Taliban's latest edicts. I imagined what it must be like to be a young man here: no girlfriends, no music, no radio, no television, no alcohol, no magazines, no books, no fun and now no prospect of ever being with a woman until you were 25. No wonder they signed up to fight.

Kabul was utterly devoid of entertainment. Ross had an illegal satellite dish hidden near a window, which enabled him to get a ghostly, smeared image of BBC World, but we couldn't go down to his house because of the night-time curfew. Tim quietly set up our shortwave radio and we listened to the scratchy reception of Voice of America.

It was bizarre to be in a world without women. All the hotel staff were men. Restaurants were full of men being served by men eating food cooked by men. All the cars were driven by men. Men were only allowed to see the faces of women who were close relatives, and only in the privacy of their own home. The Vice and Virtue Police made sure that women covered every square centimetre of their bodies when they went outside. In the name of protecting women's honour, police attacked them regularly.

'Just today we had a case where two women were beaten outside the office for wearing sandals,' Ross told us. 'Beaten by Taliban. They have an electric cord that they beat women with.'

The fervour for enforcing their laws against women made their tolerance of the heroin trade seem even stranger. Salehzai arranged for us to film and interview the Taliban Minister for Drug Control, Najibullah Shams. It was the strangest interview I'd ever done. The minister insisted we have the camera pointing at me, rather than him, so he would not be party to the sin of filming a person. For the next twenty minutes, Tim had to shoot me listening to the minister answer questions. It was going to make for odd television.

He readily agreed that the Koran prohibited the cultivation and sale of opium. 'The Islamic State of Afghanistan has put the issue of fighting against drug cultivation of poppies and drug-related plants at the top of its agenda,' he said.

'Then why do you permit it?' I asked.

'The farmers were forced by circumstances to ignore Islamic prohibition and international convention only to survive, to feed their children,' he said. The Taliban had therefore agreed to exempt them from the ban until the war was over. Once order was restored, he promised, poppy cultivation would end.

I knew this was utter bollocks. The Taliban were also taking a cut from the drug trade. 'You charge a 10 per cent tax on opium sales,' I said. 'Does that mean the Taliban are profiting from drugs?'

For the first time, the minister became loud and stroppy. 'This type of arrangement by the Taliban has been practised for hundreds of years, not only in Afghanistan but in other Islamic countries!'

After the interview, he showed me the ammunition in their war on drugs — a series of posters *suggesting* that farmers grow something other than opium. Tim followed behind, discreetly filming us both. I'm sure the minister knew but he didn't object. This was all a game.

We drove around Kabul, sneaking shots out the window of the misery to which Afghans had been reduced. Shams, our erstwhile interpreter, had talked about how cosmopolitan Kabul had once been, how educated and well travelled the people were. It was now backward and desperately poor. The war wounded hobbled on crutches or sat in the streets and begged. Children scavenged in the rubbish dumps and ruins. This was a city without hope.

Shams joined us for lunch at the Inter-Continental. As always, the meal of the day was sheep and cold fat on a dirty plate. He asked me what I thought the solution was for his country.

'Shams, I just don't know,' I said.

'Perhaps the king could come back. What do you think?'

'I don't know, perhaps.'

After so many years of war, it seemed to him — and to us — like it would never end. Neither the Taliban nor their opponents would ever make peace with each other and both sides had enough weaponry to continue their low-tech fighting for decades. The world didn't care about Afghanistan.

At the end of five depressing days in Kabul, we had filmed enough in secret to make a story. But we still had no idea if we could get it out. While it was safe to smuggle heroin, the Taliban had cracked down hard on videotape. We managed to buy seats on a UN flight to Islamabad and, as we queued to board it, we saw a large sign warning that it was illegal to take camera tapes on board. The Taliban Customs officers gave us a full search, rifling through our bags, feeling our pockets and even checking our shoes. But Tim had sewn the tiny digicam tapes beneath the ceramic plates in our flak jackets. The officials let us through.

As the plane took off from the ruins of Kabul airport, I felt a profound sense of victory. We had beaten their stupid system and lifted the veil on their grotesque hypocrisy. Arriving at Islamabad, I saw something I now found exotic, refreshing and slightly startling ... a woman's face.

Three days later I was in a village outside Moscow at a birthday party for Eve Conant, my Ukrainian-American friend from NBC. She had hired a dacha and twenty of us — men and women — were together in a sauna. We were all drunk and completely naked. It was a very good day. I realised that the fundamentalists might conquer Afghanistan but they would never take Moscow.

Boris Yeltsin Must Die

I had done six obituaries for Boris Nikolayevich Yeltsin and he still wasn't dead. Every time he went into hospital or had another embarrassing public collapse, we would haul out the archival tapes and update the Yeltsin legacy for broadcast as soon as any one of a dozen rumoured illnesses finally killed him. The obituary was getting longer and stranger each time. The defining moments of his second term had been appearances in his pyjamas, checking into or out of clinics. Occasionally the Kremlin would release heavily edited tapes of him meeting officials, minus the audio, but mostly he was 'studying documents at his residence'. His staff once tried to explain his absence by suggesting he was 'hunting bears'.

But just as the world had written him off as the sick man of Europe, Boris bounced back. In August, the Kremlin announced that Yeltsin would visit the southern city of Saratov on the Volga River. It invited Moscow-based correspondents to accompany him.

If this were a US presidential tour, the media would fly on specially chartered jets, stay in a five-star hotels, shoot carefully choreographed photo ops, record set-piece speeches, and attend well-organised press conferences. But this was Russia.

The only details the Kremlin would give us about the trip were that we had to go there by train. There was no explanation as to why we had to take a train to a city with direct flights from Moscow. The press office said simply that accreditation would only be given to journalists after they delivered a cash payment to the Kremlin to buy the train tickets.

The price of the tickets was unusually high but gave hope it would be a renovated luxury train fit to transport a president.

Instead it was like a refugee camp on wheels and Boris Yeltsin wasn't on it. We travelled 40 to a carriage and four to each compartment in suffocating heat. The windows could only be opened using a special wrench kept in the train attendants' compartments, which they refused to give us. The vinyl bunks were sticky with sweat. As far as I could make out through the thick clouds of cigarette smoke which soon filled the carriage, not a single Kremlin official had come on the train. For no apparent reason the dining car was closed. In a country that still had an excellent train service, the Kremlin had managed to put all of us on a stinker.

None of this seemed to bother the Russian journalists, who had come prepared with suitcases full of vodka, cigarettes, bread and pickles. I passed a couple of hours wandering between compartments and bludging food and drink. The Russians didn't seem to have any more idea of why Yeltsin was going to Saratov or what he'd be doing when he got there than I had. But we were all curious to see him in the flesh.

After twenty stifling hours we arrived dishevelled and malodorous in Saratov for the presidential tour. Driving from the station to the hotel, we could see frantic final preparations for Yeltsin's arrival. City workers were painting the front of every building on the route of his town tour. Others were hammering in new fences. The gutters had been swept clean and, judging by the absence of people lying in them, the town drunks had been swept out.

At the hotel, an official finally handed out the details of the following day's program: the president would arrive at the airport; meet the governor; tour a wood factory; inspect a glass factory; and converse with Saratov residents. Because of the large number of journalists covering the tour, we would be split into two groups. Group A would cover the president's arrival at each venue; Group B would cover the departure. I had been placed in Group A and Tim, my cameraman, had been placed in Group B. I explained to the official that this would make it impossible to work. 'We are a camera crew,' I said. 'We have to be together. Tim carries the camera. I carry the tripod and the microphone. We can't do any of this if we are not in the same room.'

'Security has been given the lists,' the official said dismissively. 'They cannot be changed.'

'This is ridiculous. He is a cameraman, I am a television reporter. I can't work if I don't have a camera.'

With an expertise honed by years of bureaucratic service, he ignored me completely.

The next morning we waited on the runway for Boris to descend from the clouds. The airport had seen better days. Dozens of rusting, disused planes lined the tarmac in the distance. Aeroflot, once the national carrier of the Soviet Union, had sold off most of its ageing fleet to regional airports. There were now over 500 different Aeroflots, many with only one functioning plane.

A commercial flight from Moscow landed. It was full of journalists arriving clean and fresh to cover Yeltsin's tour. They were bussed over to where we were standing. I asked a colleague from a news agency how she'd managed to avoid taking the train.

'I paid for the ticket but I told them I'd be flying,' she said. 'Don't tell me you actually *went* on the train?' It seemed we had endured twenty hours in a rolling sauna so some Kremlin official could pocket a hefty commission.

Minutes later, the presidential jet landed and taxied to just 50 metres from where we were standing. Boris Nikolayevich walked out unassisted — a headline in itself — and accepted bread and salt from local women in frilly white dresses embroidered with local patterns. He then strode over towards us. This wasn't part of the program and a hundred or so microphones were excitedly thrust out to greet him.

He happily took questions, praised the reforms of the Saratov governor and promised that all soldiers' wage arrears would be paid by the end of the month. He was not a vision of health. He did not look likely to run a marathon and he was not going to pose much threat to any bears he might be hunting. But for all that, he didn't look too bad. He had slimmed down considerably since the elections and his face was much less puffed and blotchy. He sounded coherent and his voice was strong. Striding off with his bodyguards in tow, he left us wondering whether the unthinkable had happened … that the Russian president had not only regained his health, he'd also stopped drinking. Then I got on bus A and Tim got on bus B.

The tour was an utter shambles. At every stop, packs of bodyguards herded us into the wrong rooms, shoved us into the right rooms, made us wait for no reason then ordered us to hurry up. When we finally found ourselves in the same venue with Yeltsin — a wood factory — he wandered erratically towards any point that interested him, flanked by officials and bodyguards. The media pack scrambled to keep up with him, knocking over work stands, workers and each other as they struggled to change positions each time Yeltsin changed direction. Several photographers unwisely climbed onto portable ladders to try to shoot above the mob, wobbling perilously as the crowd stirred beneath them.

I escaped the throng as a photographer toppled in front me, retreating into a side room. There was no point in being part of the madness when I couldn't film. Seconds later Yeltsin himself walked in, surrounded by officials. He gave me an odd look and his bodyguards scowled at me as they filed past, followed by the heaving mass of media. I sneaked out the back to where group B was waiting to shoot the departure and managed to slip over, unnoticed, next to Tim.

We needed to shoot a piece to camera with Yeltsin in the background. At the next venue, a glass factory, we tried a dozen times. Tim would force his way through the pack to get a close shot of Yeltsin, then pull back from his head to reveal me attempting to explain the significance of the trip, surrounded by jostling cameramen and photographers falling off ladders.

Despite the chaos, it was remarkable to actually see the man, who could have been a computer-generated television effect for all the world had seen of him in public of late. We proceeded to a meet-the-people walk where he displayed the popular touch that had first propelled him to power.

'They've come to see their president alive,' he said laughing. 'Everything is fine with me. I'm in good health. I'm working well.' I managed to get next to him and noticed for the first time that he was missing a thumb and finger from his left hand — the legacy, I learned later, of playing with a hand grenade he stole when he was eleven.

He wandered through the crowd shaking hands and patting shoulders. 'We've stabilised the economy,' he declared, waving his five-fingered hand for emphasis. 'Already for the third month there's been no rise in prices.'

For a few short weeks it looked as if Russia finally had a full-time president again. But it was to be only a brief respite. Yeltsin would continue to disappear for long periods while the Kremlin denied he had any problems. In December, a month after a Kremlin medical check-up found he was in excellent health, he was back in hospital with a 'viral infection'. He was sick again the following March, cancelling all appointments and postponing a regional summit. The next month the French leader, Jacques Chirac, let slip that Yeltsin had a 'liver problem', which, considering his past drinking, was like saying the Atlantic had a problem with damp.

Throughout it all the Kremlin insisted he was in good shape, periodically releasing tapes of him at work and play to prove it. But the footage was now so highly edited that the jump cuts suggested Yeltsin was incapable of finishing a sentence. On one of these his minders strapped him into a snowmobile and sent him racing towards the camera to show how sprightly he was. The vision cut out before he stopped.

When he had to meet foreign officials — in front of foreign cameras — there was no way to conceal his physical (and, many suspected, mental) decline. At a summit with Jacques Chirac and Helmut Kohl, his behaviour was plain weird. He mistook the photo call for the press conference, inviting startled photographers to ask questions until an aide whispered that he had to have the meeting before he could talk about it. Later he grinned inanely as he tried to hand gifts to his fellow leaders, forgetting which present was for whom and almost dropping them before the aide again came to his rescue.

At a banquet in Uzbekistan he ended his speech by explaining he had to drive back to the Kremlin. He was 2800 kilometres from it.

There were constant fears that the man who controlled the world's second-largest nuclear arsenal could die at any time, but perhaps the greater worry was what he might do with that arsenal while he was alive.

Exactly what was happening to Russia's 5000-odd nuclear weapons wasn't clear. Everyone hoped fervently that every missile and every container of fissile material was accounted for. However, forgotten plutonium kept turning up in unguarded warehouses, while disturbing claims were filtering out about nuclear submarines dumping radioactive waste at sea. Some feared it was only a matter of time before disgruntled nuclear workers or impoverished military officers smuggled plutonium out of the country and sold it to terrorists.

Despite several Hollywood movies depicting nuclear missiles heading out by the truckload, there was no proof it had actually happened. But that didn't mean that former soldiers weren't desperately trying to make money out of nuclear weapons. We found just such a group operating in almost total secrecy in a disused missile base halfway between Moscow and St Petersburg.

They were trying to sell nuclear tourism. A few years earlier, the base had been one of the most restricted sites in Russia. It was only decommissioned in 1994, under the Strategic Arms Reduction Treaty (START) with the United States. The 100 missiles were gone but one of the silos that housed them was still there. So were some of the soldiers, who had nowhere else to go.

The soldiers had made a deal with the local government and the local military command to try to keep the base going as a tourist attraction. It had been spectacularly unsuccessful. With no money to advertise, or to instal tourist-standard facilities, they had seen only three groups of paying guests in the past year — a Russian news crew, a Japanese newspaper journalist and now us.

I was tagging along with a crew from Associated Press Television (APTN) which had done a deal with an army 'video unit' to get permission to film the base. All the security organs now tried to make money on the side from foreign media. Every few weeks a police or military video unit would come to the office offering 'exclusive' footage for sale. One month it would be a 'secret' submarine base in the Arctic, the next month 'real' action footage of Russian soldiers fighting in Chechnya. Two policemen once came to the Radisson Slavyanskaya hawking tapes of a man drinking blood. He'd been attacking people and biting their necks under the deluded belief that he was a vampire. The video showed local police bringing a bucket of cow's blood to his cell and making him drink it as they recorded the action on an amateur camera. The policemen couldn't understand why we wouldn't buy it.

The other sideline was selling permission for television crews to shoot in sensitive areas. Viktor, from the army video unit, had a good record with the news agencies and promised we could film anything. He drove to the base with us from Moscow to make sure it went smoothly. APTN sent its best cameraman, a Russian named Denis, to shoot it.

The base was a six-hour drive from Moscow, not far from the main highway to St Petersburg. We arrived on a beautiful summer afternoon with a clear blue sky, a warm sun and a cool breeze. It was hard to imagine the base as one of the places that could have ended the world. It looked more like a run-down scout camp than a nuclear missile base. There were a few single-storey concrete buildings with cracked linoleum floors and broken windows. Inside, half a dozen former soldiers were waiting for us, dressed in a mixture of their old, threadbare uniforms and cheap tracksuits.

Their leader, judging by the volume of his voice and the fact that he rarely stopped talking, was a large, beet-faced man called Alexander

Glazov. 'You have come to a very important place,' he told us. 'There is no place like this in the world. You can see things exactly as they were. You can see where the most destructive war in the history of mankind could have been fought!'

Alexander was convinced that the base was potentially one of the most important tourist attractions in Russia and could not understand why nobody was coming to see it. 'They could experience life exactly as it was for the soldiers,' he said. 'They could eat the same food and sleep in the same beds.'

I didn't have the heart to suggest that that was perhaps the problem.

The men on the base had been surviving on occasional pension payments and odd jobs. We'd agreed to pay them $300 to spend the night there, which was more money than they would have seen in months. An ex-army cook was preparing a huge meal for us but, judging by the number of vodka bottles in the kitchen, the rest of the money appeared to have gone on alcohol. (At less than $2 a bottle, $300 can buy you a lot of vodka.) It was early afternoon and the drinking was already under way.

Alexander said he would give us the full VIP tour. 'I will take you to parts of the base that no Westerner has ever seen before!' He led us across a field away from the headquarters. Post-Cold War poverty did not seem to have left Alexander starving. His ample belly wobbled over to what looked like a giant tin-can lid propped open at an angle. Beneath the half-open lid, we looked down into a 100-metre-deep cylindrical chamber. 'This was where the missiles would have been launched from,' Alexander explained.

It was mid-summer, but I could see a layer of snow at the bottom of the chamber. It was so deep the sun never shone on the snow long enough to thaw it.

Next he showed us a nearby bunker where soldiers had been positioned to guard against sabotage. 'They were under orders to stay here until the missile was launched in case Americans tried to storm the base,' he said. 'They were never told they would die from the heat and fumes as soon as the missile took off. Now, come with me and I'll show you how the attack would have been launched.'

We walked back into the base and through the soldiers' cramped dormitory. The only sign of its former nuclear potency was a display of old photographs and some Soviet propaganda posters. But at the end of the soldiers' quarters, a stairway led down to an underground passageway. 'It was all designed so we could get to the control centre without having to go outside. We could launch an attack without having to go out into the rain,' Alexander said smiling.

We ambled down the tunnel followed by a coterie of missile veterans. Several hundred metres later we came to an elevator and descended 35 metres into the command centre. Its depth protected it from surface attack. Narrow and dimly lit corridors led off in all directions. This was the nerve centre of the Soviet Union's nuclear capability.

A former major in the rocket regiment, Sasha Finyov, surveyed it with pride. 'The whole country worked to create this,' he said. 'Millions of people from the whole Soviet Union. It was the pinnacle of our industrial achievement.'

Even so, it looked like a decrepit old power plant that had been built on the cheap. It was 1950s technology — needle meters, cathode-ray tubes and snaking cables wrapped in electrical tape. Still, Sasha assured us, it had all been in working order when there were missiles here to fire. He took us to an even smaller lift down to the control room that would have given the final order. We spilled out into a room with two chairs facing a panel of buttons. One of them, under a glass panel, was THE button. It was red and labelled *Zapret 2*.

Pushing it ten years earlier could have triggered the destruction of civilisation as we knew it.

I couldn't resist. 'Can I press it?'

'Yes, of course, please.'

I pressed it. It felt like a cheap plastic button.

Sasha explained that it wouldn't have actually fired the missile. It would have given the signal confirming the order to launch it. The end of the world wouldn't have got under way until about two minutes later.

We took turns photographing each other launching World War III. I was briefly caught up in a grand sense of history, being at the heart of the insanely risky superpower policy of MAD (Mutually Assured Destruction). But Alexander and the other military men were now impatient to get back to the surface. It was time for the daily *banya*.

Every evening they relaxed with this peculiar Russian institution, similar to a sauna but much more intense. Just behind the base, the soldiers had built a primitive wooden shack with a tub of hot coals that turned water into suffocating steam. I imagined we'd just sit down with towels round our waists drinking vodka, but the men had in mind the full traditional version. We stripped off completely and Alexander told me to lie down on a towel on the bench. Then he started whipping me with a birch branch. It was starting to feel like a prison movie. Afterwards Viktor lay down and told me to whip him. The soldiers took turns whipping each other. This was not part of the Australian tradition of what men do together, and I couldn't feel comfortable.

'Don't worry, it just makes your blood run faster,' Denis the cameraman said, looking amused.

There was no shower but I towelled off the sweat and went back to the base to eat. It was authentic military slop, with a heavy emphasis on boiled cabbage, greasy potato and grey meat. The other soldiers had already made huge inroads into the vodka but there was still plenty left to make obligatory toasts. Alexander filled our glasses to the brim.

'To friendship between Australian television and Russia's atomic soldiers,' I began, now fluent in Russian alcohol vocabulary.

Clink went the glasses, down went the vodka — and everyone dived for *zakuski* (food items, usually pickles, to kill the taste and help absorb the alcohol).

'To the friendship we have forged here today and the memories we shall always cherish,' said Alexander.

Another round of clinks, another glassful skolled, and more munching of pickled cucumber and bread.

'To a successful story and our future cooperation,' said Viktor.

'To your future success and may thousands of people visit your base,' I slurred.

'To beautiful women,' said Denis.

There was still light in the sky when we downed our last toast at midnight. The soldiers said we should sleep in the dormitory to continue the experience, but Denis found two slightly cleaner and more comfortable beds in what must have been the officers' quarters.

Much later, a military analyst told me I'd been conned. The base had only been used for training and had never had a real missile. But that night, as I drifted off to sleep, I thought what a waste it was that 'rich American tourists weren't sampling its history. I decided I would quit reporting, use my savings and advertise 'Adventure Cold War Trips of a Lifetime', to save my new soldier friends and make us all a fortune.

I'd definitely drunk too much vodka. No foreigner in his right mind would want to start a business in Russia.

My neighbour in Moscow, Nick Lazaredes, was an Australian journalist who came to Russia to report in the early '90s and drifted into business. For a time, he did relatively well navigating the bureaucracy, death threats, extortion attempts and bank failures that came with trying to make money here. In his early thirties, he had a large apartment, a renovated office, a staff of five and a modest but steadily rising income.

His business was distributing Western television programs to regional television stations throughout the former Soviet Union. Thanks to Nick, Siberian collective farms and Armenian salt factories were tuning into dubbed versions of *Neighbours*, *Flying Doctors* and *Cop Shop*. But his downfall began with what should have been his crowning glory ... bringing the children's series *Bananas in Pyjamas* to Russia. Nick rang me to ask if I'd be interested in covering the publicity launch.

'They've sent us two banana suits and I've hired some actors so we can take B1 and B2 up to Red Square,' he said.

The ABC series, featuring two bananas called B1 and B2, had been phenomenally successful around the world, for reasons only fully understood by children under the age of four. It sounded like an upbeat change from the usual stories I did about starving pensioners and contract killings. Plus there was the possibility of filming B1 and B2 being arrested. Red Square, which begins at St Basil's Cathedral and adjoins the Kremlin, is the most heavily policed patch of Russia. We arranged to meet on a Saturday afternoon opposite the cathedral.

Nick pulled up in a van with his Russian sales director, Igor Vassiliev, and two men dressed as bananas, minus the yellow banana heads. They climbed out, strapped on their heads and walked up to the cathedral. Groups of passing children immediately mobbed them. Some advance screenings of *Bananas in Pyjamas* had already won a small cult audience in Moscow, and a few children started singing the theme tune in Russian.

'*Banani v'pijami …*'

The crowd followed B1 and B2 as they walked into the square and headed towards Lenin's tomb. The spooks took just seconds to pounce. Two plainclothes police blocked the way, demanding to know who the bananas were and what they were doing there.

'There is no problem, they are characters from a children's television show,' Igor explained. 'They are just meeting some fans.'

'*Zapresheno!*' the first policeman shouted, 'Forbidden. You do not have authorisation.'

For a moment it seemed B1 and B2 might be hauled in for interrogation, but we quickly agreed to leave and never return.

A few weeks later Nick had to fly to Australia for the funeral of his closest friend. He returned to Moscow to find that Igor had stolen everything — including the banana suits. What's more, he was demanding a ransom for them.

'The bastard's trying to sell them back to the ABC for $2000 each,' Nick said, shaking his head in disbelief.

Igor had always struck me as a little too smooth for comfort. He was the son of a former high-ranking party official and had a great sense of his own importance. He wore expensive clothes, drove a BMW and had a vacuous platinum-blonde girlfriend with the pouting air of a spoilt princess, who also worked for Nick.

They had taken advantage of his absence to strip the office and editing suite bare — taking the computers, furniture and company records. They were trying to break down Nick's apartment door when he returned early and stopped them. Nick later found out that they had been selling programs on the sly and pocketing the money.

In almost any other country, you could go to the police and have them arrested. But Nick's attempts to get justice foundered on the chaotic commercial court system and the susceptibility of officials to bribes. Each time Nick won a victory in court, Igor launched a new appeal sending the case back to the beginning. He was finally found guilty of criminal fraud, forgery and piracy but was handed a suspended sentence. Police raided Igor's home and dacha and found no trace of the equipment. They also found that all his property was in his mother's name, meaning it would take another long court battle to reclaim it. With the core of his business destroyed, Nick had to leave Russia. When he tried to return to pursue the case, he found his name was on a computer blacklist, meaning he couldn't get a visa. Nobody could explain why.

Nick eventually returned to his true calling — reporting — and was far more successful than he'd ever been at business. But he never got back the money Igor owed him or the equipment he stole. The ABC refused to pay Igor's ransom. B1 and B2 have never been found.

Chapter 11
Belgrade, September 1997

Premature Election

It's not often you get invited to a social gathering with a mass murderer, let alone someone accused of genocide. And I wasn't really dressed for it. I had been in Belgrade less than 24 hours and I still hadn't managed to even iron a shirt. But suddenly I had an invite to drop in on Slobodan Milosevic at his palace.

It wasn't exactly a personal invitation, but I'd just bumped into the new Australian ambassador to Yugoslavia, Chris Lamb, who was about to present his credentials to the president. A meeting with Milosevic was normally as hard to get as a weekend away with the Pope. The ambassador managed to get me onto the invitation list, and I raced back to the hotel to grab a tie. You can't be too polite with important war criminals.

Tim and I were in Belgrade to cover what had once been expected to be Milosevic's downfall. During the street protests of the previous winter, the opposition had imagined they would sweep to power when Milosevic ended his constitutional term as president in September. But nothing had worked out the way it was supposed to. Milosevic was now stronger than ever, and the opposition had disintegrated.

Not long after the protests ended, the gigantic egos of the opposition leaders, Vuk Draskovic and Zoran Djindjic, collided with cataclysmic force. Djindjic decided the presidential elections would be rigged, so his party decided to boycott them. Draskovic, who had been convinced he could win, suddenly found half the democrats were campaigning against him, making him a certain loser.

Milosevic, meanwhile, pulled a constitutional swiftie. Forced to step down at the end of his second term as Serbian president, he organised his rubber-stamp parliament to appoint him to the purely ceremonial position of Yugoslav president, a meaningless post given that Yugoslavia no longer existed except in a sham federation between Serbia and the tiny state of Montenegro. But Milosevic simply decreed that it was now the supreme post in Serbia and continued running his mafia state from the federal presidential palace.

When Milosevic had been Serbian president, new ambassadors had to present themselves to him. Now he was Yugoslav president, new ambassadors still had to present themselves to him. Power went wherever he went.

Milosevic's new palace was a grand, ornate mansion at the end of a long, tree-lined drive, and had once been occupied by the Yugoslav king. Ceremonial guards, dressed in sky-blue pantomime soldier uniforms with shiny bayonets, greeted the Australian delegation. It seemed to symbolise Milosevic's rise from grubby Communist apparatchik to international statesman, at least in his own mind. Self-important aides hustled us into a waiting room, to wait.

Eventually they led us into a formal reception room, where Milosevic's official cameraman was waiting to record the meeting. It was guaranteed to lead the evening news that night.

The door opened and the Serbian strongman swept in. He looked short and strangely koala-like but he oozed charm, welcoming the ambassador in fluent English and shepherding him to seats for the official photographs.

While the official cameraman filmed from the official position, Tim and I waited to pounce. At the first break in conversation, I planned to stride forward and ask a series of polite but probing questions about, for example, his war crimes. When the moment came, I managed to take two steps before his aides blocked my path and hustled me out of the room. Tim and I waited outside with the pantomime soldiers until the diplomats could give us a lift back to the city.

Belgrade was now a gloomy place. We had driven in from Bosnia, where Tim and I had been shooting a story about continuing communal violence. After a day driving past the burnt and shelled remains of Bosnia's ethnically cleansed villages, Belgrade turned out to be even more depressing. The manic energy and excitement of the winter marches had disappeared.

We met our old interpreter, Miroslav, outside the philosophy faculty. A few students sat on the steps trying to sell old textbooks. Miroslav was reading an archaeology book, trying to catch up on the months of study he had missed while caught up in what he now saw as pointless protests. He had grown cynical, even for a Serb.

'In those days we were full of energy. We believed we could change things,' he said bitterly. 'Now we see we can't. We marched all winter for these guys and for what? For nothing.'

Campaigning was in full swing in Knez Mihailovo, the cobble-stoned pedestrian mall where the nightly protests had faced down paramilitary riot police. Draskovic's party workers and Milosevic's socialists were handing out leaflets encouraging people to vote while Djindjic's people were handing out leaflets urging a boycott. Most passers-by ignored them all.

The election was important in one sense: the constitution gave formal power to the Serbian president, meaning Milosevic had to make sure one of his socialist underlings was elected so he could continue ruling by proxy from the palace. Djindjic's party was aiming to invalidate the election by getting the turnout below 50 per cent, forcing it to be reheld. Miroslav supported the boycott but thought the socialists would eventually win. 'This is our great Serb democracy,' he sniffed. 'Milosevic is stronger than ever.'

He was too busy studying to guide us around Belgrade this time, so he introduced us to a friend called Sanja, who was majoring in English. Contemplating Serbia's future, she made Miroslav seem cheerful.

'It's like we're living in some horrible black hole,' she said. 'Everyone's only interested for themselves. Nothing changes.'

Sanja was petite and pretty with a shock of dyed red hair. She was only twenty but, like many young people in Belgrade, had the maturity and world-weariness of someone far older. Her mother was Serb, her father Macedonian, and she was deeply proud of what Yugoslavia had been: a harmonious, multi-ethnic state that had found a balance between the excessive materialism of the capitalist West and the grey orthodoxy of the Soviet East. At least that's how she remembered it. 'It was *superbe*,' she said, smacking her lips on her fingers like a chef extolling a soufflé. 'Everything peaceful, life so good. My mother could fly to Italy with her friends to shop.'

The breakup of Yugoslavia shocked and appalled her. She had spent her teens watching the country destroy itself. The winter protests felt like a turning point. A classically trained dancer, she had started each student march by pirouetting through the snow in front of the riot police, wearing a pink tutu. Like Miroslav, she now wondered why she'd bothered. 'The worst thing that happened is people lost their energy to fight,' she said. 'They're tired. It took them six years to do something, to get their energy to protest, and when they didn't get what they wanted they lost their energy.'

In fact, they were about to get something even worse.

Lurking on the sidelines was another presidential candidate who made Milosevic's thugs look like sensitive human rights activists. Vojislav Seselj (pronounced Sheshel) was one of the nastiest war criminals to have emerged from the breakup of Yugoslavia. His neo-fascist Serbian Radical Party had always been on the far fringe of extremist politics, but with the democrats in disarray he was starting to look like a strong contender to beat Milosevic's man.

Seselj didn't have charisma in the conventional sense. He was fat, pasty-faced, sweaty and mean. Notorious for having led a paramilitary group called the White Eagles on murderous rampages through Bosnia against Muslim and Croat civilians, his campaign promises included destroying the independent state of Bosnia and retaking 'traditional' Serb land from Croatia. But while the democrats had been battling each other, Seselj had been quietly accruing power and popularity.

He was mayor of a poor district of Belgrade, where his nationalist rhetoric went down well with impoverished Serbs looking for outsiders to blame for their misery. He had also shown himself to be a capable administrator, cracking down on corruption and freeing up public funds for effective public works — novel concepts for 'socialist' Serbia.

At a press conference he rattled off his priorities like a military commander. 'We will bring order and discipline to Serbia!' he barked. 'Wipe away the state and financial mafia! Tidy up finances and carry out privatisation! Pay out all the arrears! Any questions?'

Essentially, he was an honest, can-do, violent sociopath.

Miroslav lived in Seselj's district and told us he had already started a mild form of ethnic cleansing. 'People of Croatian nationalities, of Hungarian nationalities, are getting beaten up. They get papers telling them to get out of their flats, to get out of their shops and everything. That is not the way. He even tried to make a Jewish synagogue into a disco club, which in any country is unthinkable. But here he can do it. And I'm afraid of that. I'm afraid if he comes to power this can only be worse. He'll probably make war to all the countries in the world. That's how he is. He's a great Serb nationalist. I don't like him.'

But an increasing number of people did like Seselj. He had a campaign rap video to appeal to young voters, with a homeboy dude singing:

> Who is saying, who is lying, that Serbia is tiny?
> Ugh! Ugh!
> Thank God it's not tiny, as long as it's got the Radicals!
> Ugh! Ugh!

There was also a caring video chasing the family vote, showing Seselj with his wife and three sons, with Seselj saying:

Mihailo has just learned to walk and he loves his dad best.
The first word he ever spoke was 'Daddy'.

And there was a patriotic campaign video for the nationalists, proclaiming:

> From the early days Dr Vojislav Seselj has bravely and
> resolutely defended the interests of the Serb people ... in
> all Serb lands!

There was no video showing how he'd defended them, but his paramilitaries tended not to film themselves raping Muslim women and burning villages.

As expected, Draskovic suffered a humiliating loss at the elections. He came a poor third in the vote for president and his party, the Serbian Renewal Movement, won only 45 of 250 seats in parliament. However, the beneficiary was not Milosevic's Socialist Party.

Seselj's Radical Party doubled its seats to 80, putting it within striking distance of forming a government. Seselj himself won the most votes for president. He was now odds-on to win a run-off two weeks later with Milosevic's proxy, Zoran Lilic.

Instead of uniting against the common threat of neo-fascism, the democrats continued to fight each other. Sanja took us to interview the man she blamed more than anyone for the opposition's collapse. Vuk Draskovic was in the same office above Knez Mihailovo where I'd interviewed him in January, but his office now featured a gigantic wall-sized picture of his own head.

Draskovic sat in front of it, slightly obscuring the giant nose. The giant eyes stared down at both of us. It was like interviewing an egotist with his alter ego looking on.

I asked him how relations were with his old comrade Djindjic.

'He is a man without honour,' he snorted. 'It is not possible to work with such a man.'

Across town we spoke to Djindjic, who had a different take on what had happened. 'Mr Draskovic ran for president because he wants power,' he told me over coffee. 'It's nothing to do with principles or ideals. He wants to use power the way Milosevic does.'

However, Djindjic was fast becoming as irrelevant as Draskovic. One night Sanja invited me to join some friends at a jazz cellar in Knez Mihailovo. The music was good and the beer was cheap, which it would have to be considering how little money anybody had. None of the students talked politics this night or had much interest in the opposition squabbles. The main topic of conversation was getting out of Serbia. It seemed that everybody had a plan to live and work somewhere else, no matter how menial the job or the pay. They weren't bitter about it, just matter-of-fact. Their country no longer had anything to offer them. What's more, it looked as if there was going to be another war.

'We don't know what's going to happen in Kosovo but it's probably going to be bad,' Sanja said. 'None of my friends want to fight.'

Serbia's southern province of Kosovo had long been a Balkan powder keg. There were now ominous signs that it was about to explode. Ninety per cent of the population was ethnic Albanians, deeply opposed to Serbian rule. After years of peaceful resistance, the opposition was turning violent and Serbian police were responding in kind. A shadowy Albanian guerilla group, called the Kosovo Liberation Army, had begun attacking police posts. A week earlier, police had used tear gas and water cannon to crush a demonstration by Albanian students.

Tim and I had time to kill before the second round of the elections between Seselj and Milosevic's stooge. So we drove down to Kosovo to meet students there. Miroslav volunteered to come with us. Like most Serbs, he had never been there and was curious to see it. While Kosovo held a mythical place in Serb mythology as the birthplace of the nation, few bothered to make the five-hour journey from Belgrade to the Kosovo capital, Pristina — there was little to see except resentment and misery.

Pristina was like a Third World city. The ubiquitous concrete tower blocks suggested it had once been like the rest of Yugoslavia but everything was now crumbling. The roads were rutted and neglected. Unemployed Albanian youths lounged around the parks and squares. We checked into the inappropriately named Grand Hotel, which had more broken windows than guests. 'Another place to cross off the holiday list,' Tim said.

However, Kosovo could be a privileged place to live in if you were a minority Serb. Milosevic's first act to project himself as a nationalist hero in 1989 had been to strip Kosovo of its autonomy and impose direct rule from Belgrade. Albanians were sacked from almost all senior positions in state industry, the civil service, hospitals and schools. Serbs took over their jobs. The most dramatic change was at Pristina University. Albanian language classes were abolished, 800 Albanian lecturers were dismissed and more than 22,000 Albanian students were expelled. The Albanians responded by setting up an unofficial university in private homes where they could study in Albanian.

Our first stop was the 'law faculty', where we had arranged to meet Alby Kurti, the main organiser of the recent protests that the Serb police had crushed. More than 100 students were crammed into a small room of a private house. A lecturer, hemmed into a corner, was holding forth on the niceties of international treaties. It was stuffy and claustrophobic but the students listened attentively. Alby was waiting outside. With a long mane of hair, a five-day beard and a checked flannelette shirt, he looked an archetypal student activist, but he met Miroslav coolly — it seemed a Serb was a Serb. I explained that Miroslav had helped organise the anti-Milosevic protests. Neither reacted. Finally Alby broke the silence.

'Yeah, we were going to meet the students in Belgrade, but nothing ever came of it,' he said, continuing to talk to me while ignoring the still silent Miroslav.

The Serbian authorities were now allowing Albanian students to return to the university to study in Serbian, but 23,000 doggedly continued to study in private homes. 'We have our own language,' Alby shrugged. 'Why should we study in Serbian language?' They had originally thought it would be only a year before the authorities relented but nothing had changed. 'That's why after six years we've decided to start protests. They are really non-violent, peaceful protests for freeing the university buildings so we can get back there like we did in the '80s.' As we were talking, a nearby student collapsed in a fit of choking. 'A few months ago the Serbs poisoned a lot of the students,' Alby explained. I nodded sympathetically, thinking he must be making it up.

We drove up to the Serb university, a sprawling concrete complex that was eerily empty. We wandered down silent corridors past vacant classrooms looking for people we could talk to. It was ten minutes before we even found any Serb students, and they didn't want to be interviewed.

There was almost no mixing between the communities. The Albanians had set up a shadow society, completely separate from the Serbs. They ran their own crowded, ill-equipped health clinics — doctors and nurses working unpaid and surviving on outside donations. They held their own unofficial elections for their own unofficial representatives, whom the Serbian Government didn't recognise. Serbs and Albanians had their own cafés, restaurants and clubs. There was an Albanian-language newspaper, *Bujku*, which was published daily amid constant threats to close it down.

I'd arranged to meet a *Bujku* reporter named Evlijana Berani at an Albanian café. She was also hostile to Miroslav and unimpressed by his involvement in the Belgrade protests.

'Serbs do nothing about Milosevic for years while their army is butchering women and children, and then they march in the street because their pensions and wages are late,' she said angrily. Miroslav's eyes narrowed but he kept silent.

She lectured me when I mentioned we were planning to film at a mosque. 'What does that have to do with your story?' she snapped. I suggested one of the reasons for the communal tensions might be that the Serbs were overwhelmingly Orthodox Christian, while the Albanians were overwhelmingly Muslim.

'That is the kind of shit we hear on CNN,' she said. 'What does it matter what religion we are? I'm a Christian if you need to know. This isn't about religion. It's about apartheid.'

Evilijana took us to the paper's run-down office to interview the editor-in-chief, Avni Spahiu. He was a moderate intellectual in his thirties, deeply pessimistic about Kosovo's future.

'People have been patient for so long and it seems that they cannot take it any longer,' he said. 'Things are about to erupt.'

Back in Belgrade, Kosovo's rebelliousness was fuelling support for Serb extremists. A few days later the ultra-nationalist Vojislav Seselj was elected president of Serbia. Milosevic had finally been beaten — and by someone who was even more appalling.

But the victory was shortlived. The socialist-controlled electoral commission invalidated Seselj's win, claiming the vote fell below 50 per cent. It was impossible to know if the opposition boycott had been successful or if the commission simply falsified the returns. At a re-run in December, Milosevic's man won convincingly. It was business as usual for the Serbian dictator, who would continue to rule from the gilded luxury of the Yugoslav presidential palace. The chance for democracy in Serbia had passed. Nationalism was again on the rise. It seemed only a matter of time before Milosevic led the region back into war.

At home in Moscow I had a visitor. Her name was Kim Traill, an Australian who had learned Russian studying classical music in St Petersburg, teaching English in Kazan and picking cotton on a collective farm in Uzbekistan. She had taken up filming in an ABC series called *Race Around the World*, which gave promising novices a camera and a round-the-world ticket to make short reports. She was now trying to shoot her own documentaries.

I was utterly fascinated by her. She was just 28 but had lived in twenty countries and become so used to travelling that she could no longer sleep in a soft bed. She had holey jeans and a few grungy tops and I couldn't take my eyes off her. She was filming some stories in Russia, and for a few weeks she camped on my floor. I wanted her to stay with me but she already had plans to move on. It would be some months before I realised that those few weeks would change everything.

Chapter 12
Kalmykia, February 1998

Checkmate

Four hundred years ago a tribe of Buddhist Oirat Mongols wandered across the great Asian steppe, wound up on the eastern edge of Europe, decided they liked the place and stopped. Their descendants have been there ever since. Called the Kalmyks, they live in what is now a small Russian republic on the shore of the Caspian Sea, to the west of the mouth of the Volga River.

Kalmykia has always been an unusual place: the only Buddhist republic in Europe, the only desert in Europe and home of the only indigenous camel in Europe. Stalin didn't like the place and deported the entire population to Kazakhstan during World War II, fearing they might side with the German Army in neighbouring Stalingrad. (Half the population died before they were quietly allowed back in the 1950s.) Until recently, even fellow Russian citizens knew little about Kalmykia, where sheep outnumbered people by ten to one. But in 1993 a young tycoon vowed to put his native Kalmykia on the map. He decided to make it the chess capital of the world.

His name was Kirsan Ilyumzhinov. He was a Kalmyk entrepreneur, chess fanatic and ambitious politician. He became president of Kalmykia in its first post-Communist elections and three years later skilfully used his connections to get himself elected president of the World Chess Federation, FIDE. By 1998 he was preparing to stage an international chess Olympiad on the barren, windswept steppe of his remote republic.

Just 35 years old, Ilyumzhinov was a man who had everything — international prestige, his very own republic, a private fortune estimated to be tens if not hundreds of millions of dollars, and a presidential jet, aboard which we were now filming him en route to Kalmykia.

Tim had transferred to the Brussels bureau and it was my first shoot with the new bureau cameraman, Tony de Cesare, another Tasmanian getting as far away from Hobart as possible. Ilyumzhinov had agreed to let us follow him around for a profile we were filming for *Foreign Correspondent*, the ABC's international affairs program and one of the few programs on Australian television that allows reports to run as long as 30 minutes. Normally a Russian politician would see a chance to appear on Australian television as being about as useful as an interview on Tongan radio. But Ilyumzhinov judged our lengthy profile to be in his interest. He was about to fly to Sydney, which was preparing to host the 2000 Olympic Games, to lobby for chess to become a full Olympic sport. Perhaps a little publicity could smooth the way.

He was tall, slim and handsome in a pockmarked sort of way, with Mongolian features and a sharp suit. He was too busy to talk to us on the flight, but handed me an English translation of his autobiography, modestly titled *The President's Crown of Thorns*. In addition to likening himself to Jesus Christ, the book gave a potted history of his rise to greatness.

Ilyumzhinov had been a model young Communist, which won him entry to an elite language university. This landed him a job with a Japanese trading company during perestroika. The book was vague on the source of his huge fortune, concentrating instead on the boundless humanitarianism that had made him decide to run for president.

After consulting a clairvoyant in Bulgaria, who assured him he was destined for public office, he travelled to India to seek the Dalai Lama's blessing to run. The book didn't mention whether he got it, and also left out his winning campaign tactic — he promised to give $100 to anyone who voted for him.

As we touched down at the airport in his capital, Elista, a dozen assistants stood in the snow beside the runway to greet him, all wearing matching black cashmere coats and traditional Kalmyk fur hats — bowl-shaped with a spire on top. A gold Rolls-Royce arrived to collect him, along with a convoy of Humvees with sirens and flashing lights. Business appeared to be going well. He drove off as a crew from the Kalmyk television station came to interview us.

'What are your impressions of Kalmykia?' the reporter asked.

'Very beautiful,' I said, gazing at the concrete runway.

'Why did you decide to come here?'

'Um, President Ilyumzhinov is an extremely interesting and important figure,' I said.

Even the reporter rolled her eyes at that but I figured it would make our shoot easier.

The rest of Kalmykia didn't appear to be doing nearly as well as Ilyumzhinov. Elista looked desperately poor. We checked into the only hotel, near the main square and Ilyumzhinov's office. Later that afternoon we went out to take some pictures around town and couldn't help feeling we were being followed. That night our arrival in Elista was the lead item on the television news, stating we had come all the way from Australia to make a documentary about the president. It was followed by glowing reports on the president. This time the news format was Ilyumzhinov and the weather.

Running a Russian republic is similar to being an Australian state premier or a US state governor, but in Ilyumzhinov's case there were no messy checks and balances to bother about. He controlled the media, the republic's finances, the police force, the courts, even the electoral authority. His critics claimed he'd made far more money out of his position than he'd spent buying it.

But in fairness, it wasn't all about money. It was also about chess. His first directive as president had been for chess to be made a compulsory subject in school.

The next morning a carload of officials arrived at the hotel to take us to film a school chess class. This was not like a basket-weaving class or a gym lesson. It was part of the core curriculum. Each school now had full-time chess professors. We sat in on a class with students lined up in rows playing as the professor walked up the aisles drilling them in tactics.

'You must be resourceful, brave and persistent in any kind of difficult situation,' he told them.

Ilyumzhinov's decree meant that chess was taught from kindergarten to university. Chess appeared to be the chief focus of development. Most of Elista was falling apart, and even the government buildings were in serious need of repair, yet the main buzz of construction work was just outside town at a place called Chess City. It was the new venue and players' village for the upcoming 33rd World Chess Olympiad. Ilyumzhinov had used his clout in FIDE to ensure that the national chess teams would have to make the long trek to his republic. Rather than billeting the players, he was building 80 luxury villas for them, next to a specially constructed four-storey playing hall.

We watched bulldozers ploughing through the snow as teams of workmen raced to complete the work. It was quite an extravagance for a two-week chess competition — Kalmykia was one of the most impoverished republics in Russia. Most of its population of 350,000 worked on bankrupt collective farms. They were already providing Ilyumzhinov with luxury cars and a jet. Now they were paying for his global chess ambitions.

'What's going to happen to all this after the Olympiad's over?' I asked his press secretary, a short and pudgy man named Anatoly Bugatov.

'It will all be sold off as luxury housing,' he said.

'Really? Who's going to buy it?'

'Oh, there are many wealthy people in Kalmykia.'

I had a feeling they all had friends or relatives with the surname Ilyumzhinov.

Apart from Chechnya, Kalmykia was the first place I'd been to in Russia where officials insisted on escorting us everywhere. When we did manage to slip their company, there was a nagging sense that we were being watched. The same car would drive past twice, or a man walking behind us would stop to look at nothing in particular if we turned around.

That night we took a taxi to a run-down apartment block to see a woman whom Ilyumzhinov's people definitely didn't want us to meet. A short, matronly woman in her fifties met us at the door. Larisa Yudina had a kind smile and a gentle manner. She seemed an unlikely nemesis of the all-powerful president.

Larisa was the editor of the republic's only independent newspaper, *Sovietskaya Kalmykia*. Sitting at a desk in front of a photo of her grandchildren, she told us of the steps that Ilyumzhinov had taken to try to silence her. He had sent thugs to confiscate her equipment, evicted her staff from a series of offices and refused her access to the republic's printing presses. But she continued to publish in a neighbouring province and to pursue him with allegations of corruption.

'Our life has become noticeably merrier,' she said sadly. 'We have lots of festivals, contests, dances, visiting celebrities, so on the surface life is merrier. But in reality life has got worse.'

Larisa was an ethnic Russian and an old-style intellectual, the sort who'd supported Gorbachev's reforms and believed it was still possible to improve the mess that Russia was in. She was a prominent member of the liberal political party Yabloko, which campaigned against kleptocracy and human rights abuse.

Her main allegation about Ilyumzhinov was that he had stolen $10 million in federal funds intended to buy wool from Kalmykia's impoverished farmers. 'The money from Moscow was redirected to his corporation in St Petersburg and to its subsidiary in Nizhni Tagil,' she said. 'That's why our sheep and wool industry is facing such a crisis now.' Larisa said she had taken her evidence to the federal authorities but they refused to act.

Even though most Kalmyks toiled on sheep farms, Ilyumzhinov's people kept fobbing off our requests to visit one. Instead, his press secretary insisted we visit a horse stud to watch several horses running round in a circle. Bugatov assured us the horses were top quality; bred for export to Arab states. The president was planning to give some of them as prizes to the winners of the Chess Olympiad.

'This is most interesting,' I said. 'Thank you very much for organising it. But when can we go to a collective farm?'

'That may be possible,' he said evasively. 'We shall see.'

After several more requests he told us a suitable farm had been found for us. We drove for more than two hours across the bleak snow-covered steppe to a specially selected model farm. There was a wind chill factor of about −30°C as we walked across the snow to the farmhouse. A lone shepherd was bringing a flock of merino sheep back to the pen. He explained that merinos had been imported from Australia in Soviet times. Now they made up most of Kalmykia's herd.

The shepherd, Valery Adudov, and his wife, Nadia, worked the farm alone, visiting their children in a nearby town once a week. The herd had fallen 70 per cent since the state ceased purchasing all their produce. The farmhouse was little more than a hut. They appeared nervous about our visit, constantly muttering to each other in their Kalmyk dialect. I asked them how they were faring.

'Very well,' Valery said. 'Life has got much better under our president. Everything is more prosperous.'

The press secretary smiled.

'And what do you think of President Ilyumzhinov?' I asked.

They paused. The husband broke the silence. 'He is very good. He is always travelling everywhere, promoting Kalmykia.'

There was another pause. His wife cleared her throat and said softly, 'Of course, we don't get any benefit from it.'

'When was the last time you were paid?' I asked.

They looked at each other and muttered quietly. 'We don't remember,' Valery said.

The press secretary suggested we eat lunch.

Ilyumzhinov was all charm when he finally summoned us to his impressive suite of offices for a formal interview. He gave me a guided tour, pointing out an ornate chess set kept ready in case there was ever a chance of a game. I offered to play and he checkmated me in four moves. Next he showed me round his private office, where I couldn't help noticing a large model pyramid on a conference table. He told me his next project after Chess City would be building a giant pyramid in

Elista. Then he explained that he was a disciple of many religions and New Age philosophies, and employed astrologers and fortune-tellers to give policy advice.

'That is why, knowing that I'll live a second and third life, I consult in all my actions with God, the stars. I frequently make astrological maps and forecasts,' he said.

I asked him about his treatment of critics. He professed surprise that Larisa Yudina was continuing to complain. 'The task of the authorities and the mass media is to improve society, so that society is more educated and more stable,' he said. 'We have a common task and therefore we work to achieve this task.' His voice rose. 'Those who want to work together receive help, but others want to destabilise society and we don't understand them.'

It was time to chill the atmosphere. I asked him about her claims that he had stolen millions.

He assured me it was all lies. His wealth was all his own money, earned honestly through private business. He was only in politics to serve the Kalmyk people. He didn't even draw a salary. 'My attitude to wealth — I never paid attention to it,' he said dismissively. 'I never counted the money when I was in business or now. You can eat one bowl of soup or two, but you wouldn't eat ten bowls of soup. And you can't wear ten suits at the same time.'

Ilyumzhinov was still smiling, the increasing tightness of his lips the only hint that he was getting annoyed by my questions.

Afterwards, his press secretary gave us an archival tape of Ilyumzhinov carrying out his presidential duties. There was a television clip of him opening the World Chess Championship, when he leaned over and made Anatoly Karpov's first move for him, producing a surprised and filthy look from the world champion. There was also a clip of him meeting Saddam Hussein in Baghdad. Ilyumzhinov was an unabashed admirer and had brought him Kalmykian caviar as tribute. 'You can eat it every morning and always remain strong and defeat your enemies,' he told Saddam.

The next morning an anonymous caller rang us at the hotel. He didn't want to say too much on the phone but said he could tell us the real story of what was happening in Kalmykia if we came to his house that night. He dictated the address and hung up.

We caught a taxi, being careful to check that we weren't followed. We knocked conspiratorially. A large, red-faced man smelling of alcohol welcomed us loudly and invited us in. A family of seven sat in the kitchen of their tiny cottage, eating dinner. After introductions, I told them we were doing a story on President Ilyumzhinov and asked what they thought of him.

'He's an excellent president,' the father said. 'He does great things for us.'

'Life is much better now,' his wife enthused. 'He is the best.'

I thanked them and we left. Kalmykia didn't just feel weird. It was starting to feel creepy.

We visited Larisa Yudina again at her latest office. It was a disused hall and she was stacking up piles of newspaper with her five co-workers. This was their seventh office in a year. 'They occupy our rooms, break the doors, instal new locks,' she said. 'One day they broke into our computer room and I called the police. The police came and did nothing, so our doors were broken under police supervision.'

I asked her if she ever feared for her safety. She shrugged. 'We have to fight for this freedom,' she said. 'Maybe even paying for this with our lives and the lives of our families.'

She said it so casually that I didn't register its significance. Ilyumzhinov's last real opponent, this mild-mannered grandmother, feared she and her family could be murdered for what her paper was doing. I didn't even include her comment in the script for broadcast. I had no idea of how much danger Larisa was in or the risk she was taking in talking to us.

The story went to air in Australia around the time Ilyumzhinov would have been in Sydney lobbying Olympic officials.

* * *

Four months later a stranger called Larisa's apartment claiming to have incriminating documents about Ilyumzhinov. She agreed to meet him outside. Neighbours saw her being driven away in a car with an official number plate.

She didn't come home that night. Her family waited with increasing dread. The next morning her stabbed and battered body was found dumped in a pond.

I read the news in the office in Moscow, staring at her name on the computer screen and feeling shocked and nauseous. A woman I knew had just been murdered and it might have been for what she had told me. Anger welled up inside me — at Ilyumzhinov for what he did (I had no doubt his administration was behind the murder) and at myself for putting Larisa in danger.

Larisa had never been interviewed on Russian television so we gave our footage to the main network, NTV, which produced a half-hour story. It had an unexpected effect. President Yeltsin, momentarily back at work, condemned the murder, vowing that the killers would be found. Not trusting Kalmykia's police, the prosecutor-general sent federal investigators to take over the case. It took less than a week for two of Ilyumzhinov's former aides to be charged with murder. While the investigations were under way, Ilyumzhinov announced he would run for the Russian presidency.

The two men were convicted of murder but their boss denied any involvement. In an interview with Russian television, Ilyumzhinov claimed, 'The charges are unfounded and part of a Moscow plot to discredit a powerful regional leader.'

His pawns went to prison for life but the chess master remained free. He's still Kalmykia's president, he still heads the World Chess Federation and he even held the Chess Olympiad in Elista as scheduled, less than four months after Larisa's death. Few players saw any need to withdraw from it. Moral bankruptcy was not confined to Kalmykia.

Chapter 13
Armenia, March 1998

Zhirinovsky's Flying Circus

I'll start by squeezing the Baltics and other small nations. I
don't care if they are recognized by the UN. I'm not going to
invade them or anything. I'll bury radioactive waste along the
Lithuanian border and put up powerful fans and blow the
stuff across the border at night. I'll turn the fans off during
the day. They'll all get radiation sickness. They'll die of it.
When they either die out or get down on their knees, I'll stop
it. I'm a dictator.
— *Vladimir Zhirinovsky making a name for himself in 1991*

If there is impeachment, we will play golf together. We will
recall our sexual experiences. He will not be alone.
— *Zhirinovsky on President Clinton's troubles, 1998*

Vladimir Volfovich Zhirinovsky was barking mad. As leader of the
Liberal Democratic Party, which was anything but, he had at various
times threatened to retake Alaska, annihilate the United States and
launch a nuclear strike on Japan. He regularly assaulted fellow deputies
in parliament and had a habit of asking female interviewers to have
group sex with his bodyguards.

He was not a man with whom you would choose to share a
confined space. But as war clouds starting gathering over Iraq once more,
he became every Moscow correspondent's fantasy travelling companion.

In February 1998 America looked poised to bomb Baghdad yet
again as punishment for obstructing UN weapons inspections and every

foreign correspondent wanted to be there. Baghdad is less than a four-hour flight from Moscow. However, the UN sanctions committee wasn't letting any planes fly there and the Iraqi embassy wasn't giving visas to journalists. It looked hopeless until Vladimir Zhirinovsky suddenly announced he could solve all our problems. He could get us instant visas and he could charter a plane to take us to Baghdad. The only catch was that he'd be coming with us.

Zhirinovsky, while being virulently anti-Muslim, was another long-time admirer of Saddam Hussein, whom he called his 'dear friend'. It was a useful way of playing to anti-US sentiment. Zhirinovsky also seemed to have genuine respect, even awe, for someone who actually did the things he could only talk about ... like invading neighbouring countries and exterminating minority ethnic groups.

His plan was to fly a chartered plane to Baghdad to deliver humanitarian aid and show Russian solidarity against the evil aggression of America. He was offering seats to 100 Duma deputies and just as many journalists, all expenses paid by his Liberal Democratic Party.

I sent my passport round to his office and it duly came back with an elusive Iraqi visa, specifying it was only valid as part of his group. The trip clearly had the sanction of Baghdad, which always welcomed sympathetic psychopaths. There was still the small matter of the UN flight embargo, but most of the correspondents I spoke to thought it was worth a try.

Few of us had the slightest intention of actually reporting Zhirinovsky's mission. We were hoping to use him even more than he was using us. A colleague had a contact for an agency in Baghdad which we could bribe to extend our visas, so we were planning to bail out of the Zhirinovsky circus as soon as we hit the tarmac at Saddam International Airport.

We were trapped from the moment we arrived at Vnukovo Airport in Moscow. More than 100 journalists had signed up for the mystery tour and as soon as we passed through security we were locked in a waiting area. Two hours later, Zhirinovsky arrived with a flourish, just visible through the cloud of cigarette smoke now choking the waiting area. Surrounded as always by a coterie of bodyguards and theatrical extras ... today a Cossack and a Chechen shepherd, as far as anyone could work out ... he sailed through Customs without even a passport check and assembled us for the first of many, many doorstops.

'Today we are going to Baghdad to stop Clinton and his evil degenerates' plan to subdue the world in humiliating slavery,' he thundered. When pressed, he admitted the UN had not yet given permission to fly but dismissed that as a technicality that would soon be resolved.

We boarded the Ilyushin 86 jet; the media in economy class and Duma deputies in business and first class. The flight attendants began distributing free vodka. After an hour, the engines fired up and we taxied down the runway. Then we stopped.

The UN was still refusing to give clearance to fly to Baghdad so the plane sat idling at the edge of the runway while Zhirinovsky began 'negotiations'. This consisted of ringing Russian radio stations on his mobile phone to berate America and the UN and to demand that Yeltsin restore Russia's honour by getting clearance to fly.

The vodka was still flowing, and almost everyone was chain-smoking, the plane was filling up with an odorous fug, while Zhirinovsky continued to scream down his mobile. By now some of us were beginning to have second thoughts but there was no going back. The engines were idling to keep the plane warm, we were stuck at the end of the icy runway and armed security guards stood by the exits. Nobody was leaving the circus.

As the Duma deputies finished their business-class lunch, Zhirinovsky announced they would begin a hunger strike to force the UN to back down. Within minutes, news organisations around the world were reporting the Russian parliamentarians' fast. For almost four hours, the Duma deputies consumed nothing but vodka, beer and cognac. Then they interrupted the hunger strike to have dinner, bravely resuming it once the dessert was cleared away.

We had been sitting on the tarmac for eleven smoke-filled and alcohol-sodden hours when Zhirinovsky announced a breakthrough. 'We are going to Iraq!' he proclaimed. The plane started taxiing again, and the flight attendants ran through the safety instructions, ending with the words 'Flying time to Baghdad will be three hours and 45 minutes'. The plane took off.

Three and a half hours later, we landed in Armenia.

No announcement was made of what was going on. We were told only to get off the plane and take our luggage with us. Evidently, the UN had still not succumbed to Zhirinovsky's charms so the plane had landed at the nearest former Soviet country to Iraq to have another crack at it the next day. Zhirinovsky's people told us it was safe to leave our technical gear on the plane. Just in case, we lugged it off, leaving nothing but the box marked 'Humanitarian Aid' which we'd brought to help extend our visas — a case of scotch and several cartons of Marlboro Red cigarettes.

There were no passport or Customs checks, even though we'd arrived uninvited in another country in the early hours of the morning. Instead, there was a fleet of buses to take us to a hotel.

By two in the morning, we had found our rooms and crashed out, a few hacks staying up to file the first instalments of their 'Flight to Nowhere' pieces.

The next morning I wandered down to the restaurant and found scores of grumbling journalists debating our chances of getting to Baghdad and tossing up ideas for stories to do in Armenia. I asked a waiter for a cup of Turkish coffee and he froze. 'We have "eastern coffee",' he said. A *Sunday Times* journalist whispered that they were still a little sensitive about the Turks massacring a million-odd Armenians in 1915.

A few of us killed time wandering around the city of Yerevan, one of the sleepy outposts of the former Soviet Union which normally only drew the press pack if there was a good natural disaster. There was a strange sense of lost potential about the city. It was more European than most former Soviet cities, the Bolshevik monuments and concrete-slab architecture even more ill-fitting. It had been one of the intellectual centres of the Soviet Union but that meant little now. Lacking the natural resources of its neighbours, Armenia was condemned to poverty. It also seemed to lack any obvious story except for Zhirinovsky.

We arrived back at the hotel to find him holding an impromptu press conference on the staircase. Wearing a pale grey tracksuit, he launched into a fresh attack on the forces of darkness stopping the flight.

'The delay is humiliating and outrageous,' he shouted. 'If we do not get permission for the plane to leave I will demand the Russian Government's resignation. It will mean America has declared World War III!'

By now, the rumblings of mutiny were stirring. Why, many asked, didn't we just fly to Jordan and *drive* in? We could do it in one hard day. 'No, that is not the point,' Zhirinovsky shouted back. 'We must fly!'

Show had always been far more important than substance for Zhirinovsky. He'd come out of nowhere after the fall of the Soviet Union, suddenly appearing at elections and challenging Yeltsin with an arresting mixture of bravado, showmanship and mental instability. He'd begun by presenting himself as a sensible alternative to the failed policies of the Communists and the scorched-earth economics of the democrats. Once that faltered he threw the switch to vaudeville.

It soon became apparent that there was nothing behind his rhetoric. There were no massed ranks of paramilitaries ready to seize power, no brigades of young fanatics marching across Mother Russia towards the Pacific, and no real threat to Yeltsin either, at least not from Zhirinovsky. He knew where the serious money lay in Moscow and he wasn't about to upset the system. His strategy was simply to be as outrageous as possible to ensure maximum publicity. Some months earlier he had appeared naked in a threesome in a soft-core porn movie and it had only boosted his electoral rating. His crude but entertaining populism had won him a large bloc in the lower house of parliament, the state Duma, which he could sell off to the highest bidder when it came to crucial votes. Yeltsin depended on the Duma to pass key legislation. So

Zhirinovsky voted for the Kremlin every time it mattered and became extremely rich in the process.

Ignominiously driving into Baghdad on a bus was never going to be an option for him. So for the next three days, we wandered the streets of Yerevan, lounged round the bar with the Duma deputies and packed or unpacked our bags with each new announcement that the flight was approved or denied.

On the third day, Zhirinovsky made his definitive announcement. 'Tomorrow, we fly to New York to confront the UN!' It was time to leave the circus.

I went upstairs and packed again, planning to catch a commercial flight back to Moscow the next morning. At dawn, I was woken by the sound of panicked movement. People were running down the corridors hauling suitcases. The foyer was full of people frantically trying to check out. 'I don't know what's going on,' an American photographer told me. 'But apparently Zhirinovsky left an hour ago.' We jumped in a taxi and sped off to the airport. At the terminal, a bevy of guards blocked our way. An official told us no more people would be allowed on the plane.

We were shattered. After four days with this lunatic, we were not just going to miss out on Baghdad; we would have to explain to our news desks why the rest of the media got in.

Minutes later the other Western reporters came trooping out of the terminal building, swearing. The UN had only approved Zhirinovsky flying in with 30 people, which meant culling all the foreign journalists. They were ordered off by security, some clinging grimly to the armrests until they were dragged away. Some claimed Zhirinovsky punched the Russian ambassador to Armenia for not securing a better deal. Others said he threw a glass of water at him.

We boarded our jet to Moscow just as Zhirinovsky's diplomatic mission soared off into the sky. The prospects for peace looked bleak indeed.

Chapter 14
Moscow, 1998

Meltdown

The call came just as we arrived back in the office. 'We've got a burglary and stabbing, one man dead,' said the voice on the phone. 'We're heading there now. It's Kutuzovsky Prospekt, Building Eleven, ninth floor.'

We were following one of Russia's most popular television programs, *Dorozhny Patrol* (Highway Patrol). It was an imitation of American reality police shows, only it went much, much further — graphically showing naked corpses, stab wounds, mutilations and all-round gore on prime-time television.

We'd asked the program makers to let us know when they were racing off to the next crime scene so that we could film them filming the dead and injured. We'd expected it to be a gruesome event — that was the program's trademark. We hadn't expected it to be in the building next to our office. Tim and I picked up our camera gear and walked next door.

On the ninth floor, we found a freshly stabbed body in the doorway, slightly obscured by the *Dorozhny Patrol* cameraman painstakingly shooting close-ups of the entry wounds.

The police were in the next room interviewing the killer, who in this case was considered the victim. It was his apartment and he'd caught a man breaking in, so naturally he'd stabbed him. It was a perfect ingredient for the next day's episode, which would screen in the early morning for kids to watch during breakfast before they went to school. It would be repeated in the afternoon so that kids who'd missed it but had heard about it at school could catch up on the latest suicide, car smash or serial killing. And it would be rebroadcast in the evening so that all the mums and dads could watch it too, over dinner.

'We see ourselves as a documentary program,' the director of *Dorozhny Patrol* told me. 'We're also a public service program, warning of the dangers of crime and bad driving.'

Russia was no longer catching up on the excesses of the West — it had overtaken them. While pornography had been banned until recently, *babushki* now sold X-rated videos and magazines in the metro. Posters advertised bare-knuckle boxing matches called 'Fight Without Rules!' They were soon supplemented by posters spruiking: 'Fight Without Rules — For Children!'

Television, which once consisted of syrupy love stories set on collective farms interspersed with men with bad teeth reading news reports on wheat harvests, now showed the world's pick of Z-grade sex and violence. It could make for engrossing viewing. Barely a night passed without at least half a dozen on-screen murders — and that was before the kids went to bed.

One game show called *Intercept* featured high-speed car chases around Moscow. Contestants were provided with expensive cars, which they were allowed to keep if they could outrun the police. The show became quite popular before it was quietly withdrawn. Somehow nobody was killed in the high-speed chases — but if they had been they would have wound up on *Dorozhny Patrol*.

Sociologists sometimes pondered the implications of all this, suggesting it was due to social alienation, the spiritual vacuum left by the end of Communism, or a Nietzsche-like nihilism engendered by reading too much Dostoyevsky. I suspected it was far simpler. Everyone was lapping up sex and violence simply because the boring Communists had banned it for so long. It wouldn't be long before the novelty wore off. But for now it was the age of excess — a little like schoolies' week before the hangover sets in.

★ ★ ★

By early 1998 Moscow's mad frenzy of consumer and social excess was reaching a climax. Novi Russki, never renowned for their taste or reserve, were constantly searching for new ways to spend their wealth. At one restaurant in Moscow, patrons tired of eating overpriced meals on boring white plates could pay extra to eat them served on naked women.

Even after death, the quest to outdo your Novi Russki neighbour — the one with the four-storey lime-green dacha — continued. Impoverished embalmers, who had once dedicated their lives to preserving the corpse of Grandfather Lenin, now moonlighted to pickle slain gangsters.

It took more and more to shock the public. Among the few crimes to get people talking were the notorious Auto Shop Murders in May 1998, and this was only because they were as ludicrously stupid as they were excessive. Some would-be gangsters got the idea of opening a car-repair shop so they could kill the customers and steal their luxury cars. This crime spree ended with police finding ten bodies buried under the shop floor.

Every age of excess eventually ends. And after a long, hot summer, Moscow's mindless orgy ended sooner and with greater pain than almost anyone predicted.

In March Boris Yeltsin sacked the discredited prime minister, Viktor Chernomyrdin, appointing a 35-year-old reformer called Sergei Kiriyenko to revitalise the economy. Chernomyrdin had run the gas monopoly, Gazprom, in Soviet times. He was reputed to have siphoned off hundreds of millions of dollars through family companies. Under his stewardship, thousands of Moscow crooks had grown extremely rich at the expense of the rest of the country.

The short, bespectacled Kiriyenko, who resembled a high-school swat doing work experience, laid out some of the bad news of Chernomyrdin's economic legacy. More than a quarter of the country was living below subsistence level, more than a third of the budget would be spent on repaying foreign debt.

Investment in the country was plummeting, as foreign businesses finally faced up to the fact that the emerging market of Russia was a financial black hole. The stock market plunged 20 per cent. For seven years politicians had allowed Russian industries to fall apart while their cronies devoured oil and gas holdings. Now that commodity prices were falling worldwide there was nothing to keep the bubble inflated.

Many kept pretending that everything would sort itself out. The IMF continued to believe it could help Russia by putting it deeper into debt, lending to the same government crooks siphoning out money to Swiss bank accounts. In July the IMF approved a new $22.6 billion bailout package to boost the economy. US and Russian businesses in Moscow greedily stuck their hands out for more.

Charlie Ryan, an executive with the United Financial Group, told journalists, 'We're also hoping there's a possibility that there will be additional support, because at this point a lot of the economic fundamentals in Russia haven't changed, but the crisis of confidence and the psychology of the market has only deteriorated.'

You heard that a lot in those weeks — there was a crisis of confidence but the 'fundamentals' were still sound. Russia had lots of natural resources and, thanks to weak labour laws, unlimited slave labour. You just had to ignore the massive theft of state resources, rampant tax evasion, criminalisation of business and all-pervading corruption.

Russians in the provinces couldn't afford to ignore them. For the first time in years unemployed and unpaid workers began staging mass protests around the country. In May coal miners began blockading railway lines in the Arctic and Caucasus. Miners in the Siberian province of Kemerevo followed suit, blocking the Trans-Siberian railway. Pensioners, teachers and doctors joined them on the tracks. Scientists in Vladivostok closed off roads leading into the city to protest about wage arrears. On 12 June the unrest came to the capital. About 150 angry coal miners from Vorkuta arrived by train after a 40-hour trip. Linking arms and demanding Yeltsin's resignation, they marched on the government headquarters, the White House, then set up camp on the lawn beside it.

The next day we went to film them settling in. Dozens of tents stood beside the seat of government. Miners sat on the forecourt in the glaring summer sun, banging their helmets on the concrete. One of them declared that the capital could no longer ignore the troubles of the regions. He looked oddly familiar. Then it clicked. He was Vladimir, the hunger-striking miner I had met in Vorkuta and the only owner of a toy koala in the Russian Arctic.

'So, my friends from Australia,' he said. 'You are following me across Russia!'

Things had not been going well for Vladimir and his friends since we left. Some of the miners were so desperate for money they had taken the mine manager hostage, only releasing him when he agreed to pay their back wages.

'Everything is very bad,' he sighed. 'We are on the *Titanic.*'

He perked up when he saw the Communist leader, Gennady Zyuganov, arrive to express his solidarity with the workers. 'Your socialism is shit,' he shouted.

The party continued for those who could afford it. While the protesters slept in tents, restaurants a few hundred metres away in the upmarket Arbat Street served $500 meals to *biznesmen* and their model girlfriends, their bodyguards parked illegally in black Mercedes-Benz jeeps on the footpath outside. Nearby casinos like the Golden Palace charged $100 to walk through the door, while Western expatriates sipped on $10 pints of Guinness in fake Irish pubs. The bubble of excess stretched even tighter.

The Reserve Bank, following the wave of currency collapses that had swept through South-East Asia months earlier, was spending billions of dollars to keep the rouble artificially high at 6.3 to the US dollar. Now the government's reserves were running out.

On 14 August, as Yeltsin went on holidays, he ruled out any devaluation. 'No, there won't be, that's loud and clear,' he promised. 'Everything is going the way it ought to.'

The devaluation started three days later. The Reserve Bank announced it would 'widen the exchange corridor' up to 9.5. That meant the rouble would be allowed to lose a third of its value. At the same time the government announced a three-month freeze on foreign debt repayments. In other words, it was broke. The rouble began slipping into freefall.

The first sign I saw of it was at a money exchange across the road. Like all Moscow's exchanges, it advertised its rate on large cards hung above the kiosk. As I walked to the office in the morning, a man with a ladder was taking down the 6 from 6.3 and replacing it with a 7. Further up the road, another street trader was doing the same thing, except that he stuck up an 8. Within a few days, the rouble was trading at 10 to the dollar. The city went into panic.

Everybody wanted to get rid of their roubles before they were worthless. Overnight there was a run on the banks as Muscovites queued to withdraw their savings. As soon as they got them out, they headed straight to a money exchange to buy dollars. Within days, banks were rationing dollars or closing their doors.

Shop shelves were swept clean. Anyone with spare cash bought everything they could, knowing prices were about to skyrocket. Because local production had collapsed, Moscow was heavily reliant on imports, which traders had to buy with hard currency. As the rouble continued falling, the suppliers stopped selling. Soon people were queuing outside stores for food, as they had in the bad old days of perestroika. I was working so hard reporting the crisis that I had no time to stand in a queue. I soon ran out of toilet paper and food. The only place I could eat at was a nearby McDonald's, which rallied heroically to serve junk food to the starving masses. Day after day I lived on *Beeg Meki*, *Chikinbergeri* and *Frees*.

Boris Yeltsin's reaction to the mounting financial crisis was to sack the government again — thereby plunging the country into a political chaos. On 23 August he dismissed the new prime minister, Sergei Kiriyenko, and his cabinet, announcing the reappointment of the recently sacked prime minister, Viktor Chernomyrdin. At first it seemed as if Yeltsin was simply confused and had mixed the names up. But he wasn't skipping his medications — he was serious. In a nationwide address, he said that only Chernomyrdin had the experience and honesty to restore economic stability — a bold statement considering that Chernomyrdin was a crook who had been sacked for ruining the economy.

The public reaction was disbelief followed by shock. The Communists' response was jubilation. The last real power of the Duma was to approve or reject the appointment of a new prime minister. And the Communist Party, still the dominant force in the lower house of parliament, made it clear it would not accept Chernomyrdin. Russia was facing its biggest crisis since the 1993 coup and there was no sign of when it might even have a functioning government. The rouble kept tumbling, now thirteen to the dollar.

As the political order collapsed, President Clinton arrived for a prearranged summit with an increasingly unstable Boris Yeltsin. It was excruciatingly bad timing but Yeltsin managed to make it even worse. At the photo call, he couldn't work out which way he was supposed to face and turned his back to the cameras. Clinton gently turned him around the right way. The next day at a joint press conference, Yeltsin started in good form until he was asked if he'd sack parliament if it didn't approve Chernomyrdin. Yeltsin paused. And continued to pause. And went on pausing. The clock ticked as he sat open-mouthed, saying nothing, with Clinton wincing in embarrassment beside him. Finally, after more than a minute, Yeltsin said, '*Vsyo!*' (That's all).

The Novi Russki found it hard to believe the party of the century was ending. Soon after devaluation began, *Vogue* magazine launched its Russian edition with a soiree for 4000. It was held in Petrovsky Passazh, a restored Tsarist-era shopping arcade behind the Bolshoi Theatre. Twice as many people turned up as the organisers expected, the crowd spilling into the designer jewellery and fashion stores to escape the crush. The cream of Moscow's elite were there — *biznesmen*, high-class hookers and corrupt politicians. Around them swirled the beautiful people — pop stars, models, designers and media celebrities.

Earlier that day, the rouble had fallen 22 per cent.

'It's like a feast in a time of plague,' a pop starlet told me, using a phrase from the Pushkin poem 'Little Tragedies'. I was just as happy to be there, eating my first finger food in days that didn't have processed cheese, pickles and sauce on a sesame-seed bun.

Vogue appeared to have brought in a job lot of models to add glamour. We started filming a young couple who turned out to be ex-models. Vlad was setting up a designer clothing store and his wife, Natalia, was working as the receptionist at Moscow's most famous modelling agency, Red Stars. They were unconcerned by the crisis sweeping the country. 'Nobody said life was going to be easy,' Vlad commented, all cheekbones, suaveness and charm. 'Anyway, there's always Australia. We'll come to visit you if we have to. But everything will be fine.'

I caught up with Vlad and Natalia a week later. Their designer shop was on hold. Natalia looked likely to lose her job. Ninety-five per cent of Red Stars' business had evaporated. 'Versace, Cerutti, Dior cancelled their shows, the jobs just disappeared,' Natalia said. 'People are afraid of the crisis. They don't want to come here.'

'The mood is horrible,' Vlad said. 'Everyone's losing their jobs or their contracts, people are escaping abroad if they can. Everybody who kept their money in securities or banks lost everything in one hour. A friend of mine who had $800,000 lost everything but a thousand dollars he kept in cash.'

While the banks were collapsing, claiming they'd been wiped out, new banks, strangely, were opening just as fast. The über-rich bank owners were transferring all the assets to the new banks, leaving customers to try to sue the bankrupt shells left behind. Tens of thousands of Muscovites lost everything. The new middle class was almost done for.

The Communists' mad *babushki* and ageing trolleybus drivers wheezed back into life, dusting off their red flags and staking out the Duma. The deputies voted to reject Chernomyrdin as prime minister.

In the midst of all this chaos, Kim Traill, the woman who had stayed in my apartment and had such an effect on me, arrived back in Moscow to do some more filming. I invited her to stay with me again. She agreed to come for a few nights but didn't reciprocate my interest in her. I tried to hide my disappointment when she insisted on sleeping on the lounge-room floor.

Meanwhile, I was facing my own Russian crisis — with my teeth. A month-long diet of McDonald's appeared to be taking its toll. I was suffering shooting pains in the sides of my mouth and downing painkillers to keep going. Finally I went to a dentist, who informed me I had to have my wisdom teeth taken out immediately. Five hours later I was lying at home, heavily drugged but still in agony, when the dentist rang. 'There's nothing to worry about,' he said reassuringly. 'But you've probably noticed we accidentally cut some of your tongue out.' I hadn't, but it was good to know. 'We also accidentally drilled into the bone,' he continued, 'so it might be a bit painful. Please come back again any time if you have a problem.'

The problem of the Duma also seemed unresolvable. Yeltsin kept refusing to back down on his nomination of Chernomyrdin and threatened to dissolve parliament and call new elections. That would leave Russia with neither a parliament nor a prime minister and cabinet during an economic meltdown.

One day, as we were filming at the Duma, the protesting coal miners from Vorkuta led by Vladimir stormed the building. They bashed the stairs with their helmets as Vladimir made a dramatic call for the Duma to fight Yeltsin.

'We don't want this government of killers, we don't want this government of thieves!' he shouted. 'We want the Duma to protect the people. And if they defend the people, the miners will defend the Duma.'

For a moment, it really looked like the start of a new revolution. But in the end, as usually happened in Russia, it all fizzled out. Catastrophe was averted by last-minute compromise. Yeltsin withdrew his nomination of Chernomyrdin. The Communists, fearing an election that could see them lose their offices, cars and subsidised apartments, approved an alternative candidate, Yeltsin's foreign minister, Yevgeny Primakov, as prime minister. Primakov had been a Middle Eastern correspondent for the Soviet news agency, Tass, meaning that he was a former spy. He'd later headed the foreign intelligence service, and enjoyed strong Communist support. This didn't do much to reassure investors, but at a stroke the political crisis was over.

My dental crisis was worsening, however. I was taking so many painkillers I was dispensing with water and just chewing them down. Later, I steeled myself to go with Kim to a Shostakovich concert at the Conservatorium — a stirring symphony about the siege of Leningrad. Just as the Nazis attacked, the tooth pain invaded my chest. I staggered outside in agony and chewed some more painkillers. But it became worse than anything I had ever known. I was suddenly afraid of what could be happening. 'Oh Jesus,' I thought, 'I'm having a heart attack.'

Kim found me groaning in the foyer. I whispered that we had to get to the medical centre. She dragged me outside and tried to flag down drivers, telling them it was a medical emergency. The first three wouldn't take a sick person and the fourth said it was out of his way. Finally, a van driver agreed to take us through the grid-locked traffic.

The people at the European Medical Centre couldn't work out what was wrong but did several expensive tests and kept me in overnight for observation. The diagnosis was: 'Severe pain. Recommend further tests.' I drank some water and after a while the pain went away. The bill was more than $2000.

I was slightly cheered by how worried Kim had seemed when it looked as though I might die. We were friends, of course, and that was still as far as she wanted things to go. She had by now moved out to house-sit for a friend.

The other crisis — Russia's economic collapse — continued. A month after devaluation began, the rouble was trading at 24 to the dollar. Western firms were shedding staff or pulling out; an estimated

100,000 had been sacked in Moscow alone. Scott Blacklin, president of the US Chamber of Commerce in Russia, put it like this: 'The business community feels like it was hit by a neutron bomb, and we've all been irradiated. The rest of us will recover, but we'll have to lay around and throw up for a while.'

I went out to the countryside to visit the first family I'd become acquainted with in Russia. Back in 1996, Boris and Masha and their two daughters had been full of optimism. Boris was a former scientist who had joined the new middle class ten years earlier by getting a job as a driver for a foreign company. Now they were hoarding food in case there was a winter famine. I found them pickling cucumbers and burning the ends of onion stalks to preserve them. The cellar was crammed with cases of potatoes, buckwheat, tomatoes, beetroot and berries.

'Many people are now talking about famine, and we have a big family,' Boris said. 'I've decided we need to stock up on the basic minimum to get us through if there's no food in the shops. It's not a matter of prices going up. I'm scared food may disappear altogether.'

It never came to that in Moscow, where there would always be enough dirty money sloshing around for some of it to trickle out to the masses. Once the panic died down, the rouble went from freefall into slow decline. Imported food eventually came back to the stores, Novi Russki regrouped with money from their Swiss bank accounts, the government continued to plod on in a dependably incompetent way, and something approaching normality returned to the city. But there was a sense that things would never be quite the same again.

Kim was busy shooting a story about a rescue service so I decided to go back to Australia for a holiday and to check out my suspected heart attack. It seemed a cheaper option than spending another day at the medical centre in Moscow. In Sydney, I talked through the chain of events with a specialist who listened in silence. After I'd finished he said, 'And you were taking painkillers without water?'

'Yes, a dozen or so.'

The doctor stared at me for a moment, sighed, then explained that if people take too many pills without water they can lodge in the oesophagus and produce a haemorrhage, causing excruciating pain. In future, he said, I should read the instructions on the packet.

I felt strangely disappointed. I hadn't had a dramatic heart attack. I had just been a dork. My crisis was over.

Chapter 15
Moscow, December 1998

Party Central

I returned to Moscow just before Christmas, a time when Russians traditionally shake their lethargy to do what they can still do better than any other nation — drink. The binge begins on the Western Christmas Eve and goes on until the Orthodox New Year, 14 January.

I was expecting the city to have a pall of gloom as oppressive as the weather. But with New Year approaching, the mood seemed to have turned around. People were celebrating with a fierce determination despite the economic crisis, or perhaps because of it.

Some of the cheer was government directed. Moscow Mayor Yuri Luzhkov had ordered every store to put up Christmas and New Year decorations at their own expense or face hefty fines. While most of the population had to choose between buying presents and eating, some were still shopping as though money flowed like water. The Novi Russki had stripped some more assets and regrouped for another consumer orgy.

The Expocenter shopping mall on the banks of the Moscow River was offering traditional Novi Russki gifts, such as plastic Christmas trees for $695, and $6900 fur coats. The corridors weren't packed but there were still plenty of customers.

The manager, a Swiss man with a natty tie and handlebar moustache, was relieved. The crisis hadn't stopped the Christmas spirit of giving. The stores had merely had to lower the prices from astronomical to absurd. 'They do not buy any more for twenty-five thousand dollars,' he explained. 'They buy them for six or seven thousand dollars. This time they buy more specific goods and even more quality and less mess.'

Two platinum-blonde women walked past wearing the classic uniforms of Novi Russki girlfriends — imported tight black boots, imported tight black pants, imported tight black tops and bright pink lipstick. They were laden with shopping bags. I asked one of them what presents she'd bought.

'I bought a really nice $2000 dress,' she pouted. 'It's a present for me.'

'But there's a crisis,' I said. 'How can you spend $2000?'

'Because I've got my boyfriend,' she purred.

'Yeah? What does your boyfriend do?'

'I think it doesn't matter,' she snapped. 'He's a *biznesman.*' She walked off to buy herself more Christmas gifts.

Kim had now moved into an apartment down the road from mine but we continued to see each other most nights 'as friends'. A Russian television presenter I knew kept asking her out and I kept insisting he was a notorious sleaze and she should have nothing to do with him. For now she seemed content to hang around with me. Fortunately there was some event on almost every night. The mere masses were partying as hard as the fallen elite were.

The new bureau cameraman, David Martin, had just arrived and wanted to see 'the real Moscow'. We took him to the Hungry Duck. It had lost none of its unique style and class. After queuing in a line of men 100 deep we were let in just as the male strip show was ending. Hundreds of women had been drinking free alcohol for three hours. David watched the ensuing orgy in slack-jawed disbelief. Moscow wasn't the grey, crisis-ridden place of food queues he'd been expecting. It was ancient Rome.

We kicked on to Trety Put, a small club in a former *kommunalka* (communal apartment) popular with impoverished artists and students. You had to know exactly where it was to find it. The building wasn't numbered, the place wasn't signposted and there was no indication of which apartment door to knock on. But tonight you could hear it from the street. I opened the door and it was more crowded than I'd ever seen it.

In the first room, hundreds were dancing in a miasma of heat and sweat that extinguished the −10°C draughts blowing through the cracked windows. In the next room, drugged-out artists were playing tapes of avant-garde music at full volume, randomly bashing cymbals, drums and triangles in accompaniment. In another room, people were arguing about art and sex, shouting above the din. Young women in bizarre retro space-age clothing promenaded through it all in what was apparently an organised fashion show.

The manager, Boris Raskolnikov, was surprised when I asked him how so many people could be out spending money when they had so little to spend. 'Don't you know the world's ending?' he asked.

I thought he was joking but he wasn't.

'The world is ending when the second millennium finishes next year. Everybody knows that. You *really* didn't know that?'

Pharmaceuticals appeared to have fuelled his conviction but there was definitely an end-of-everything feeling. Everyone was spending their last roubles on going out and having fun rather than staying home and wasting their roubles on, say, food.

It was now two in the morning and the place was getting even more manic. I asked a petite red-haired girl named Sveta why everyone was so happy. 'If we don't have fun it'll be hard to survive the crisis,' she said. 'We'll cry, suffer, sleep, stay at home and watch TV. But now we go to clubs and it's not so bad.'

The following night we went to a press conference in a strip club. Vladimir Zhirinovsky, the politician who had taken me on the trip to nowhere a year earlier, had hired the notorious Dolls 'gentlemen's club' to launch his latest book. It had nothing to do with politics. As with everything the self-promoting demagogue did, it was designed solely to get publicity and money. His book was called: *The A–Z of Sex.*

With surgically enhanced strippers dancing around a pole to the tune of 'Girls, Girls, Girls' to introduce him, Zhirinovsky came on stage, flanked by a woman in a leopard-skin bikini doing extraordinary things with a python. He began offering tips from his book. Young men, he said, should store their semen in jars and give it to their girlfriends as facial treatment. The crisis hadn't hurt him. The man was still one of the most powerful politicians in Russia. It had just made the public more susceptible to his cheap entertainment.

The next night Kim and I went to a classical concert. It was a performance of the Mozart Requiem held in the Pushkin Art Gallery, conducted by a famous viola player, Yuri Bashmet. Moscow's extraordinarily rich classical music scene also seemed unaffected by the crisis. Musicians were paid such low wages anyway — they were used to living hand-to-mouth. The only drawback with the concert was that we had to stand, despite having tickets to the best seats in the house. Scalpers had sold the seats several times over and people were already sitting in them. The Moscow spirit of entrepreneurship was alive and well.

The corrupt traffic police, the Gaishniki, had also retained the commitment to private enterprise that was making Russia great. On New Year's Eve I picked up some friends at Leningradsky railway station. As we drove home, the traffic police pulled us over. I had done absolutely nothing wrong. I hadn't drunk a thing. I had all my documents and the car was in perfect working order.

'How much?' I asked.

'Ten dollars,' the fat Gaishnik replied.

I thought of arguing and threatening to report him but it was New Year's Eve and I was in a hurry. 'OK, I'll give you 300 roubles,' I said.

The Gaishnik was aghast. 'You don't have dollars?'

One thing the crisis *had* changed — nobody wanted bribes in roubles.

There was a New Year's Eve party at my friend Eve Conant's new home. After years of bumming around doing lowly jobs for lofty networks, Voice of America had just hired her as its youngest ever correspondent. It gave her a huge pay rise plus a monstrous apartment. Her expatriate and Russian friends arrived to trash it.

I stayed far too long, drank for too much and felt queasy when I left with Kim to go to a different party. My last memory was lying in the snow outside, looking up at two policemen looming over me.

Another year was over. Moscow was still insane. And I was home.

Kim had by now decided to stay in Moscow and found herself a miniscule one-room flat to rent. I offered to help her move from the flat she had been minding and take her shopping to get some basics for the new place, which was completely empty. Just as we had loaded everything into the car, a friend called to invite us to a party that night. 'Let's just dump everything at my place and I'll take you there tomorrow,' I suggested.

To my surprise she agreed.

She never did move to her new flat. Perhaps it was fear of cockroaches and shopping for cutlery. But suddenly we were both happy to be together. And at last she stopped cluttering up the lounge-room floor.

We were soon both hit with a new health scare. It began with a mysteriously bad cough and progressed to a hacking bark that made it impossible to finish a sentence. I had vowed never to return to the overpriced expatriate medical centres in Moscow, but in the end we decided to go to the American Medical Centre, which boasted a new doctor from Kansas. 'A cough,' he said. 'I see. And you're from Australia? Are there any endemic diseases in Australia?'

Kim thought for a minute. 'Well, there's dengue fever,' she said.

'Hmm, maybe we should get you tested?'

We assured him there was no way we could have dengue fever but he put us through a series of tests 'just to be on the safe side'. One hour, two chest X-rays, two blood tests and two Mantoux TB tests later, came the written diagnosis.

'Cough.'

The bill was $1250.

Chapter 16
Vladivostok, March 1999

Saving Mashka

Even after three years of travelling in the region, it was difficult to comprehend what a tiny dot Moscow was in the vastness of Russia. In early spring, I flew to the Pacific port of Vladivostok with my cameraman, David, and Slava the office translator. It was a ten-hour flight due east, crossing nine time zones, and we were still in Russia — with jet lag.

Vladivostok had been a closed city until 1991, restricted even to other Russians. It was the headquarters of the mighty Soviet Pacific fleet and foreigners were not permitted to spy on its strategic might. At least that was the official reason. Looking at the rusting, decrepit fleet in the harbour it seemed more likely that they just hadn't wanted the world to know how bad things were.

We had come here to do some stories about economic collapse in the provinces. But I also wanted to show a rare good-news story by revisiting the most extraordinary Russian I'd ever met. Viktor Yudin was a zoology professor from Vladivostok University who was single-handedly rearing four ferocious tigers. They lived in a ten-hectare enclosure belonging to a now penniless biological institute. When state funding ceased, Viktor took it on himself to keep the tigers alive. He moved into a shack behind the enclosure in order to feed and guard them, as well as continuing to study them. Every day he drove round to collective farms in a barely functioning truck to scrounge any leftover meat. At night he slept with a rifle in order to protect the tigers from poachers. They were Amurski, known in the West as Siberian tigers, and they were close to extinction.

'The tiger is like a president of animals,' Viktor told me when I last visited him in 1997. 'He governs not by decree but by his actions, by his mere presence. The loss of the tiger would be a catastrophe.'

They were magnificent animals. When he called their names, they strode up through the heavily wooded enclosure and roared until he threw them chunks of meat to devour. It was not like watching animals dozing in a zoo. There was a grace and savagery to Viktor's Amurski that made them seem as though they still lived in the wild. After our first story went to air, hundreds of viewers rang wanting to donate money. A Sydney woman, Hazel Barker, set up a Save Viktor's Tigers fund and collected almost $9000 to send him. Around Russia's Pacific rustbelt, that buys a lot of meat. Two years later, I thought it would be a good time to find out how Viktor was going.

It was a scratchy phone line when Slava called Viktor from Moscow to organise our visit, but between the static and the crackles he picked up the words 'sure, come over', 'bought truck' and 'Moscow circus'. Viktor was clearly still alive, if unable to buy a decent phone. After a few more calls, Slava filled in the gaps and learned that things hadn't being going well for Viktor or his tigers.

He had used the money we raised to buy a replacement truck for collecting meat from nearby farms, which helped feed the animals for a while. However, one of the tigers had given birth to a pair of cubs. By then it was getting too much even for Viktor. He tried to find a zoo to take the cubs, without success. In desperation, he gave three of his tigers to the Moscow circus. A Vladivostok *biznesman* who saw his plight offered to help, taking the second cub, Mashka. Viktor still had two tigers he was managing to keep alive and we were welcome to come and see them.

It wasn't quite the happy ending I had anticipated. We flew to Vladivostok anyway, and before heading up to Viktor's village, which was a few hours' drive north of the city, we planned to see the cub, Mashka. Slava rang the *biznesman* who was looking after her. That's when we heard the second bit of bad news.

'He says the tiger is about to have an operation,' Slava said. 'It's dying.'

We raced down to the veterinary hospital and found the *biznesman*, Pavel Samolyanov, pacing nervously outside, chain-smoking and shouting into his mobile phone. His chauffeur kept his black four-wheel-drive Land Rover running, the tinted windows rolled tightly shut. Another man with a beanie pulled over his ears stamped his feet in the snow by the car. In his early thirties and wearing a black Armani leather jacket, Pavel didn't look like a typical soft-hearted animal lover.

'She's inside,' Pavel said to us. 'I'm just getting a surgeon.'

At the bottom of the stairs, in a dingy basement clinic, the cub lay growling on an operating table. Mashka was only ten months old but already had enormous paws that could playfully scratch open a man's belly. She was a perfect specimen of a Siberian tiger cub. Or had been. She now had serious internal injuries. She was stretched out on the table, full of drips, with her belly shaved. The veterinarian stood beside her looking worried. Not only was Mashka about twenty times bigger than the average house cat, but her owner was not a man to displease.

Pavel came in looking flushed and anxious. 'The police did this,' he said angrily. 'They took her away and didn't tell me why. I collected her that night and she's been sick ever since.'

It seemed the local police had been suspicious as to why he had a tiger cub. While Pavel was out, they made his caretaker open the cage and brought her down to the station while they cleared the matter up. Soon after, the police called their children in to play with the cub in the cell. Thinking she must be hungry, they fed her sweets and pies. At some point, she swallowed a rag that lodged in her stomach, rupturing her intestines.

'I brought her here and got some vets, but as usual they just charged money and didn't do the job properly,' Pavel continued. The present vet was looking even more nervous. 'Some friends who know better examined her and said she needed an urgent operation.'

Moments later a doctor came rushing in to perform the operation. He wasn't an animal doctor. He was chief surgeon at one of

Vladivostok's hospitals. Pavel had demanded the best surgeon in town and it seemed to be a demand that couldn't be refused. The surgeon had come in such a hurry that he was still wearing his hospital gown. Slava whispered later that he had left a human patient on the operating table.

He looked as nervous as the vet did as he prepared for surgery. By now, Pavel's 'associates' had come to lend a hand, wearing matching leather jackets and dark sunglasses. It was starting to resemble a scene from *National Geographic* directed by Quentin Tarantino (the real one).

I wondered how pure Pavel's motives were. Siberian tigers are worth a fortune to poachers, who sell their bones to the Chinese to make into aphrodisiacs. A fully grown tiger would obviously be worth much more than a prematurely deceased cub. But Pavel seemed genuinely upset by Mashka's condition. She continued to growl in pain as the medical team prepared for surgery.

'Maybe you should, you know, give her some medicine or something,' he told the surgeon.

'No, hold on now, we have to operate,' the surgeon replied. 'We have to put all the intestines back again.' We left them to it.

Hours later, Mashka lay moaning groggily from the anaesthetic. Pavel fondled her ears and made Mohawks with the fur on her head. 'I think she's OK,' he said, almost in tears. 'She's a fighter.' His associates wrapped her in a blanket and carried her out to the Land Rover.

It seemed that Mashka was one lucky tiger cub. She had one of the few protectors in Vladivostok with the muscle to get what she needed. I just couldn't help wondering what had happened to the human patient the surgeon had left mid-operation.

We drove up to Viktor's town of Spassk, arriving late in the evening. There were no rich benefactors here. I remembered it from two years before as a town with nothing to recommend it. It appeared to have gone downhill. The only hotel had no heating and little power. A rotund *babushka* sat in the cold, dark foyer with a small gas lamp. There were no other guests in the hotel but she insisted we take rooms on the fourth floor. Not surprisingly, there was no lift. We hauled our luggage up by torchlight to our dismal rooms with sticky carpet and stained sheets. I turned on the tap. There was not even a dribble.

I went downstairs to buy some bottled water from the *babushka*. She eyed me suspiciously. 'We have Coca Cola, Fanta and Sprite,' she said.

'No, I want plain water,' I explained. 'To brush my teeth.'

She gave a half sneer, revealing several stainless-steel teeth and a few gaps. 'Well, we don't have any. Fanta is 20 roubles.' I bought a bottle and retired to my freezing room.

Viktor remembered us fondly. He showed us the truck which he had purchased with the money raised by ABC viewers. It had a large winch on the back — big enough, he said, to lift a whole cow carcass. Now he could scour the local area for animals to feed his tigers and be able to get them back on his own. I asked him to turn it on for the camera. The engine wheezed and died. 'It's been having some problems,' Viktor said apologetically.

We went out to the yard to see his tigers, Nyurka and Koucher. There were large snow-covered mounds by the enclosure. I noticed some birdlike feet sticking out of the top of one. Viktor grabbed them and held up a dead hen. 'These were given to us for the tigers,' he said cheerily. Sure enough, a pile of scrawny, frozen chickens was buried under the snow. Further on some sheep's hooves pointed to the sky. A number of small deer-like animals with long fangs lay by the shed. The site was one giant meat freezer.

Nyurka and Koucher were playing in the snow behind a high wire fence. They looked well. So did a whole new menagerie of animals beside the enclosure. Viktor's yard had become a dumping ground for every lost or abandoned animal in the district. He had cages full of foxes, wolves, dogs and bear cubs. Once word got out that he'd been sent some money, he also had every drunk in town turning up asking for a handout. As determined as Viktor was, it was clear that he was not coping well. He told us environmental groups hadn't given him any help for more than a year.

'There are so many nature activists now that you could feed them to the tigers without any harm,' he said. 'That was a joke,' he added. 'But many people come here promising to help and just take pictures of the tigers, or film them, and that's it. They forget about help straight away.'

We told him about Mashka's injuries and the operation and he went silent. He'd had no idea she was sick. 'When you told me about Mashka I felt like it was nightmare,' he said later. 'I feel so sorry for her. I miss them all.'

We drove back to Vladivostok that night. On the flight home, I scripted a story I hoped would bring Viktor more donations. He was a powerful if temporary antidote for the cynicism I was feeling in Moscow. For all the hardships that Russia was enduring, there were still passionate people doing extraordinary things against the odds. Unfortunately, their efforts rarely had a happy ending. Not long after we left, Mashka fell ill again and died.

Cleansing

While poachers were stalking tigers in Russia, paramilitaries were hunting down humans in Kosovo. Things hadn't been going well in the province since I'd been there with Tim in September 1997. The tensions between the large Albanian community and the small Serb community had escalated into full-scale war. Kosovo was still a province of Serbia, the larger republic (along with Montenegro), in what was left of Yugoslavia. But ethnic Albanian paramilitaries had seized large swathes of it by force.

The paramilitaries — from the self-styled KLA (Kosovo Liberation Army) — wanted independence from Serbia and thought the best way of getting it was to provoke a war that would lead to outside intervention. Serbia was determined to retain Kosovo and had flooded the province with Yugoslav soldiers, Serbian police and Serb paramilitaries. It was a particularly nasty war in which civilians were being targeted on both sides, but the main victims were Albanians. Now in 1999, NATO was bombing Serbia to make its troops and paramilitaries behave.

I had been trying to get back to Kosovo since the first fighting began more than a year before. Even though it was a place that nobody except journalists would want to go to, the Yugoslav embassy in Moscow handed out visas as sparingly and imperiously as if they were backstage passes to a Madonna concert. At the embassy, two diplomats and their resident spook grilled me about what I wanted to report in Kosovo. They seemed unconvinced by my hints that I would just be covering KLA 'terrorist attacks' on Serb civilians.

But I soon blew any chance of getting a visa by daring to ask a question of Slobodan Milosevic. In the middle of 1998 the Yugoslav dictator came to Moscow for talks on the Kosovo crisis with a sympathetic Russian Government. Happy for once to be treated as a statesman rather than an international pariah, Milosevic agreed to hold his first press conference in years.

We crammed into a Foreign Ministry briefing room moments before Milosevic walked in. Looking relaxed, he made a short speech and was supposed to take two polite questions from Yugoslav and Russian journalists before departing. But I couldn't resist. 'There have been allegations made of war crimes committed by Serbian security forces in Kosovo,' I interjected from the back of the room, 'including ethnic cleansing and deliberate murder of unarmed civilians. How comfortable are you with the conduct of your security forces?'

A murmur went through the room and his aides bristled. Milosevic looked unfazed and answered in English. 'Oh, there was no at all kind of ethnic cleansing,' he said. 'All actions of Serbian police were only against terrorists groups, not against civilians.' It was his only public comment on war crimes allegations in the lead-up to the NATO bombing, and he ended with a smile, saying, 'Next time we'll see you in Belgrade. You're all invited.'

But I could tell from the glares of his embassy officials that I had just lost any hope of going to Yugoslavia.

When NATO started bombing on 24 March 1999 I was stuck in Moscow wondering how to cover a war I couldn't get to. Tim had managed to slip into Belgrade the day before with the Brussels correspondent, Greg Wilesmith. Since program producers were screaming for war stories from as close to the fighting as possible, I decided to head for Kosovo's southern neighbour, Macedonia, and wait for the inevitable humanitarian crisis.

Macedonia had not been in the news much since it peacefully split from Yugoslavia in 1991. When it was, the reason was usually for what the country was called, rather than for what it did. In one of those disputes that make perfect sense in the Balkans but seem utterly bewildering outside, Greece was continually objecting to Macedonia calling itself Macedonia. Macedonia had long been a province of Yugoslavia called Macedonia, until Yugoslavia disintegrated. Now it was an independent country and continued to call itself Macedonia. This, Greece believed, was an act of provocation. The reason was that a Greek province which borders Macedonia is also called Macedonia. Greece regards this as the true Macedonia and the other Macedonia as a usurper of its name. Greece insistently demanded that the country Macedonia be referred to as The Former Yugoslav Republic of Macedonia. Only the Greek province of Macedonia could be called Macedonia. There had even been mutterings of war.

This was only relevant to me because I had to go via (Greek) Macedonia to get to (The Former Yugoslav Republic of) Macedonia. The day after the NATO air strikes began, (The Former Yugoslav Republic of) Macedonia closed the airport in its capital, Skopje. So I flew to Thessaloniki in (Greek) Macedonia with a freelance cameraman, Glenn Coddington, and caught a taxi to the border of (The Former Yugoslav Republic of) Macedonia — being sure to say we were going to Skopje, rather than Macedonia, to avoid giving offence. The (Greek) Macedonian taxi couldn't cross the border into (The Former Yugoslav Republic of) Macedonia, so we hauled our gear by hand across the 500-metre no-man's-land and caught another taxi to Skopje.

Skopje was the headquarters for NATO's ground forces but you had to look hard to find any. The public mood was so hostile that NATO had ordered its soldiers to stay in their camps. About a third of the population were ethnic Albanians, who supported their brethren across the border in Kosovo. However, most Macedonians were Slavs or ethnic Serbs who feared the rise of a Greater Albania and were happy to see their Serb brothers crushing Albanian separatists. The previous night a Macedonian mob had attacked and burned the US embassy in retaliation for NATO bombing.

I wasn't the only person who'd failed to get a Yugoslav visa for Serbia. Foreign media were pouring into Skopje faster than Albanian refugees, and heading straight for the border, just a half-hour drive north of the city at a village called Blace (pronounced Bluht-say).

Before Yugoslavia fell apart, the border had been just an administrative line on a map. Now it was a fortified frontier between two separate states. Macedonian soldiers lined the roads approaching it. We could see the Macedonian border guards but the Serbs were just out of sight. Smoke was still rising from the village on the Kosovo side after a fierce battle between Serbian forces and KLA guerillas, which ended with the guerillas retreating into the hills.

The bombing itself hadn't triggered a mass exodus. The few Albanians coming across the border said they were fleeing from Serb security forces. A woman clutching her baby told me that Serb paramilitaries had forced her from her home and then burnt it to the ground. She had fled to save her child's life. Another group of men said police had come through the village advising them to leave in two hours or they could not guarantee their safety. The police added a parting joke that would be recounted by refugee after refugee: 'You wanted NATO to come to help you, now you can go to NATO for help.'

It was disturbing but not the disaster that picture-hungry networks were hoping for. Frustrated producers tried to pounce on refugees first to get agreement for exclusive profiles, particularly if they were distressed-looking families with cute young children. Fierce arguments broke out between rival crews.

'Back off, this one's ours!'

'Fuck you, asshole, I can shoot what I want.'

'OK, one shot but no interviews.'

However, Milosevic was about to give them more than they could have imagined. What none of us realised was that an entire nation was being expelled.

It began on the morning of 30 March, six days after the bombing began. Hundreds came across the border at first light. By late morning it was thousands. All were ethnic Albanians and all of them told the same story: Serbs wearing black ski masks had come to their homes and ordered them to leave or be killed. They also told us that even more people were waiting on the other side to cross. Many claimed that the Serb border guards were taking people's money and valuables before letting them through, and then tearing up their identity papers. It was impossible to verify what they said because the Yugoslav side of the border was out of view, but the stories were too frequent and too similar to be dismissed.

Refugees kept pouring through as fast as the Macedonian guards could process them. By the end of the day we could see the edge of a giant crowd on the other side of the border. It was now obvious that the Albanian population was being systematically expelled. Until now Macedonia had allowed the refugees to continue on to Skopje and register with the police. But it wasn't willing or able to accept an exodus.

Two days later Macedonia closed the border. When the refugees passed the Yugoslav side, they were trapped in the no-man's-land between the two sides. As we looked on, Macedonian soldiers cordoned off a field next to the border and herded the refugees into it. The people had no choice but to sit on the ground with whatever they had managed to carry across. Everyone imagined it was just to process them. But hours passed and nobody was let out.

The field soon filled with thousands of Albanians. They sat on the ground bewildered, without shelter, water, toilets or food. Many were already suffering thirst from the hot April sun. The only way to relieve themselves was to squat in the open. A stench was already spreading across the field from people defecating. The edge of the crowd was only twenty metres away but we could do nothing to help them.

As night fell, it became clear that the open field was now a holding camp. And every hour, hundreds more people were being forced into it. Children cried and men shouted to be let out. Eventually everyone lay down on the dirt to sleep.

Worse was to come. A railway line ran beside the road through the border crossing. The next day passenger trains started arriving from Kosovo's main city, Pristina, pulling to a stop in the no-man's-land. Armed Yugoslav soldiers stood at the door of each tightly packed wagon as the Albanians were disgorged into the camp. Old people tumbled out along with teenagers, parents, babies and small children.

For the first and only time, the soldiers allowed media into the camp to talk to the refugees. Until now, most of the refugees we'd interviewed had been poor farmers. But these were from Pristina's educated middle class. Many spoke English. Even after a decade of discrimination, they were stunned by what they had just been through. Everyone said that paramilitaries had ordered them from their homes at gunpoint and marched them to the railway station.

What shocked me most was that one group reminded me of my older sister's family. The parents sat with their two daughters, aged four and six, staring into the distance, trying to comprehend the end of their world. It shouldn't make any difference, of course, if someone speaks English or reminds you of someone you know. It doesn't make their suffering any greater or any more important than the others'. But it makes it confrontingly real.

'They came with guns and tanks, for every suburb one tank,' the father, Faif, said. 'They entered the houses with guns, destroyed the documents. Then they marched us to the station. It's something terrible. Man cannot think this could happen to such a big number of people.'

The trains kept coming. Within two days more than 30,000 refugees were trapped in the holding camp. The UN refugee agency, UNHCR, predicted that up to 200,000 more Albanians were on the way. Aid agencies struggled to get in water, food and plastic sheeting for shelter. They were unprepared for this scale of crisis and the Macedonian authorities were uncooperative. By the second night refugees were dying. The next morning aid workers brought out the bodies of about a dozen elderly people and newborn babies for burial.

There was a surreal gulf between what was happening at the border and 30 minutes' drive away in Skopje. While people were succumbing to shock and exposure at the holding camp, the restaurants and nightclubs in the capital were in full swing. The local TV news showed little of the crisis, always qualifying the refugees as 'victims of US aggression fleeing NATO air strikes'. There was no mention of ethnic cleansing.

On 4 April ethnic Serbs and Macedonian Slavs held a huge rally in Skopje in support of Serbia in a plaza in the city centre. We arrived to hear thousands of people shouting 'Makedonia, Yugoslavia! Makedonia, Yugoslavia!' Speakers were cheered as they denounced NATO as fascists and war criminals. Western media weren't popular either. Aggressive young men came up to us repeatedly and asked threateningly if we were from CNN. They seemed only slightly mollified when we said we were from Australia.

We befriended a young Serb who seemed a little more Westerner friendly. Oliver Aristic was an amateur bodybuilder who claimed to have worked in Hollywood as a bodyguard for Tony Curtis and Jean-Claude Van Damme. 'I got bored so I came back,' he said with a Serbo-Californian accent. 'Skopje is a party town.' He was in his early twenties, from a rich family and spent most nights in bars and clubs with other rich young Slavs. He said the war hadn't stopped anyone going out but the clubs were playing less American music. 'Every one of my friends thinks America is doing a really bad thing with the bombing,' he said.

I met him for coffee with a Serb friend of his, Viktoria. She was slim and attractive and appeared to know it, preening as she sipped her espresso. Viktoria was studying at an exclusive American-run high school but had no sympathy for America attacking Serbia. 'I don't think Serbs are killing Albanians like they're showing on CNN,' she said.

Oliver nodded, saying the only massacres had been carried out by the KLA, who killed Albanians who refused to fight with them. 'They massacre them and after that the BBC comes and gets a picture of that and sends it to the world and says, "Hey, the Serbs did this."' He went on to describe how BBC journalists in Belgrade had been caught laying laser markers to help NATO bomb public buildings.

'You don't really believe that, do you?' I asked.

'Come on,' Oliver answered, laughing at what he saw as my naiveté. 'You don't know this?'

'Well, why do you think hundreds of thousands of Albanians are fleeing Kosovo?'

'NATO bombs!' Viktoria said at the same time as Oliver.

'So why aren't thousands of Serbs fleeing to Macedonia too?' I asked.

'Albanians are very simple people,' Oliver said. 'A lot of them, they hear a rumour that NATO is going to, like, bomb them and they run away. It's very sad.'

I drove back to the border where the number of people trapped in no-man's-land had now swelled to 45,000. Some plastic shelters had gone up but most people were sleeping in the dirt and mud. There were still no toilets and disease was spreading fast, particularly among babies and children. The Macedonian authorities refused to let anyone out. Refugees screamed at us to help them. All we could do was stand behind the cordon of soldiers and film the scene. It was distressing and dispiriting. Hundreds of journalists hovered around the holding camp like flies, filing reports that were achieving nothing.

The 'international community', if such a thing exists, seemed just as impotent. Every day, UNHCR held press conferences in Skopje appealing for the refugees to be released. Nothing happened. NATO made statements that it would target any soldiers trying to expel civilians. But its planes were flying too high to be effective and it refused to use helicopters in case one was shot down. This was the era when Western nations thought they could fight wars without suffering casualties.

I was starting to feel overwhelmed by the scale of the misery we saw each day. I was also completely exhausted, sleeping just a couple of hours a night to keep up with the story demands for news and current affairs. Glenn and I would film all day, edit until two or three in the morning, then head off to the feed point at seven to send our stories to Australia. Ten days into the assignment I rang Sydney to appeal for a night off. There were other reporters in Albania who could file and I desperately needed a break. A few minutes later, an angry television presenter rang back ordering me to send a story. He abused me for not being able to 'take the pressure'. For the first time, I felt the job and the life that came with it were not worth the trouble.

I continued filing. At least I'd chosen to come to a war. Millions of Albanians and Serbs were trapped in a conflict that was not of their making. Most of the Albanian refugees had nothing to do with the KLA. Every Serb I'd met in Belgrade detested Milosevic.

I thought of my friend Sanja, who'd taken part in the anti-government protests. After a dozen attempts to get a phone line to Belgrade, I rang her to see how she was coping with the nightly bombing raids. She was more angry than frightened. 'How can NATO do this to us?' she said. 'How can they bomb us? The West is so moral and righteous, it bombs us for what Milosevic does?'

Chapter 18
Kosovo, June 1999

Here We Come, Slobba

Serbian Customs officers turned up for work at the Blace border crossing on 12 June knowing it was going to be a bad day. For some three months they had supervised the final stage of Milosevic's ethnic cleansing and had harassed and robbed 200,000 Albanian refugees who passed their checkpoint. Today they stood watching NATO tanks and heavy artillery rumble past the duty-free store into Kosovo.

The peace deal imposed after 78 days of bombing effectively ended Serbia's control of the province and put the once impregnable border under NATO control. Now that the border was open, I couldn't help wandering up to the Customs officials and asking what they did in the war. Half a dozen officers and border guards were milling around outside, looking gloomy.

'Good morning,' I said, under the roar of a passing tank. 'I'm from Australian television. Does anyone speak English?' Two men nodded.

'Could I ask you why you stole from the refugees who came through here?'

'We did not take nothing,' one officer said indignantly.

'I've spoken to dozens of refugees,' I countered. 'They all said you stole money.'

The men denied it again, as a self-propelled gun trundled past. 'I was here all the time,' the officer said. 'I don't believe that anyone took money from anybody.'

'What about all the cars parked down there?' I asked, pointing at the hundreds of cars below the crossing.

'They had not any registration,' a guard said.

We drove on into Kosovo, weaving between the military convoys and stopping at gridlocks on the tight mountain passes. I was travelling with the bureau cameraman, David Martin, and with a 23-year-old woman called Nika, who was translating in return for a ride home. She was a middle-class Albanian, and seemed more interested in music and fashion than in politics or religion. She came from a town called Urosevac, which the Albanians called Ferizaj, 30 kilometres south of Pristina. Her family had fled to Macedonia a few days after the NATO bombing started.

'Men with black masks came to our house and told us we must go,' Nika said as we drove towards Pristina. 'I recognised one from his voice. He lived in our street. I grew up with him.'

Nika was excited about returning home but also anxious. Her father, Kodri, had raced back as soon as the border opened, to protect their house from looting. She had had no way to contact him to see if he was safe.

Our driver, a young Slav Macedonian named Marian, was even more worried. We chose him because he spoke some English and in the hope that we could use him rather than Nika to interpret for us with Serbs. I presumed most Serbs would be more comfortable speaking to a fellow Slav than to an Albanian. As he was a Macedonian, the KLA would, we hoped, not see him as an enemy. Marian was dreading the whole thing but he had a new baby and needed the money. He also had what was probably the coolest car in the Balkans — a 1967 wide-bodied Mercedes-Benz painted jet black to hide the rust. David immediately nicknamed it the Fear-and-Loathing-Mobile.

It was slow going across the mountains, stuck behind hundreds of NATO vehicles, all bearing the inscription 'KFOR' (Kosovo Force). We fell in with a group of Gurkha soldiers waiting at one of the traffic logjams — village boys from Nepal who saw it as the ultimate honour to fight for the British Army. One of them was playing Scottish ditties on the bagpipes, the music drifting down the Yugoslav mountainside.

Another was reading a copy of the British tabloid, *The Daily Star*, headlined: 'HERE WE COME, SLOBBA!'

It was a strange sort of day.

Some Albanians had already begun walking home, mostly single young men carrying the few possessions they had fled with. They strode past the idling tanks and armoured personnel carriers (APCs), but none asked for a lift. Nobody wanted to get ahead of the main body of NATO forces in case they ran into Serb security forces. The Yugoslav Army was retreating slowly, and Serb paramilitaries weren't far away.

We passed their handiwork on the road. They had burned houses to the ground, smashed shop windows and painted obscene graffiti on the walls of any buildings they left standing. Most of the villages looked empty. But as the day wore on, Albanians who had stayed in Kosovo began to venture from their homes. Children lined the roads cheering the NATO advance and chanting, 'Oo-cha-ka!' (U-C-K — the Albanian term for the KLA). Further on, we passed columns of Yugoslav troops retreating to Belgrade. They didn't look like a defeated army. They seemed proud and defiant.

We arrived in the capital, Pristina, in the late afternoon. NATO's bombs had wreaked havoc. The key military and administrative buildings were completely destroyed. A few NATO vehicles had taken up positions in the centre but they weren't yet in control of the city. The most visible military presence was Russian. The day before NATO moved in, Russian peacekeeping forces in Bosnia raced to Pristina in a grand gesture of Slavic defiance. The Serbs welcomed them as heroes. Russian APCs had positioned themselves in the centre opposite every NATO vehicle. Russian troops also took control of the airport, robbing NATO commanders of a triumphant entry into the capital.

The Grand Hotel was still controlled by a Serb paramilitary group called Arkan's Tigers. Several Rambo-like thugs strutted around, showcasing their machismo at the end of a war they had spent fighting unarmed civilians. A muscle-bound Tiger, with sleeveless black T-shirt, tattoos and shaved head, sat in an open black car with a machine gun mounted on the bonnet. Two others pointed their guns at our faces and asked where we were from. We said Australia and they motioned us inside. At Reception, we asked for three rooms. The Serb clerk told us all the rooms were taken. And no, there were no other hotels.

It was close to sunset. We drove up the hill looking for a safe place to stay. We stopped when we saw a NATO foot patrol, one of the first in the city. Eight British soldiers passed us in tight formation, constantly turning as they walked, scanning the buildings for snipers.

A group of Albanian children were playing in the street. This looked as safe an area as we'd find. Nika asked the children if they knew of a place that would take guests. They took us to a large house across the road. A middle-aged Albanian woman answered the door suspiciously. She was nervous and hesitant when Nika told her we needed a place to stay, but her face lit up when I said we'd pay $100 a night — more money than the household had seen for months. It was a boarding house of sorts, with three university students sharing four rooms with the owner and her teenage son and daughter. They vacated two rooms for us.

As we were carrying in our gear, we noticed the NATO foot patrol had returned. A British officer was talking animatedly into his radio as his troops trained their rifles at the housing estate opposite. We walked up to hear him say an Albanian across the street had just been murdered. 'They killed him,' he shouted into the radio. 'The body was in the school but they moved out. The window has been smashed.'

A black car drove slowly up the street. Nika recoiled in fear. She told us it belonged to a Serb paramilitary group called Black Hand. It turned out we had not come to an Albanian area but to a mixed suburb called Sunny Hills. As one of the few suburbs where Serbs and Albanians lived cheek-by-jowl, it was among the most dangerous places in Pristina. But it was already dark and too late to look further. David set up our editing gear in the bedroom and we went to work.

Moments later the owner, Ilera, came into the room with coffee and nearly dropped it when she saw the open curtains. She ran over and pulled them shut. 'There is a sniper across the road,' she warned. 'Keep the curtains closed.'

The three students were all women in their early twenties. They had come to Pristina to study in the parallel university the Albanians ran in private homes. The university shut down when the war and the mass expulsions began. One of the women, Tina Pantina, a short, stout medical student who spoke good English, showed me a note that had been pushed under their door. 'We wake up one morning and suddenly we find this. It says that "You have 24 hours to go from this house, so if you don't leave, then you will all be shot."'

'Why didn't you leave?' I asked.

'Because here I was born, so here I was prepared to die.'

They had bought a savage dog, which they kept chained in the front yard, then stocked up on food, stayed inside and kept watch every day for paramilitaries, praying that NATO would come first.

'I knew we would be safe in the day, we could run and hide if they came,' she said. 'But the nights were terrible. We knew we could not see them coming.'

Ilera apologised that there was hardly any food for us. The Serb shops had refused to serve them. 'Tomorrow I think we can find something,' she said.

The most uncertain times in conflicts are the very beginning and the very end, the periods when nobody is completely in control and everything is unpredictable. The women were nervous about what the paramilitaries would do that night. It was the last chance to attack Albanians before NATO arrived in force. Marian had found some whisky and got horribly drunk, moaning that he should never have come here. He passed out behind a lounge chair.

For us, the night passed quietly. We heard distant shots but nothing close enough to worry about. We stayed up until two cutting a feature about the uncertain mood in Pristina, slept for three hours and got up at dawn to finish our news piece. Not much more had happened in Pristina overnight, except for someone burning down a mosque which kept Albanians' birth and death records.

We went down to the Grand Hotel to feed our stories from a satellite dish that one of the agencies had set up on the roof. Scores of journalists were in the foyer getting ready to go out. We then heard the news that none of us ever wants to hear: two journalists had been killed. Gabriel Gruener, a German reporter with *Stern* magazine, and his photographer, Volker Kraemer, had been shot dead in their car outside Pristina. Nobody knew the details but everyone suspected they had been murdered by Serb paramilitaries.

As the NATO forces poured in, Pristina started to feel safer. The last Yugoslav soldiers were pulling out, tooting their horns defiantly and holding their fingers out in the three-fingered Orthodox salute. Ethnic Albanians who had spent the war cowering in their homes stood on the street jeering at them. The Serbian administration had already left en masse, leaving the city without running water. The remaining Serb residents sat in groups looking nervous and crestfallen. With Yugoslav forces gone, it would not be long before the KLA arrived to settle scores.

We found the first unit of the KLA at the village where the German journalists had been last seen alive. Half a dozen KLA fighters had set up a checkpoint in the centre, stopping all cars to search for weapons or Serbs. They eyed Marian curiously and he attempted a half smile. Nika assured them he was a good guy and they agreed to take us back to their base.

We followed one of their cars several kilometres down a dirt road to the village of Petrova, the Fear-and-Loathing-Mobile bouncing over the potholes as Marian grimaced in discomfort. Serb paramilitaries had 'cleansed' the town, burning most of the houses and using the mosque for target practice. The KLA had now set up a command centre in one of the abandoned houses.

Fighters were doing drills with weapons beside the building. Some of them were women. They all wore the KLA's improvised uniform of black shirt and trousers, with a bright orange pennant sewn on the shoulder, bearing the inscription 'UCK' over a black eagle. Under the peace deal, they were supposed to hand in their weapons to NATO, but this didn't look like a militia planning to disarm.

I started talking to one fighter, an intense woman in her early twenties who spoke fluent English. She said she would keep fighting for Kosovo's complete independence from Serbia. 'Every Albanian wants that, to fight for our sacred aim,' she said. 'We can't live with Serbs now. They have done too much here.'

Just inside the door an armoury of assault rifles was lined up against the wall. Wooden coffin lids were lined up on the opposite wall, decorated with the names of KLA fighters killed in battle.

The building next door had been turned into a makeshift hospital. Wounded soldiers lay on stretchers next to civilians injured by landmines. A doctor guided us around the rooms, lifting up the blankets to show recent amputations. He pointed out a young man with a bandage over his eye. 'Serbs shot him three days ago as the NATO troops arrived,' he said.

More fighters loitered outside smoking. The air was thick with testosterone. One of the fighters with a belt of bullets slung over his shoulder offered us cigarettes. I hadn't smoked in more than ten years, even while living in Russia where it was almost as popular as breathing. But the soldier was insistent and pushed a cigarette into my mouth. I was only going to have a puff, but a forgotten pleasure shot through my veins. I figured I might just have one more. In this place, lung cancer was the least of the dangers.

The woman fighter took us into the main building to meet the commander. He was dressed in camouflage fatigues with a sling around his right arm. I asked him how he had been injured. He cleared his throat and said he had fallen over. Then he launched into an account of his unit's battle deeds and their moral superiority over Serbs. 'They killed and tortured prisoners,' he said. 'We always treated our prisoners well. We never killed anyone who surrendered.'

'Will you hand in your weapons to NATO?' I asked.

'Serbs are still armed so some of our soldiers must stay armed,' he said. 'We still don't trust the Serbs.'

'Will Serb civilians be safe in the new Kosovo?'

'Those who have clean hands can stay,' he promised. We would hear this mantra many times over the coming days. Each time it was clear that the KLA believed there was no such thing as a Serb with clean hands.

We returned to Pristina to find there had been more murders in Sunny Hills. A large crowd was gathered outside an apartment block in our street. Men were shouting and several women and children were crying hysterically, one woman convulsing on the ground in tears. There were pools of fresh blood in the entranceway. The atmosphere was utterly chaotic but Nika managed to glean that four Albanians had been shot dead after an argument with their Serb neighbours.

British NATO troops arrived just as David started to film. As I tried to move out of their way a soldier shouted, 'Get your feet out of the blood, you dumb cunt!' I looked down to see that I was standing in a puddle of blood and backed out with a start, trailing red footprints around the grieving women. I felt ashamed and disgusted in equal measure, but barrelled on through the filming process as if on autopilot, finding a woman who spoke English and interviewing her for details.

'One of them took a pistol and shot three boys,' she told me. 'When my father came between, they shot my father too.'

I recorded a piece to camera with wailing relatives in the background, trying to concentrate on the story and forget how I was intruding on their grief and shock. I didn't want to be callous. I didn't even want to be doing this. But it was why we were here.

On the way back to the house, I bought a packet of cigarettes.

Nika was now desperate to get home to Ferizaj. We drove down with her the next morning, thinking it was probably as good a place to film as anywhere. The signposts to the town all said Urosevac — the Serbian authorities didn't recognise Albanian place names.

Nika was dreading what she'd find. 'When NATO began the strikes on Yugoslavia, they [the Serbs] began to destroy everything the next day. Everything in Ferizaj,' she said bitterly.

Now it was the Serbs' turn to have their lives turned upside down. The road out of town was choked with cars, trucks and tractors driven by Serbs — some heading south to Macedonia, others north to Serbia proper. Their time in exile would be indefinite. Nobody was going to bomb Kosovo to bring Serbs back.

Urosevac/Ferizaj was in the hands of American NATO troops. After bombing Yugoslavia, the Americans were now the remaining Serbs' only protection against the KLA. Yet they were having trouble just controlling the traffic. We stopped at a bottleneck on the edge of town, where an African-American sergeant was trying to sort out an argument between an ethnic Albanian and a Serb family who, the Albanian claimed, had stolen his truck.

'We just got here,' the sergeant told me, pumped up and flustered. 'From our understanding, either the truck or something on the truck is someone else's property. I'm not too sure. I'm going to get the details now. Stop that truck!'

The Albanian was a refugee who had returned just in time to see the Serbs getting into his truck. He produced his documents to the soldiers, proving he was the owner. The Serb parents shrugged, got out of the vehicle with their children and walked away.

'They will just steal another,' Nika said angrily. 'All these Serbs are taking our lorries and trucks because they want to sell them in Serbia.'

Suddenly she recognised some Albanian friends and ran over to them excitedly. She thought they had been expelled at the same time as her family but they told her they'd stayed in town the whole time.

'They go from one house to another house, again from one house to another house, to be safe,' Nika said, translating for me in between talking. 'Some of their friends are in prison still.'

We went on past an Albanian district in ruins. It was signature ethnic cleansing — windows smashed, shops and homes looted, walls smeared with graffiti. Every building was daubed with a cross and four letters, short for 'Only Unity Saves Serbs'. On the next block, the buildings were untouched.

'They are Serb shops,' Nika said.

'Who did this?' I asked her.

'Serbs, of course.'

'Yes, but who? Police, neighbours?'

'Paramilitaries, soldiers, police, everybody … This is my road.'

We turned into her street, driving past several more homes that had been trashed or destroyed. We stopped in front of Nika's house. From the outside it looked untouched. She bounded out of the car and ran through the gate. Her father, Kodri, stood in the doorway. She embraced him and broke down, the tension of the past three months giving way to uncontrollable sobs. A little while later we sat down to coffee in their lounge room.

Kodri explained that a Serb friend and neighbour called Mila had protected the house while Kodri was away. 'There were police on one side and paramilitaries on the other but Mila told them nobody was to touch this house,' Nika translated. 'He said he would kill anyone who tried to enter it.'

It was the first hint of decency between the communities I had seen. Kodri showed none of the bitterness towards Serbs I found in other Albanians. He had been the town's senior engineer before Milosevic stripped Kosovo of its autonomy and Albanians were sacked from senior positions. But he blamed politicians and the military for the persecution, not the entire Serb community. It seemed fitting that a Serb friend had protected him.

A few minutes later there was a knock on the door. It was his Serb friend, Mila, coming to say goodbye. Having protected Kodri's house, he and his family were now joining the Serb exodus. Kodri argued with him, begging him to stay. 'You will be safe here,' he promised. 'I'll make sure of that.' But Mila had made up his mind. KLA fighters were starting to arrive in town and he wanted to protect his family.

Right On the chaotic campaign trail with Boris Yeltsin. My cameraman had been sent to a different part of the city by Yeltsin's minders. I am peering over the president's left shoulder.

Left Interviewing the cosmonauts bound for Mir, who included the first Frenchwoman in space. We paid $200 to get up close and personal with them — and then conducted the interview from the other side of a pane of glass.

Right Camping out with the Nentsi and their reindeer.

Left A pensioner wearing his naval cap at a Moscow protest against the Yeltsin government. For many, the changes in the former Soviet Union had happened too quickly; they longed for a more secure past. PHOTO: KIM TRAILL

Right At the nuclear missile silo in Central Russia we were invited to a *banya*. I discovered too late that it involved being flogged with birch leaves in a sauna.

Left 'What happens if I press this?' Testing the button, which would, in a different era, have led to nuclear war. Later we were told the nuclear silo was just for training.

Right Bananas in Red Square. Russian actors dressed as B1 and B2 try to convince the Russian public they can't live without televised dancing fruit. The suits were later stolen and held for ransom.

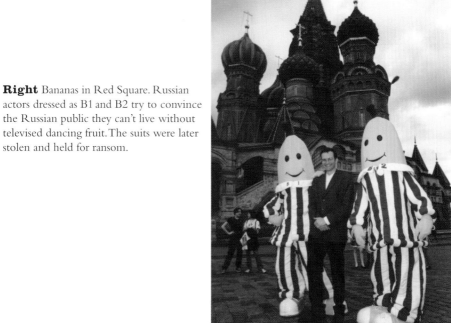

Left Outside the student protest headquarters in Belgrade during the anti–Milosevic street protests. The protests went for two months with more than 100,000 people marching in horrible icy conditions.

Right A mass grave outside Pristina. We were taken there by British troops from NATO. This was the first mass grave found in the area and a grim glimpse of things to come.

Left Files left on the floor of a police station in Pristina which had been used by the Serbian military to torture Albanian civilians. The files show the victims, many of whom looked like children.

Right In Pristina two trucks pass each other, one holds NATO soldiers coming in – the other carries Serb refugees fleeing.

Left No-man's-land: A holding camp for more than 30,000 Albanian refugees near the Kosovo-Macedonian border. The refugees were stuck here for almost a week without food, water or toilets before Macedonia let them cross.

Right Sebastian and me with the Dalai Lama in Dharamsala where he lives in exile.

Left Reading a voiceover for the news from Afghanistan. The torch on my head lit the way — without the flash from the camera taking this photo, the room was pitch black.

Right In Afghanistan, exploded shells are part of the landscape; this Hazara man squats nonchalantly on one.
PHOTO: KIM TRAILL

Below The site of the famous destroyed Buddhas in Bamiyan. Aside from the statues, the Taliban had also destroyed the mudbrick town and locals were living in former monastic cells carved out of the rock. PHOTO: KIM TRAILL

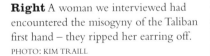

Right A woman we interviewed had encountered the misogyny of the Taliban first hand – they ripped her earring off.
PHOTO: KIM TRAILL

Left Kim, decked out in standard female uniform in the house we rented in Kabul.

Below Outside Osama bin Laden's old house in Jalalabad. We had taken stars off his security gates as souvenirs. From left, a member of Jack's fearless militia, Sebastian, Jack and me.

Left Jack insists on showing me how to fire a pistol — the first time I had ever held one.
PHOTO: KIM TRAILL

Left In front of the al-Qaeda training centre north of Kabul where the videos Jack obtained were recorded. These villagers had come back to claim their houses after the Taliban fled.
PHOTO: KIM TRAILL

Right Sebastian, with Walid, the interpreter, on the left, and Fayez Mohammed, the world's least hygienic cook, on the right.
PHOTO: KIM TRAILL

Below The only photo I have of Paul Moran. We were in Kurdistan filming the *peshmerga* who were fighting against Saddam Hussein.

We walked outside to see his son loading the last of their belongings in the car. Mila introduced him to us as Dragan, but the son was in no mood for pleasantries. He shouted something at us in Serbian and Mila intervened to calm him. His young wife stood beside the car in tears, holding their three-year-old son. Dragan shouted more abuse at us then climbed in the car. Mila asked Kodri if he would look after his house while he was gone.

'Of course,' he said. 'But you don't need to go.'

Mila shrugged and climbed into the back of the car with his wife. Dragan revved the engine and sped off towards Belgrade.

The reprisals began the next day. We were driving north when we saw a huge plume of smoke behind a copse of trees. It was a village on fire. The houses belonged to Serbs who had just fled to Serbia proper. Back near the main road, we saw NATO troops with their shirts off, sunning themselves on their APCs.

Over the next few days, Serb villages went up in flames across the province. At one village we filmed moments after the fires began, a passer-by told us that men in black uniforms had run through lighting them. Albanian civilians looted what wasn't burned. Near every fire, we'd see people driving tractors laden with furniture. None expressed any embarrassment when we filmed them stealing. 'The Serbs destroyed my home so I take this from theirs,' one man told me. A fridge, lounge suite and washing machine lay piled up on the back of his tractor.

In the northern city of Mitrovica, local Serbs were taking matters into their own hands. It was the last major town before Serbia proper and the Serb community had decided to take over the northern half, creating a Serb-only corridor to the administrative border. Vigilantes rounded up Albanians from their apartment blocks and marched them across a bridge to the southern side. A river ran through the town neatly dividing it into halves. Serbs living on the southern side abandoned their homes and moved north to take over the Albanians' apartments. We arrived to see people scurrying across the bridge with their belongings while French NATO troops stood by unconcerned, watching the enforced partitioning of a mixed city.

A group of young Serb men stood on the northern end of the bridge to stop any Albanians trying to cross back. Several of them spoke English. 'We are protecting our lives, our families,' one man said. 'Our way of life!' another shouted.

I asked them what they thought of the ethnic cleansing of the previous months. They all denied it had taken place. 'These people run from NATO bombs,' a thick-set man claimed, repeating the lie I had heard so often from Serbs in Macedonia.

David was starting to get a little nervous. We were both wearing bullet-proof flak jackets but a young tough grasped David's, pointed his fingers at David's head and said, 'This not stop shooting *here*.'

One of the men said he could show me where some Serbs had just been murdered. He seemed the most intelligent and least aggressive of the group, so we decided, a little uncertainly, to go with him. As we walked down the street, away from the bridge, I asked him what he did for work.

'I was a chemistry student,' he said. 'But there is no work.'

'Did you fight in the war?' I asked.

'Yes, of course. We all did.'

'Then you must have seen what happened to the Albanians.'

'I saw many things.'

'And what did you think?'

'I was shocked, of course,' he said. His admission surprised me. He went silent for a moment. 'I don't know what to think,' he added.

We turned a corner and came to a black hatchback car. The windows were shattered and bullet holes riddled the exterior. The upholstery was covered in blood. Bone fragments lay beside the steering column. He said KLA soldiers had opened fire on the car that morning, killing two Serb men and seriously injuring a third. 'We haven't got guns, we haven't got army, we haven't got police,' he went on. 'We are all alone.'

★　★　★

Back in Pristina, British troops were trying to deal with a new outbreak of ethnic cleansing in apartment blocks. Scores of Serbs came to the NATO headquarters complaining that armed Albanians had forced them from their homes. Harassed-looking soldiers tried to explain that they were not a police force.

'We are here to provide a security framework,' one female officer shouted to an angry crowd besieging her office. 'Not individual, not personal security. We haven't got the forces to do that.'

At a rally of Serbs in another part of the capital, a UN official came out to address the crowd. 'I plead with you to stay here in Kosovo to work together with us to build a prosperous future,' he said. The Serbs listened to his speech with as much incredulity as Albanians would have. Nobody outside the UN and NATO believed that Serbs and Albanians could ever work together again.

The images we were seeing each day were dizzying. Everywhere there was evidence of sickening atrocities against Albanians and merciless reprisals against Serbs.

In the town of Podujeve, near the administrative border, we found a shocking testament to the hatred between the two communities. Serb paramilitaries had gone from Albanian house to Albanian house to expel the residents, something they could only have done with the advice of local Serbs. In one courtyard, the walls were sprayed with bullets, as though people had been lined up and executed. Nearby, an axe lay beside what appeared to be a human leg bone. In another courtyard there was a human skull. In a ruined Albanian restaurant, a thick trail of blood ran from the table to the street, as though someone had been shot and then dragged outside. In building after building, the windows were smashed and the interiors destroyed. There was the ubiquitous piece of graffiti, the scrawled cross and four letters standing for 'Only Unity Saves Serbs'. On one building, in red paint, were smeared the Cyrillic letters for 'Seselj'. This man, the Belgrade neo-fascist who had almost been elected president of Serbia two years earlier, appeared to have found another cause for his bold paramilitaries.

The stories and experiences started to merge and blur. It seemed we could stay here for weeks delving into the dark side of humanity. However, Sydney was already tiring of the story and our reports were dropping further and further down in the news.

On our tenth day, we covered the departure of the last Yugoslav troops from Kosovo. It seemed to mark an endpoint to the conflict that I had followed intermittently for more than a year. With Nika now at home in Ferizaj, Tina, the Albanian medical student from our house in Pristina, had agreed to come with us to translate. There was at last a feeling that the worst of everything was over. Maybe that made us careless, or perhaps it was accumulated exhaustion. We drove past a British checkpoint and the soldiers waved in greeting. It didn't occur to us that they could be the last NATO soldiers before the Kosovo border. Then we rounded a corner and drove straight into the Yugoslav forces.

Marian slowed to a halt and gulped. Twenty metres ahead of us was Yugoslav blockade. A tank and several APCs straddled the road, leaving only a small gap for vehicles to pass through. With a terrible jolt I realised we had unwittingly crossed the border into Serbia proper, and had done so without visas and with an Albanian interpreter. A soldier pointed a huge machine gun directly at us. We heard the sound of rifles cocking. An officer stared at us angrily and gestured at us to come forward.

'Shit,' I heard myself saying. 'What do we do?' Nobody said a word. Then Tina shouted, 'We go!'

Marian slammed the gear into reverse and we sped backwards, lurching as we went. Through the windscreen I pointed at my watch and waved apologetically, as if to explain that we were only going back for an urgent appointment. I expected bullets to come flying through the glass at any moment. Finally we rounded the corner at high speed and continued for another 200 metres in reverse before stopping. Tina, David, Marian and I looked at each other and simultaneously screamed in relief.

Then we laughed, lit up a cigarette, coughed and went home.

Chapter 19

Moscow and Chechnya, August to December 1999

Dying for the President

Commentators took to calling Kosovo the last major war of the millennium. It seemed a sure bet just five months before the Big 2–0–0–0. Certainly nobody imagined Russia would be crazy enough to have another go at Chechnya. But nobody had counted on Vladimir Putin. In fact, few people had even heard of him.

On 9 August, Yeltsin sacked his prime minister and cabinet for the fourth time in a year and a half. Out went the latest patsy, Sergei Stepashin, a former head of the secret police. In came Vladimir Putin, the current head of the secret police.

Yeltsin even declared Putin to be the best man to take over as president. 'Russians will have a chance to value the human and professional qualities of Putin,' he said in a televised address. 'I trust him and want everyone who votes in July 2000 to trust him too.'

It seemed another sign that Yeltsin was skipping his medication. Putin had spent most of his career spying for the KGB, an organisation that evoked as much nostalgia as a gulag did. After working for the corrupt St Petersburg administration, he had moved to the even more corrupt Kremlin property office. His latest job had been running the KGB's evil post-Communist spawn, the Federal Security Bureau, or FSB. He appeared to have the charisma of an undertaker. Fellow spooks had nicknamed him the Grey Cardinal.

With a confidence and wisdom honed by nearly four years in Moscow, I sent a report back to Australia declaring that Putin could never be elected president.

'In his first appearance since being named prime minister,' I intoned with gravitas, 'Vladimir Putin looked every inch the KGB spy he once was. Cold, aloof and impersonal, the 46-year-old head of the secret service appears a curious choice to lead Russia.'

Happily I wasn't alone in being wrong. One BBC commentator decided that Yeltsin's endorsement was 'a kiss of death' for Putin. A well-regarded Russia watcher, Matt Bivens, concluded, 'The uncharismatic former KGB man Putin will probably never be electable.' The liberal *Moscow News* weekly dismissed Putin as 'hardly a figure of presidential calibre'. Boris Nemtsov, a former deputy prime minister, assessed Yeltsin's move as 'madness'.

But a few weeks later, something fortuitous happened to make Putin not just electable but the most popular man in Russia. Moscow's buildings started blowing up.

It began on the night of 31 August. I was sitting at home when Eve Conant rang to say that a bomb had gone off near Red Square. 'I'm going to check it out,' she said. 'Do you want to tag along?'

We found ambulances evacuating the Manezh underground shopping complex opposite the square. Forty people were injured, some horrifically, from an explosion in a games arcade. A publicity-seeking deputy from the nearby Duma, Vladimir Semago — famous for owning a bank and a casino as well as being a Communist — came racing down to declare it was the start of a Chechen terrorist campaign. 'It's just a hint to the authorities, stop attacking our people in the Caucasus or we'll start doing this,' he said.

It was the usual political reaction to anything going bang — blame the Chechens. The breakaway republic hadn't had the rosy future many had hoped for after the 1997 elections. The secular president, Aslan Maskhadov, had failed to control either the criminal gangs or the Islamic extremists led by his rival, Shamil Basayev. A few weeks earlier, Basayev had led 1000 halfwit fanatics across the border into the neighbouring republic of Dagestan to declare it an Islamic state. Federal troops were in the process of blasting them back into Chechnya.

On the other hand, Chechens, even fanatics like Basayev, had rarely targeted civilians. Bombs were usually planted by mafia figures to settle business scores. Police said they were investigating several possible scenarios. I filed a story on the explosion and thought little more about it.

A few days later, a massive car-bomb blast levelled an apartment block used by the military in Dagestan, killing 64 people. This time suspicion fell immediately on Basayev's militants. But the rebels denied it and the blast stirred little interest in Moscow. As far as most Muscovites were concerned, Dagestan was far enough away not to worry about.

Everything changed on 9 September. I was working late in the office when Reuters flashed a message that an apartment block in southeast Moscow had collapsed after an explosion. I woke up David and we took a cab to the site. It looked as if an earthquake had struck. The whole nine-storey building had fallen, killing everyone inside. Dust was still rising, illuminated by the searchlight of an emergency services vehicle, but no sound came from beneath the rubble. There was only one other journalist at the scene, an American friend from Reuters who had filed the flashed report. No senior officials had arrived and no one could tell us what had caused the blast. Residents from neighbouring apartment buildings stood bewildered in the dark street in their pyjamas, some weeping at the certain loss of friends.

A few minutes later, a black luxury car with a flashing blue light pulled up and Mayor Yuri Luzhkov stepped out. I walked over to ask for his reaction and he waved me away. I took a step further and two policemen grabbed me and pulled me back. The emergency services minister, Sergei Shoigu, came not long after, and the police manhandled David and me away again. For the rest of the night we watched from behind a cordon as streams of FSB investigators sifted through the scene. At dawn, police announced that the likely cause of the explosion was a leaking gas main. Later that morning, they corrected their explanation to its being a likely terrorist bombing. We didn't know at the time, but it was to be the trigger for another war that would change Russian history.

Yeltsin declared 13 September a day of national mourning for the 93 victims of the Moscow explosion and for the soldiers and their families who had died in the car bombing in Dagestan. Luzhkov immediately sent police on a rampage to harass anyone of Caucasian appearance. Squads of police descended on vegetable markets to check for residency permits and hauled hundreds of bewildered Chechens, Georgians, Azeris, Armenians and Dagestanis off to prison. Putin was more circumspect about who might be responsible. 'If it was a terrorist act,' he said, 'we are facing a cunning, treacherous and bloodthirsty enemy.'

As the day of mourning began, another Moscow apartment block was blown up. We arrived just as police started clearing the area in case surrounding buildings collapsed. This time the death toll was even worse. About 120 people were believed to be buried under the rubble. Both apartment blocks had been indistinguishable from thousands of others in Moscow and appeared to have been picked at random.

Yeltsin gave a televised address, calling for calm. He announced, 'Terrorism has declared war on us, the people of Russia.'

Overnight, Moscow went onto virtual war footing. Residents of every apartment searched for explosives and formed vigilante groups to question strangers. Many people taped up their windows and sandbagged doors. Police searched vehicles entering or leaving the capital. Foreigners were a prime target — I was stopped and questioned by police or civilians every time I went out.

The interior minister accused Shamil Basayev of organising the bombings. Putin for the first time linked the Chechen conflict to the bombings, saying, 'It is obvious to us that both in Dagestan and in Moscow we are dealing not with independent fighters but rather with well-trained international saboteurs.'

Three days later there was another fatal bombing, this time in southern Russia. A truck laden with explosives blew up outside an apartment block in Volgodonsk, killing sixteen. Fear now spread across the country.

Putin dropped any pretence of uncertainty. He announced there was no doubt that Chechens were responsible for both the bombings and the attacks in Dagestan. He ordered Russian troops to mass at the Chechen border. 'We must act decisively, grit our teeth and crush the vermin at the root,' he said.

Most Russians had been relieved when the first war in Chechnya ended, but the public was now clamouring for retaliation. Many people genuinely feared going to bed at night, wondering if their apartment block could be next. As a foreigner living in a diplomatic compound I never felt that worry. Why would Islamic militants blow up Western journalists? But the fear in the city was palpable.

I debated with other journalists whether Chechens really were responsible. Shamil Basayev had close links to a Saudi militant in Chechnya named Omar Ibn al-Khattab, who was believed to be an associate of Osama bin Laden. It was quite possible they had copied bin Laden's method of fighting infidels by slaughtering innocents. But most of us felt it was all too pat. Wiping out distant apartment blocks with massive precision explosives just didn't seem the rebels' style. It also made no sense. The bombings were jeopardising Chechnya's de facto independence. The only winner was likely to be Putin, who had a chance to pose as a strongman saving Russia from terrorists.

Two days after the Russian Army massed on Chechnya's border, there was news of another 'bomb'. Alert residents noticed two men carrying sacks into the basement of an apartment block in Ryazan, four hours' drive southeast of Moscow. Local police evacuated the building, finding a detonator device attached to the sacks. The next day, Putin declared war on Chechnya.

What wasn't revealed until three days later was that the men who had planted the sacks in Ryazan were agents of the FSB, the secret police force formerly headed by Putin. They were arrested by chance as they were trying to leave the city. The FSB director, Nikolai Patrushev (Putin's former deputy), claimed they had simply been on a 'training exercise' to test security precautions. It seemed either an extraordinary act of stupidity or something almost unthinkable — a sign that the FSB was behind the bombings. But it no longer mattered. Russia's re-invasion of Chechnya was already under way.

It started with bombing runs on Grozny's airport and oil refinery and with strafing of outlying villages. Air strikes then spread to the television tower, fuel depots and administrative buildings. 'We will pursue the terrorists everywhere,' Putin said, adding in tough-guy street language: 'If we catch them on the toilet, we will waste them in the outhouse.'

Hundreds of thousands of terrified civilians were now fleeing Chechnya. The Russian Army swept into the republic, encountering little opposition. Journalists in Moscow had no choice but to follow the story. Few of us wanted to go. It wasn't the fighting that frightened everyone; it was the risk of being kidnapped.

Chechnya had become kidnap central. The few foreigners who were game enough to go there risked abduction and torture, followed by execution if ransoms weren't paid. Not long before, a New Zealander and three British telecom workers installing a mobile phone system had been kidnapped and beheaded. The rebel leadership claimed that the FSB was kidnapping foreigners to destabilise the republic. The reality was that abduction had become one of the few profitable industries in Chechnya's postwar ruins.

Eve and I decided to go to the neighbouring republic of Ingushetia to report on the refugee crisis and to slip into Chechnya if it seemed safe. However, even Ingushetia was now dicey, with kidnap gangs targeting foreign construction workers there, after running out of foreigners in Chechnya. The ABC gave David and me permission to travel after the Ingush authorities assured us that six well-armed bodyguards would be waiting for us at the airport.

There was, in fact, a man in a suit. He was a petty official and he explained that the guards would be waiting for us at the Hotel Assa in Nazran, the Ingush capital, 30 minutes away on a road notorious for kidnappings. They weren't, but at least there was an elderly policeman with a rifle. Together with Eve, we drove off to a nearby camp where refugees were flooding in from Chechnya. Angry women mobbed us as we got there, shouting their stories of indiscriminate bombing and shelling. 'They say they are bombing terrorists,' one woman yelled as she clutched a small boy. 'But they bomb civilians because of terrorists. Are we to blame? Is this child to blame?'

The only way to try to verify the claims was to drive into Chechnya. The next morning we spent an hour arguing with Ingush officials before they agreed to provide us with two soldiers. Timur and Rustam looked like armed school students. They were more polite than fearsome, and insisted that Eve and I sit in the front seat of the van while they squatted in the back. Unfortunately they had a habit of resting their Kalashnikovs on their knees, the barrels pointed at our backs and heads as the van bounced over the potholed roads. After more argument, we moved into the back with David.

Less than 20 kilometres into Chechnya we came across a refugee camp. It was a dire place. Women and children who had not eaten for days queued in front of a bread truck as a harassed Ingush man threw loaves out into the crowd. There wasn't nearly enough food to go around and this was just the beginning of the war.

We had only been there a short time when Timur and Rustam insisted that we go back across the border. 'There are kidnappers coming,' one of them said. 'They heard there are foreigners here. You must come now.' I asked him how he could know there were kidnappers. He replied, 'They are coming. It is very dangerous. We must go now.' He was clearly worried so we left.

At the hospital in Nazran the wards were already filling with wounded civilians. Many were children with heavily bandaged burns and shrapnel wounds. A sixteen-year-old boy lay in shock; doctors had amputated his leg. In the next bed an old man lay trying to wave the flies away from burns and blisters that covered most of his body. He said he had been taking the garbage out when a shell landed beside him.

Outside the room, the doctor told us the man had just days to live, adding that the hospital was almost out of medicine. 'I don't know what we'll do if the war goes on,' he said.

We flew back to Moscow the next day. I hoped I would never have to go near Chechnya again.

It was nearly the end of my four-year posting in Russia and I was feeling overwhelmed by the misery I had reported on. For the past seven months or so, I had been continually confronted with suffering and death. One incident in particular had left me wondering if it was all taking a greater toll than I could handle.

Not long after we covered Kosovo, David and I were scrambled to Turkey to report on a massive earthquake which was believed to have killed 20,000 people. We travelled all night without sleep to get to the earthquake zone, stopping at the first collapsed building. A woman was sitting next to the rubble of her home, screaming. Her child was buried beneath it and she wailed and banged the rocks hysterically. As we rushed back to Istanbul to file a TV story, I kept hearing her screams in my mind. For the first time since I'd become a correspondent, I couldn't focus on the story. The Foreign Desk in Sydney rang, asking for radio coverage as well. I told them I didn't have time. The desk rang again at the feed point saying that Radio was insistent. I yelled, 'They can fuck off, I can't do it.'

I pulled myself together a few hours later and we went back to the earthquake zone. Over the next week, in scorching heat, we filmed rescue workers digging decomposing bodies from rubble while their anguished families looked on. Every night I would stand in the shower trying to wash off the smell of death. But it never quite went away and I was sure I could smell the corpses as I lay in bed.

In the middle of it all, a friend rang to warn me that I was in serious trouble. Radio executives had complained about my swearing and my refusal to file, and demanded that I be punished. I rang Sydney and was told to write an apology. A senior executive said I would be formally counselled; a first warning before dismissal.

Back in Moscow, every time I went to buildings that had been blown up, I remembered the woman in Turkey screaming and thought of the child in the rubble. The conflict in Chechnya brought home still more grief.

Kim and I were due to leave Moscow in February and I thought if I could just keep a distance from war and calamity I'd be fine. A month after the trip to Ingushetia and Chechnya, though, I had to go back.

Learning from the mistakes of the previous war, the Russian Army was demolishing the Chechen resistance. Rather than risking its own soldiers, the army was shelling every town or village thought to harbour fighters. It had given an ultimatum for civilians to leave the capital, Grozny, before it launched an all-out assault to seize it. The Russians had sealed the Chechen border to stop journalists going in, so the press pack was descending on Ingushetia.

This time Kim flew down with David and me to translate for us. Security had now become a money-making racket for the corrupt Ingush administration. An official assigned us a soldier, a rusting car and a sleazy Chechen driver called Ruslan for the extortionate rate of $150 a day. Ruslan seemed as trustworthy as a funnel-web spider. He talked nonstop about how he could smuggle us into Chechnya for the right price, take us to some Chechen rebels for the right price, even take us to meet some kidnap gangs at the right price. The last bit I believed; there was an unspoken hint that we had better look after Ruslan if we wanted things to go nice and safely.

There were no vacancies at the Hotel Assa, so Ruslan took us to some 'friends' in town. It was a small private house. The owner demanded $100 from each of us to sleep there plus $20 each per meal. We had no choice but to pay. Then the guard told us we'd have to pay him extra to spend the night with us. I was feeling just so glad I'd come back to Ingushetia.

About 170,000 Chechen refugees were feeling the same way, but they didn't have the option of sleeping in a house. The camps in Ingushetia were some of the worst I'd seen. The lucky ones were sheltering in disused railway carriages. Most were in tents in the mud and snow. The campsites were freezing and putrid. The children were traumatised. But it was better than the conditions across the border. The Russian authorities refused to allow the UN refugee agency to operate in Chechnya, and almost all the foreign aid groups had pulled out because of the twin risks of fighting and kidnapping.

This was my last trip in Russia and it seemed a bad way to be finishing up. I wanted to leave on a positive note, but everything I could see around me was disillusioning and depressing. At least in the first war many Russians had questioned the conduct and strategy of their military. This time nobody seemed to care.

The war had transformed Vladimir Putin from a shadowy bureaucrat to a national hero. In Moscow, it was extraordinary to see how many people admired him. Liberal intellectuals were as enthusiastic about his invasion of Chechnya as nationalist bigots were. The Russian television coverage, which had been fearless and independent in the first war, was now overwhelmingly jingoistic about the exploits of 'our boys'. One TV station showed a story I'd done about Chechen refugees as an example of 'anti-Russian propaganda' being spread by Western journalists.

I knew all the theories about why people's opinions had changed — disillusionment with reform, innate longing for a strong leader, the shock of the apartment bombings — but I couldn't understand how it happened so quickly and completely. After four years in Russia, trying to understand the place, I realised I was still a naïve foreigner trying to penetrate the edges.

But Boris Yeltsin understood his people completely. The appointment of Putin proved to be a masterstroke. Yeltsin was due to step down the following June at the end of his second term and there weren't any friendly faces lining up to replace him. Likely successors included the egomaniacal Mayor Luzhkov and the wily Yevgeny Primakov, whom Yeltsin had unceremoniously sacked as prime minister when he started looking too popular. Both men had been muttering about criminal prosecutions of the Kremlin entourage who'd grown rich on Yeltsin's largesse, a group that included Yeltsin's own family. The loyal bureaucrat Putin was a much more dependable successor. He'd just needed a successful war to give him electoral appeal.

By December 1999, when a new political party endorsed by Putin won the parliamentary elections, his ascendance to the presidency seemed assured. But some Russians cautioned that it was still unpredictable. The war could turn bad for Russia very soon and a winter of heavy casualties could damage Putin's aura of invincibility.

There was fear about another possible catastrophe and it had nothing to do with Chechnya. It was Y2K. Millennium Bug experts predicted that Russia would be among the countries hardest hit by the possible collapse of the world's computer systems, as their clocks ticked over to 2000. New Year's Eve could see power blackouts across the nation. Even the centrally controlled heating system could cease to function, leaving millions at risk of freezing to death.

The Australian embassy in Moscow was so alarmed that it flew most of its staff out of the country. The ABC recommended that we leave our office and apartments and move all our gear, plus wives or partners, to a five-star hotel with an emergency generator — adding that we should stock up on food and water and stay there for ten days. This looked like being enjoyable, but I knew it would be a waste of money. Whoever it was in the Department of Foreign Affairs who had gone along with the idea of Y2K chaos in Russia had obviously spent too much time in Canberra. Chaos was the natural order of Russia and the few computers installed at power plants and offices were broken more often than they were functioning. There could be a Millennium Bug disaster and you'd hardly know it, given the daily catastrophes.

But still, on the morning of 31 December, Kim and I packed our bags ready to move to the hotel later that day. We planned to meet some Russian friends for dinner before joining the masses celebrating in the city centre. I was confident there'd be no work to do.

Then Boris Yeltsin spoiled everything. With no warning, he appeared on state television to make a special announcement. I half expected him to sack the government again. Instead, he sacked himself.

I could hardly believe it was happening. Looking like a remote-controlled corpse, Yeltsin growled something about choosing this symbolic date to end his presidency early. And that was it. The tumultuous Yeltsin era was over and the Putin era had begun. As prime minister, Putin now automatically assumed the post of acting president until the elections. With the full powers and resources of the presidency, he would be an unbeatable candidate. History had changed in five minutes.

We cancelled dinner and left for the hotel. Hundreds of thousands of people were heading to Red Square for the fireworks display promised by the Kremlin. The streets were already littered with bottles. People lurched and swayed, singing arm in arm. They weren't necessarily celebrating Yeltsin's departure, but his resignation didn't seem to have spoiled their day.

By nightfall, any sign of sobriety had disappeared completely. We headed out with our camera and tried to find people to comment on Yeltsin's resignation — in English. It was my last story on Yeltsin and I wanted it to be easy viewing. With hundreds of thousands of people to choose from it shouldn't have been hard to find an English speaker. But I hadn't banked on the newfound patriotism of the inebriated masses.

'We're in Russia, so speak Russian!'

Drunken youths waved sparklers in my face. Firecrackers exploded at our feet. Bottles smashed at our ankles as we pushed deeper into the crowd, now sliding on a sea of broken glass. A group of drunks came up and said they'd talk to us in English. They were Americans working for NASA in Moscow.

As the hands on the Kremlin Tower clock edged closer to midnight and the temperature fell below minus ten degrees, champagne corks began to fly, some narrowly missing us. Eventually we got a few mildly coherent sentences on tape. And the legacy of Yeltsin's years? Nobody really cared.

'I'm glad he's gone. I don't have to be embarrassed any more.'

'All will be well.'

'I thought he was already dead.'

The final countdown to the millennium began, the assembled masses slurring the numbers backwards from ten. The sky exploded in fireworks, the crowd erupted in screams and cheers. Everyone started kissing friends and strangers, and drenching themselves in cheap champagne. It was a spectacular end to Boris Yeltsin's anti-climax of a resignation.

I'd arrived in Moscow as he began campaigning for his second term and I was leaving just as it ended. In between, I'd seen one of the strangest times in Russian history. I had lost a marriage, found love, crossed the Arctic, met cosmonauts, fled from the Taliban, caroused with bandits, witnessed wars and revolutions and known extremes of good and evil. I'd found a life I could not have imagined and experienced things I never thought possible. I felt as though I'd come to the end of a spectacular ride and I wasn't sure if I was ready to get off. But it was New Year's Eve and a new century and I was in Red Square in a sea of drunken Russians living for the moment. I would worry about the future when it came.

Part Two

FURTHER EAST

Chapter 20
Sydney to Beijing, May 2001

Enter Mr Pu

I had a sinking feeling that I'd made a terrible mistake. It started with a polite but firm phone call from the Chinese embassy's political counsellor. 'I should very much like to meet you in person,' Madame Ren Xiaoping said. 'In Canberra. On Tuesday.'

I had just been chosen as the ABC's new China correspondent and the embassy was already sizing me up. Five years earlier I'd gone to the Russian consulate in Sydney and told the counter official that I was going to be the ABC's new Moscow correspondent. He gave me an uninterested glance before returning his attention to his cigarette and newspaper. It was the start of a wonderfully free posting, where there were hundreds of rules for foreign journalists none of which the authorities could be bothered enforcing. It appeared, now, that Chinese officials would be watching my reporting closely.

Madame Ren was charming and flattering when she greeted me in the embassy foyer. Immaculately dressed and speaking perfect English, she even praised my mangled attempt to say 'Pleased to meet you' in Mandarin, and ushered me into a meeting room for a little chat over a pot of tea.

'I'm so glad we are going to have a journalist of your seniority and experience to report on our country,' she said, then proceeded to go through the faults of the other Australian correspondents in China by name. They were variously 'sneering', 'biased', 'distorted', 'inaccurate' and 'hostile'. Some were even 'cynical'. 'I know you will be different,' she said. 'I'm sure we shall be friends.'

It was a year since I'd nominally moved back to Australia but I'd spent most of that time overseas, doing long trips reporting and producing for *Foreign Correspondent*. It was a perfect job but I missed the experience of being immersed in a different society. Moving to China seemed like a good idea, though the conversation with Madame Ren left me wondering.

Kim was shooting a documentary in Afghanistan, so I packed up to fly to China on my own. Beijing airport felt like Singapore. It was clean, modern and efficient, the Customs officers were professional, taxis had meters and no one asked for a bribe. As I drove into the city, I looked in vain for any relics of Communism. The city seemed to have already leap-frogged to hypercapitalism — the highways full of advertising billboards, neon signs, shopping centres, luxury hotels, elaborate flyovers, imported cars, garish restaurants, designer stores and crowded construction sites for massive office blocks.

The diplomatic compound where my office and apartment were located was reassuringly Soviet — tower blocks that looked as if they'd been flung up in the 1970s from prefabricated ferro-cement. But outside it was a market-economy feeding frenzy. A whole world of pirated Western goods was literally thrust in my face as I stepped out of the car.

'Hello — DVD.'

'Hello — Rolex watch.'

'Hello — socks.'

Across the road from the compound were a Starbucks Coffee franchise, a Delifrance, a Baskin-Robbins and a Pizza Hut. Further down the road were a McDonald's and a KFC. Every few blocks there were department stores filled with Western and Chinese goods. An adjoining alley called the Silk Market sold imitation Fendi and Prada handbags, fake North Face jackets and copied Hugo Boss and Armani clothes to throngs of Western tourists.

It was a raw and pulsing capitalism, encouraged by the world's largest Communist Party that seemed about as Communist as Ronald Reagan. But Big Brother was still watching.

The morning after I arrived, the ABC radio correspondent, Tom O'Byrne, took me out on the balcony. 'This is about the only place we can be sure they're not listening to us,' he said quietly, over the roar of the traffic twelve floors below. 'We assume every phone call is monitored. They can also intercept faxes. And don't send anything sensitive by email. They can probably hack into it.'

Tom seemed a patient man, but after eighteen months in China he was developing the testy twitch of someone undergoing water torture. 'See the guards at the gate,' he said, pointing to ramrod-stiff paramilitary soldiers at the main gate below us. 'They're just the ones they want you to see. The spooks are in the offices beside each entrance. They videotape everyone coming and going, 24 hours a day.'

He explained that the Chinese staff were also expected to spy on us. All employees had to be hired through the DSB (Diplomatic Service Bureau), which took a large cut of their wages and required them to attend regular meetings to report on what we were doing. But in this respect at least, Tom believed the system was breaking down. Most news bureaus were illegally hiring people outside the DSB so that they could trust them. And long-term DSB staff employed by the bureaus generally felt more loyalty to their co-workers than to the DSB officers they had to report to.

The ABC bureau was one of the best. The DSB driver, Lao Zhang, had been with the ABC for six years and was as adept at navigating the Chinese bureaucracy as he was the streets of Beijing. He had a round, smiling face and was always giggling or making incomprehensible jokes. The chain-smoking, hard-drinking researcher Li Bin was only in his twenties but had an extraordinary understanding of Chinese politics and a great contact list of both officials and dissidents.

Then there was my new cameraman, Sebastian Phua. He was a Singaporean-Chinese hippie. 'Hey, bro, you gotta chill out,' he said, sensing my discomfort with China. 'Come and have a Margarita.'

He took me across the road to a Mexican bar where we sat watching the pollution turn the sunset golden red over the crowded skyline. Sebastian had found his favourite style of dress, music and living in the 1970s and stuck with it blissfully ever since. He was wearing a tie-dyed singlet, tie-dyed trousers, a Mongolian vest and an Indian headband over his shoulder-length hair.

As we downed Margaritas he filled me in on the important things to know about Beijing. 'You gotta be careful, bro,' he advised. 'There's a lot of Irish pubs here, but only some have real Guinness. I always stick to Durty Nellies. Shoot a bit of pool, knock back a few pints, hear some music. Hey, you like Pink Floyd?'

'No.'

'You know, it depends on the mood,' he continued. 'Sometimes I like Jethro Tull, Gentle Giant, King Crimson, but for me, you know, any time is right for Pink Floyd. A bit of "Lucifer Sam", "Interstellar Overdrive", bit of "The Body". Roger Waters, he is, you know, the thinker, but Syd Barrett is the MAN.'

I had no idea what he was talking about but I was fascinated. Sebastian was from a legendary family of cameramen who had been filming for the ABC and BBC in Asia since the 1960s. Despite decades of shooting wars, coups, massacres and rebellions, he was one of the most positive people I had ever met.

'Hey, mate, don't worry, it's going to be cool,' Sebastian assured me, lighting up his fortieth Marlboro Red for the day as he put down his fourth drink. 'You leave the cops to me. And you gotta come and hear our band. We play every couple of Fridays, if you and me aren't travelling. Man, we gotta go to Tibet! You're gonna love this place! The main thing is you gotta chill. Take it easy. Smile! Another Margarita?'

Before I could do any reporting, I had to get a residency permit. As a foreigner, I was not just an object of political suspicion. The first requirement for residency was to be tested for AIDS.

The Chinese embassy had already made me undergo an extensive medical check in Australia, titled 'Physical Examination Record for Foreigner'. It included the following question:

Do you have any of the following diseases or disorders
endangering the public order and security?
- Toxicomania
- Mental confusion
- Psychosis (including one or more of — Manic
  Psychosis, Paranoid Psychosis, Hallucinatory
  Psychosis)

Fortunately, I didn't. But I also had to prove that I didn't have cholera, yellow fever, plague, leprosy, venereal disease or opening lung tuberculosis — as well as certify the state of my various attributes: development (normal), nourishment (normal), neck (normal), vision (normal), corrected vision (6–5/6–5), eyes (normal), colour sense (normal), skin (no abnormalities), lymph nodes (no abdominal enlargement), ears (normal), nose (normal), tonsils (not enlarged), heart (no abnormalities detected), lungs (no abnormalities detected) and abdomen (no abnormalities detected).

On top of all that I was immunised for Japanese encephalitis, rabies, hepatitis A and B, typhoid, polio and tetanus, and had a Mantoux test for tuberculosis.

I had everything covered. I had attached a photograph in the space provided, and the doctor at the medical centre in Sydney had signed and stamped the form. When I arrived in Beijing, I gave it to the driver, Lao Zhang, to pass on as proof of good health for the residency permit. He gave the amused, embarrassed half giggle of a Chinese dealing with a silly foreigner. 'Is no good,' Lao Zhang said. 'No chop on photo.'

A chop is an official stamp that needs to mark every photograph attached to a form. My chop wasn't over the photo, merely next to the doctor's signature at the end of the three-page form. Without this, Lao Zhang explained, there would be no way of proving that I hadn't stuck my photo on somebody else's medical examination form, albeit somebody who looked identical to me and had the same name and birth date. There was no alternative but to go to a special clinic set up to test arriving foreigners.

I couldn't shake the fear that one of the best ways to catch HIV in China would be to have a needle shoved in your arm for an AIDS test. But it was that or return to Australia. So I queued behind the other nervous foreigners at a testing clinic. The needles had already been removed from their sterile packets and were stacked on a stand. I closed my eyes as the nurse drew a vial of blood.

The next step for official registration was to take a Chinese name. Western names are often impossible to write in Chinese so the bureaucracy insists that resident foreign journalists adopt a new identity. You can call yourself whatever you want. But the office told me they had already chosen a name for me to get the paperwork started. It was Pu Rui; *pu* being a vague allusion to the last Chinese emperor, Aixinjueluo Puyi, and *rui*, meaning good or fortunate. In combination, it meant I was a noble, honourable man. At least that's what the office staff told me. I could never be sure it wasn't some huge practical joke and they'd actually named me Pig Nose or Duck Fart. But from now on, on every document, at every press conference and on every official trip, I was no longer Eric Campbell. I was Mr Pu.

Once I was officially a resident, I was given accreditation as a journalist. This meant I could report. Sort of. There were just a few rules I had to follow, set out in a booklet called *Handbook for Foreign Journalists in China*. The foreword described it as 'authoritative and handy, the handbook is designed to serve journalists' — which was a friendly way of saying 'this is how we're going to fuck up your stories'.

Among a bizarre series of restrictions was the catch-all Article 14.

> Foreign journalists ... shall observe journalistic ethics and
> shall not distort facts, fabricate rumours or carry out news
> coverage by foul means. Foreign journalists ... shall not
> engage in activities ... which endanger China's national
> security, unity or community and public interests.

I asked Tom what it meant. 'Basically any real journalism you do is illegal,' he said.

He explained that it was illegal to speak to any critics of the government or the Communist Party (such critics, by definition, distorted facts). It was similarly illegal to film any protests (which, by definition, endangered national security). And it was just as illegal to expose problems like epidemic disease or corruption (which were only rumours unless the authorities confirmed them).

As the authorities controlled the satellite feeds, the only way to get controversial stories out was to try to courier them overnight to Sydney, which made it rather a challenge to cover breaking news. That was also technically illegal.

Chinese media followed all the rules. Every newspaper, magazine and television station in the country was state-controlled and portrayed China as a happy and prosperous land under the wise rule of the Chinese Communist Party.

For the benefit of foreigners, TV news reports were broadcast in English on CCTV 9. It was compulsive viewing.

The news bulletins began with pacy American-style breakers and punchy jingles, mixing to handsome, square-jawed presenters in flash suits. While the opening was slick and packaged, the content would have fitted comfortably into the Brezhnev-era Soviet Union. The top news story was always something involving President Jiang Zemin, such as an important meeting with the president of the Ivory Coast. There would be much shaking of hands, followed by shots of the two leaders perching uncomfortably on enormous yellow velvet-upholstered chairs. The reporter would describe breathlessly how the leaders had declared their ongoing friendship and desire to establish future trade and cultural exchanges with mutual respect for each other's sovereignty.

The second story would always be about the premier, Li Peng, who was ranked second in the party hierarchy. Then came news of bumper wheat harvests.

The general programming reflected a manic desire to show people how great China was and how much the world respected it. A multitude of documentary programs showed the superiority of Chinese civilisation. I watched one about how China discovered the world, including Australia. Another showed how the Chinese had invented the wheel.

The pinnacle of the evening's entertainment was a series in which foreigners would sing Chinese popular songs, in Chinese. It was always a mega pop concert spectacular, with a large in-house audience, stage, orchestra and accompanying dancing troupes who changed costumes for every number. Cameras on cranes swung round endlessly zooming in on hapless Pakistanis or Americans struggling with lyrics in Mandarin, which were subtitled in English at the bottom of the screen.

One memorable number included the following:

Every year we're getting richer,
Our houses are getting bigger,
Our children are taller,
Our mobile phones are getting smaller.

Watching CCTV 9, you could imagine that China was paradise. But it didn't take long to find the dark side of the economic miracle.

Chapter 21
Masanjia, Northeast China, May 2001

Work Makes You Free

Officials in Moscow had ignored my arrival in their country in 1996; the Chinese authorities, however, decided to welcome me by sending me to a re-education camp. After just four days in Beijing, I was invited to join the first ever media tour of China's gulags for dissidents and low-level criminals.

I had no idea why the authorities had chosen me, the least experienced China watcher in China. Many other bureaus had longstanding requests to film labour camps. Tom spoke good Mandarin and enjoyed considerable respect, even from officials. But the honour was going to the ABC's Mr Pu. A long-time BBC correspondent, Rupert Wingfield-Hayes, had a theory. 'They probably thought you were new enough to take it seriously,' he told me later.

The State Council — the government wing of the Communist Party — had invited a handful of other foreigners for the historic first visit: a text reporter from Associated Press, a camera crew from Japan, and an American reporter from NBC, who was effectively just coming for the ride because his head office didn't think it was a story. There was also a throng of Chinese journalists as well as Beijing officials in matching smart suits, white shirts and dark ties. A trip as important as this couldn't just be left to the local yokels.

We flew to the city of Shenyang near the North Korean border. Before economic reforms began in the 1980s, it had been a centre for heavy industry. Now it was a rustbelt of bankrupt factories. But we weren't here for a town tour. The bus took us quickly to a five-star hotel to be met by another throng of Communist Party officials.

The numbers swelled further as we sat down for a banquet. The tables were laden with exquisite regional cuisine, including whole fish and whole birds, right down to the half-cooked eyes. Some places like to disguise the origin of animal dishes, but the idea here seemed to be to make a feature of it. There was an endless supply of beer, wine and *maotai*, a near lethal Chinese rice wine. Even cigarette packets were laid at every place setting. As in Russia, small talk gave way to increasingly exuberant toasts. We drank to friendship, cooperation between nations, closer relations between Australia and Shenyang, world peace and global understanding.

In the morning an air-conditioned coach took us through paddy fields and poor rural villages to Masanjia — a 2000-hectare prison colony with nine 're-education through labour' camps. It was set up in 1957 during Chairman Mao's anti-rightist campaign, when he began imprisoning party colleagues in one of his many fits of Machiavellian paranoia. It was still being used to lock up dissidents without trial for up to three years. The camp to which we were being taken was exclusively for women members of the banned religious sect Falun Gong.

To its many supporters, Falun Gong was a form of meditation and controlled breathing, somewhat similar to Tai Chi. To China's Communist authorities it was an evil cult led by a ruthless criminal mastermind, Li Hongzhi. The authorities claimed they were imprisoning Falun Gong members to protect their human rights.

A handy reference book called *China Facts and Figures 2000*, which the government had sent the ABC bureau, put it like this: 'The Chinese Government cannot sit back and do nothing about Falun Gong, a cult organisation that has seriously endangered society. To indulge this cult would be tantamount to rejecting science, blaspheming civilisation and trampling on human rights.'

Falun Gong is, arguably, a little on the weird side. Its website, clearwisdom.net, claims to be able to 'eradicate all evils, expose and dispel all lies and strengthen righteous thoughts'. Li Hongzhi has written often about how aliens from outer space walk among us and how he can make himself invisible. But what scares the Chinese Communist Party most is the threat Falun Gong poses to the party's authority. It banned the movement in 1999 after Falun Gong staged a mass demonstration outside the Beijing headquarters of the party leadership to protest police harassment. It was the only mass movement in China not subservient to the party and had shown itself capable of organising mass actions without the security services knowing. That made it public enemy number one.

There were no reliable statistics on the numbers of Falun Gong members arrested since the crackdown. The group's website was blocked in China but, before leaving Beijing, I arranged for Sydney to email me its contents. (The authorities were able to read emails but hadn't yet worked out how to stop them.) The website claimed that tens of thousands of people had been imprisoned, and described Masanjia as 'a living hell' where inmates were routinely beaten and tortured with electric shocks. It also claimed that prisoners were forced to work fourteen hours a day and were regularly slapped in the face or forced to squat the entire night as a punishment for minor transgressions. The website named the captain of the women's unit, Madame Su Jing, as the worst tyrant.

Human rights groups had long condemned China's suppression of the movement. Allowing us to go to the camp seemed a relatively daring attempt by the Chinese authorities to answer their critics.

The bus pulled up outside Masanjia's Second Women's Unit, a complex resembling a minimum-security prison with steel gates and barbed wire. There were no watchtowers or heavily armed guards. But given that it was a prison within a prison colony, there wouldn't be much point in trying to escape the compound. The officials led us into a courtyard where inmates were playing basketball. Before we could speak to anyone, we were ushered into a room for a one-hour press conference.

The camp commandant sat at the centre of a long table, flanked by his senior wardens, all wearing jet-black uniforms with silver buttons. Next to the commandant sat Madame Su Jing. She was in her mid-forties with tightly groomed hair and a slightly fanatical glint in her eyes. I could imagine her being equally adept at running a tank regiment.

I asked her about ill-treatment of prisoners. 'We police officers treat them like sisters,' she said indignantly. 'We get close to them and make friends with them. This enables them to realise how they have disrupted public order and violated laws. As a result, they willingly accept re-education through labour. In order to express their gratitude some take the initiative to actively assist police officers to redeem other followers.'

We were then taken to meet some of the 483 female inmates in a second building housing classrooms and dormitories. I had not been allowed to bring an interpreter but planned to use Sebastian to speak to inmates away from the officials. Growing up in Singapore, he had picked up five Chinese dialects, as well as English and Bahasa Malaysia. (Although in typical Sebastian style, he hadn't learned to read or write a single Chinese character. 'I'm a really slack Chinaman,' he told me, politically incorrectly.)

It made no difference. The officials were never more than a few steps from us. In the canteen, a group of prisoners were lined up wearing clean, matching tracksuits.

'When we came to Masanjia the police used their love and patience and the party's principles to educate us, help us and rescue us,' one inmate said. 'I totally changed my opinion of Falun Gong and now know it seriously endangers me and our society.'

Another said, 'The police officers treat us as their own children. They patiently persuade and educate us, so we mentally understand Falun Gong's counter-revolutionary characteristics.'

It was obvious the place had been tarted up for our visit. The dormitories were freshly painted, with comfortable bunks, fluffy pillows and cosy blankets. In one room the inmates were sitting in neat rows watching subtitled Australian science videos.

'This is to teach them to think rationally,' Madame Su Jing said. Having once worked on the ABC science program *Quantum*, I wondered if my reports on large bacteria of the Great Barrier Reef or poisonous birds of Papua New Guinea were helping their re-education.

In another room a group of women stood in a horseshoe formation waiting to be interviewed. I asked if each one could tell me what they thought of Falun Gong. One after another they replied robotically, 'Falun Gong is a cult', 'Falun Gong is a cult', 'Falun Gong is a cult', 'Falun Gong is a cult' ...

None of the Chinese journalists had asked any questions since they had arrived. A camera crew followed us from room to room filming everything we did. I assumed they were shooting our material to save having to ask awkward questions themselves. But as we entered the courtyard, the Chinese journalists began conducting their first and only interviews — with us. Yu Tingting, a pretty reporter from one of the state television networks, asked if she could talk to me. It seemed polite to say yes. And I expressed my feelings about the camp as diplomatically as I could.

Then the tour was over. The minders ordered us to stop filming and shepherded us onto the bus. It wasn't just that they wanted to control what we shot. They had organised another banquet at the hotel and they were getting hungry.

The next day the national *People's Daily* and several other Chinese newspapers carried a front-page article about our trip to the camp.

FALUN GONG RE-EDUCATION CAMP EXPOSED
TO FOREIGN MEDIA
'What do you think of Falun Gong?' a journalist with the
Australian Broadcasting Corporation (ABC) asked two
rows of 'students' at a re-education camp for female Falun
Gong practitioners. 'I think it's an evil cult.'

The article described how good the conditions were and how grateful the inmates were for being saved. Then it talked about how impressed the foreign media were, starting with me.

'"It [the camp] is extremely open, and I am surprised that we are allowed this close access to the re-education camp," said Eric Campbell from the ABC.'

For the benefit of foreign readers, they used my real name. After less than a week in China I had already become part of the government's propaganda campaign to discredit its dissidents. Watching closely from the Chinese embassy in Canberra, Madame Ren Xiaoping must have been proud of me.

When she finally arrived to join me, Kim was more enthusiastic about China than I was. She'd spent several months travelling around western China some years earlier and had been fascinated by the place. The reality of Beijing, though, was less magical.

As summer approached, the temperature soared to 40°C, which made the pollution even more stifling. Most days the city was shrouded in heavy smog, making it difficult to see more than a few hundred metres from our ninth-floor apartment. Some days giant dust storms blew in from the Gobi Desert, which crept ever closer to Beijing, as decades of environmental mismanagement turned more and more pastureland into desert.

In the headlong rush to modernise, the city authorities were erasing what was left of the old Beijing. National monuments were preserved as museum pieces but the living old city was falling under the wrecker's hammer. Our compound was surrounded by *hutongs* — narrow alleyways of courtyard houses crowded with Chinese families gossiping, gambling or drinking in the stifling heat. It was another world compared with the noisy expressways and glitzy shopping centres on the main thoroughfares. You could walk 200 metres from the compound and feel that you were at last in the real China, with stallholders barbequing scorpion and frog kebabs, children playing shuttlecock and streetside barbers plying their trade as they sat on wooden stools. But every week another *hutong* would disappear, demolished to make way for high-rise apartment blocks or commercial centres.

It was still possible to ride around Beijing by bike but it was getting ever more hazardous as the Chinese middle class bought cars by the millions. Kim and I used to ride to Tiananmen Square every night, sticking to the few bike lanes that wove around the expressways. There were wonderful rides along canals and street markets and the moats of the Forbidden City, but when you re-entered the traffic it was remarkable how little heed car drivers paid to cyclists' vulnerability. Occasionally a clear stretch of bike lanes let you pelt full speed and enjoy a cooling breeze and the momentary sense of being in a people-friendly city. But we stopped riding as often after a passing rider blew his nose, sending a giant glob of sputum at high speed straight into Kim's face. She spent a week in bed with flu.

Most people were friendly, giggling good-naturedly as we tried to shop in markets with our limited Mandarin. I could sense that there was a vibrant culture under the commercial surface, but I couldn't yet see how to penetrate it. I spent most of my free time with expatriate journalists and occasionally knocking back pints with Sebastian. I figured I'd make more Chinese friends once I learned more of the language.

Then I discovered how dangerous a casual social contact can be.

Chapter 22
Beijing, May to July 2001

New Beijing, Great Olympics!

Dissidents continue to be imprisoned or sent to labour camps
for peacefully commemorating the anniversaries of Tiananmen
[where] hundreds of unarmed civilians were killed and injured.
— *Amnesty International Report, May 2000*

Beach volleyball and triathlon will compete on the historic
Tiananmen Square should Beijing play host to the 2008
Olympic Games, Beijing Mayor Liu Qi confirmed.
— People's Daily, *25 November 2000*

By May of 2001, China was entering the home straight in its bid to win
hosting rights to the 2008 Olympics. The venues were all on track,
Beijing had passed the technical inspection with flying colours and the
bid committee was on side about sport fostering peace and global
understanding. Just to be on the safe side, police were also locking up
and torturing anyone likely to criticise or embarrass the bid.

The first Chinese friend I made disappeared in the security
crackdown just a few weeks after I met him. He was having a night out
with a group of acquaintances when police appeared from nowhere,
threw them to the ground, handcuffed them and drove them away. My
friend, whom I'll call Jiang, was a young computer buff who lived at
home with his mother. The police wouldn't tell her where they had
taken him, what he was accused of or when he might be released.

Jiang hadn't done anything wrong. The problem was the company he
was keeping. One of his dinner companions had been shot and crippled

when the army massacred student protestors near Tiananmen Square in 1989. (He had only gone to the square to try to find his younger brother but was cut down in a hail of bullets.) It was now just before the 4 June anniversary of the shootings and the authorities were terrified that survivors of the massacre might mark the day with a protest. The usual security paranoia was heightened by a determination that everything should look nice during the bid for the Olympics. So for weeks the Public Security Bureau had been tailing and arresting anyone they suspected might cause trouble, as well as anyone who happened to be with them.

Police didn't need to justify their actions and detainees had no right to speak to lawyers or relatives. Suppressing protest was regarded as a 'matter of national security', meaning that any accused person's legal protections were dumped. For all I knew, Jiang could have been secretly sentenced to three years in Masanjia.

The slogan for the Olympic bid was 'New Beijing, Great Olympics'. It was accompanied by a catchy advertising campaign, a terrific film clip of athletes and historic sites, and show-stopping promotional performances including 2000 schoolchildren singing and dancing in Tiananmen Square. The square hadn't seen that many students since the 1989 massacre.

Memories of the bloodshed had been a little fresher the last time Beijing made a bid for the Olympics, in 1993, when it lost by one vote to Sydney. This time around, Australia and China were on the same side.

All through May and June, a battalion of Australian politicians, business leaders and sporting figures passed through Beijing to cheer on its bid. The city was facing tough competition from Paris and Toronto, so Australia was lending it high-profile support. And Beijing was lapping it up, giving red-carpet treatment to even minor dignitaries like the chief minister of the Australian Capital Territory, Gary Humphries, who announced after a meeting with the Beijing mayor that 'China is a very, very appropriate host for the Games in 2008'.

The reason for Australia's support was simple — money. Having staged the 2000 Games in Sydney, Australia was hoping to cash in on its

Olympics expertise. There was clearly more chance of contracts with a developing Asian neighbour than with Europe or Canada, particularly if China felt at all indebted to Australia for winning.

Not long after my friend Jiang was arrested, a delegation from the Australian Government trade agency, Austrade, arrived in Beijing touting for Olympic business. The star speaker was Sandy Hollway, the former chief executive of SOCOG (Sydney Organising Committee for the Olympic Games). He was full of enthusiasm for how Australian companies with experience from the 2000 Games could help China. 'There were at least 300 Australian companies who stepped up to the mark and showed remarkable innovation and who I'm sure could help friends in China if they do win the bid,' he said.

At the Austrade cocktail party, diplomats and officials enthused about how much better China would become if it hosted the 2008 Games. 'I think it will open up the country to new ideas,' one diplomat told me. 'And it will put the government on its best behaviour.'

'Well, they're locking up anyone they want to while they're bidding for the Olympics,' I said, a little too loudly. 'So why would they be any different once they get them?'

The diplomat smiled indulgently.

The treatment of my friend Jiang had left me a little testy about my country's possibly sincere but definitely self-serving attitude. Jiang was released two weeks later. He had not been charged with any offence but he had been beaten and given electric shocks. I met him in a café the day after his release. He sat stunned, nursing a giant bruise on his chest and still bearing marks on his wrists from the handcuffs. Even today he is frightened that if I mention his real name he will be re-arrested.

I couldn't believe the Communist Party was pushing to get the Olympics in order to improve democracy and human rights. It seemed more likely it wanted to boost its own popularity. And Australian expertise was seen as the key to victory. The Beijing Bid Committee had hired Sandy Hollway and several other executives from the Sydney Games as consultants. In an interview, the Bid Committee's director, Liu

Jinming, told me: 'Many professionals and technicians who worked on the Sydney Olympics are now working here in Beijing. The foundation of Beijing's Olympic bid is built upon the success of the Sydney Olympics.'

One of the Australians' contributions had been to rewrite Beijing's bid document, throwing in lines to soothe any image problems for the dictatorship. The document presented to the International Olympic Committee (IOC) included the extraordinary statement that journalists would enjoy complete freedom during the Olympics. This was like promising that turkeys would have complete freedom on Christmas Day. The idea that Beijing's paranoid authorities would allow several thousand foreign journalists to roam the city covering demonstrations, Falun Gong, heritage demolition, corruption and anything else that caught their interest was beyond ludicrous.

(A year later, China's senior Olympic official, IOC member He Zhenliang, admitted it was untrue. He told me, not surprisingly, that accredited sports journalists would only be allowed to cover sport.)

The ruling Communists simply didn't countenance the Western concept of public debate. There was only ever one correct position — the state's. To find a Chinese critic of Beijing's Olympic bid I had to look outside China.

Wei Jingsheng was a prominent dissident living in exile in Washington DC. He was expelled from China in 1997 after spending a total of eighteen years in prison for peaceful protests. His first offence, in 1978, was calling for democracy, for which he was imprisoned as a counter-revolutionary. The authorities released him in 1993 as a PR gesture while Beijing was bidding to host the 2000 Games. After Beijing lost to Sydney, he was thrown back in jail and sentenced to another fourteen years. President Clinton brokered his early release.

I arranged for a crew to interview him in Washington, faxing a list of questions. Understandably, he was less than enthusiastic about Beijing hosting the 2008 Games. 'If it wins, I'm afraid it would be a great disaster,' he said. 'The Chinese Government is used to turning sporting games and other international events into political events and using them to show to the people of China that the international community is supporting the one-party rule by the Chinese Communist Party.'

He thought the Australian Government's argument that the Games would improve human rights was ridiculous. 'The Chinese Communist Party violates human rights from its fundamental theories. When given tolerance by the international community, it would only do more, not less.'

It seemed unlikely that Wei Jingsheng would get any speaking engagements with Austrade.

The Beijing Bid Committee set up a giant screen at a concert stadium called the China Millennium Monument to broadcast the IOC's announcement, on 13 July, of the winning bid. We arrived to find acrobats, dragon dancers, pop stars, laser lights and wildly coloured banners. In addition, the authorities had thoughtfully bussed in hundreds of English-speaking Chinese students after coaching them on what to say to the media. They stood in columns with matching T-shirts waving national flags.

'We believe Beijing can give the world a beautiful, wonderful Olympic Games,' said a student from the group in red T-shirts.

'I want to speak to all the world,' said another from the blue shirt faction. 'Now Beijing is ready. Come to Beijing.'

When the IOC's announcement of Beijing as the winner flashed up on the screen, the arena erupted with joy. Red T-shirts hugged blue T-shirts, students and performers shrieked and wept, and enough beer and champagne were splashed around to leave everyone wet and sticky. Then the fireworks began. For half an hour the Millennium Monument was dazzled by pyrotechnics. The sheer volume of fireworks reflected how confident the authorities must have been of winning. It would have been a huge loss of face if all of it had to be quietly packed up and removed.

We left the orchestrated fun to hit the streets. The feeling was just as electric but there was nothing for anyone to do. The city hadn't organised any celebrations for the public so crowds milled around happily but uncertainly. Eventually people started heading for Tiananmen Square. It was the natural meeting point for large crowds, but there hadn't been an unauthorised mass gathering there since the 1989 massacre. By midnight, tens of thousands of jubilant Beijingers had spontaneously marched down the broad boulevard in front of the Forbidden City to converge on the square. The authorities were taken completely by surprise. Police rushed in to keep order but the crowd was friendly and well behaved. We wandered through it, startled at being able to film freely in the square. There was a heady sense of victory, a love of country and delight that the world had finally given China the respect it deserved. And for one night only, as people savoured the win, the city belonged to the masses.

It was five in the morning before the riot police were sent in to disperse the crowd.

Chapter 23
Qinghai Province and Dharamsala, July 2001

Tibet Express

'It's illegal'; 'It's against the law'; 'It's against China law'; 'It's banned'; 'It's prohibited'; 'It's not allowed'; 'It's not permitted'. 'I'm afraid we'll have to detain you temporarily'; 'I'm afraid we'll have to take you to the police station for questioning'. 'Don't pretend to be innocent'; 'Don't try to fool us'; 'Don't play any tricks'.

— *From* Olympic Security English, *the official language handbook for police for the 2008 Beijing Games*

In most countries, being an accredited journalist gets you privileges. In China, it gets you home detention. Any tourist with cash and a Lonely Planet guide can travel freely around the People's Republic. But resident journalists can't report outside Beijing without permission from the provincial Foreign Affairs bureau, known as the Waiban. If the Waiban approves the visit, it sends an official to accompany you for the entire shoot. The official will make sure you don't film anything that could make the authorities look bad or interview anyone who might criticise them. Then they will charge you a fat fee for ruining your story.

The most sensitive areas, like Tibet, are completely off-limits. Beijing-based journalists can't even go there on holidays. Limited access is only allowed with special approval and it's rarely granted.

This was a particular problem in May, as every foreign journalist was trying to get to the Tibetan capital, Lhasa. The reason was that Tibet was 'celebrating' the 50th anniversary of 'peaceful liberation'.

The Communists are highly sensitive to any suggestion that they 'invaded' Tibet or any hint that they've been 'occupying' it for the past half century. When 40,000 Chinese troops stormed into the region in October 1950, crushing the Tibetan Army, killing thousands of people and generally shooting up the place, it was not even a conflict, according to official parlance. It was the start of 'peaceful liberation'. On 23 May 1951, Tibetan officials signed an 'agreement' on 'peaceful liberation', meaning that they surrendered. Fifty years on, according to state television, Tibetans were still joyously celebrating it.

'People's lives have been through evident improvement in the last 50 years,' one Tibetan told a Chinese TV crew. 'Personally my life is happy and beautiful. I celebrate this peaceful liberation anniversary from the bottom of my heart.'

Other media around the country joined in the spontaneous outpourings of gratitude to the People's Liberation Army (PLA). Newspapers paid tribute to the PLA soldiers who had 'died fighting' in the 'peaceful liberation'. But the closest any of us could come to seeing the celebrations was watching them on Chinese TV in Beijing. Despite the apparently universal joy of the Tibetans, every one of us was barred from going to Tibet to report on the happy anniversary.

The Chinese Government argues that it's quite normal for journalists to have less freedom of movement than tourists. 'Every country has restrictions on media,' one official told me, ending the discussion. But sometimes there are chinks in the wall of secrecy.

A few weeks later, the Foreign Ministry unexpectedly announced a tour to the province of Qinghai to show off its burgeoning investment potential. Qinghai is historically the northeast of Tibet, but is now administered separately. And it's almost as politically sensitive as Tibet proper. It has a large Tibetan population and some of the most important Tibetan monasteries. It is also the birthplace of the exiled Tibetan leader, the Dalai Lama. The most extraordinary thing about the proposed tour was that it included one of China's most controversial construction projects — a railway being built from Qinghai to Lhasa.

For decades the Communists had been trying to extend the railway line to Tibet, but the mountainous terrain, high altitudes and unstable soil had defeated every effort. Now they were confident they had the technology to make it work. Chinese media were hailing it as a new chapter in Tibet's 'peaceful liberation', a project that would bring economic prosperity to the grateful Tibetan people. Tibetan exiles were condemning it as the final chapter in the invasion, claiming that the railway would flood Tibet with millions of additional Chinese migrant workers.

Given the controversy, it seemed unusual that the authorities were inviting us to film it. But it wasn't necessarily a sign of openness. Judging by the trip to the Masanjia re-education camp, Foreign Ministry tours were more like portals to a parallel universe, where all were happy and owed their joy to the Chinese Communist Party. I could just imagine how many Tibetan yak-herders were waiting to tell us how excited they were about the railway.

Sebastian and I flew to Qinghai along with 30 other journalists and a squadron of minders from the Foreign Ministry in Beijing. The provincial capital, Xining, lies on the edge of the Tibetan Plateau, a vast dry landscape of barren rock and mountains 3000 metres above sea level. As we got off the plane, I was struck by how thin and clean the air was. Another squadron of minders from the Xining Waiban was waiting for us, bringing to more than fifteen the number of people controlling our moves.

'Xining welcomes our foreign friends from many lands,' an official squawked through a PA system as we drove into the city. 'We hope you fall in love with us and never want to leave.'

We had been split into two large buses to accommodate the burgeoning ranks of officialdom. The large number of minders represented both the political sensitivity of the area and the tour's extensive banqueting opportunities. The seven-day itinerary had a heavy emphasis on buffets, formal dinners and official lunches. This would ensure that we had minimal time to film anything and maximum time watching our minders shovel down food and drink, all of which we were paying for, because the fees paid by journalists for the tour covered all the costs of the officials.

There was little of interest to anyone in Xining, a generic Chinese city of white-tiled buildings with blue glass windows. But the local Waiban had organised a full-day tour. Attendance was compulsory.

The first stop was a scenic lookout. Xining from above looked as dull as it did on the ground, but there was an exciting-looking cable car snaking off into the distance. I asked one of the minders, a young woman from the Beijing Waiban who went by the name of Isadora (Chinese officials often adopt Western names when dealing with foreigners), if we could go on it to film some aerial shots.

'No, not possible!' she snapped.

'Why not?'

'It is not in the program.'

The other correspondents seemed less fazed about the minders wasting our time.

'Don't worry, 90 per cent of these tours are always bullshit,' the BBC reporter Rupert Wingfield-Hayes told me. 'The main reason for coming on these trips is so you can sneak off at the end of the day and get the real story.'

The tour progressed to the main tourist attraction in Xining, the fourteenth-century Dongguan mosque. Xining has a large population of Chinese Muslims, known as Hui. Old men with wispy goatee beards and wearing skullcaps worship at one side of the mosque and women with multicoloured scarves at the other.

I was about to get back on the bus when Rupert explained the mosque's real significance. Eight years earlier, it had been at the centre of the biggest protests since Tiananmen Square, sparked by the publication of a Chinese book showing a Muslim praying next to a pig. When police tried to raid the mosque to arrest protest organisers, tens of thousands of Hui came out onto the streets to defend them. Crowds rioted, burned cars and attacked police stations. 'The Chinese sent in the army to storm the mosque,' Rupert said. 'Then they tried to cover up that it had ever happened.'

We asked the Muslim guide who had taken us through the mosque about the protests. A dozen other journalists huddled in to hear his answer.

'This Muslim event took place,' he said carefully, watched by our minders. 'But the government solved this problem very well. We did not kill anybody; neither did the government.'

There was still palpable hostility between the Hui Muslims and other Chinese. One of the foreign journalists in our group was a Chinese-American photographer, Chien. As he was getting back on the bus, he took a photo of a Hui woman. She jumped in after him and bit him on the arm. I tried to pull her away but she refused to let go. It took a concerted effort by several people to prise her off his arm and off the bus.

Ethnic tensions were increasing as Chinese migrants flooded into the province. More than 94 per cent of China's population are from a distinct ethnic group called Han Chinese. The 55 ethnic minorities, including the Tibetans, Hui and Mongols, are relatively few in number but are spread over vast areas. As a means of increasing control over the minorities, the central government had, since 1950, been encouraging Han Chinese, often at gunpoint, to settle these areas. Vast numbers of them were sent to labour camps in Qinghai. In recent years, even more Han Chinese had come voluntarily as migrant workers. In 1999 President Jiang Zemin launched a development plan called 'Go West' to send workers and state enterprises to impoverished western areas. The idea was to stave off separatism by boosting the local economies as well as changing the demographics. But many believed that only the Han were benefiting. One of the main claims of exiled Tibetans was that the Chinese were plundering the region's natural resources while taking all the jobs and profits.

The next day we boarded the train that runs to the end of the existing railway line near the administrative border with Tibet. It was packed with Chinese migrant workers heading west to the frontier town of Golmud in search of jobs. I planned to film them to show the phenomenon of migrant workers. If this many were going to a dusty, isolated town like Golmud to try their luck, how many more would travel to Tibet once the line was extended to Lhasa?

The minders placed us in a separate carriage from the Chinese passengers but once we were under way, Sebastian and I strolled into an adjoining carriage of workers. We had gone just four steps before two uniformed police sprang up in front of us, six plainclothes police appeared behind us and a group of minders came running up to stop us.

A police officer pushed us back, saying, 'It is forbidden to film.' Our loudest minder, a skinny, short-sighted man named Stanley, shouted that we were breaching railway regulations.

'What regulations?' I demanded.

'A new regulation,' he said.

Stanley ordered us back to our compartment.

We retreated, deciding to try again later, but the carriage doors were immediately locked. Police were stationed at each exit. We now had a sixteen-hour train journey ahead of us under carriage arrest.

'I can't believe we've just been locked up for trying to film on a frigging media tour,' I said to Sebastian.

He smiled gently, concerned I was getting worked up over something that would never change.

'OK bro, time to relax,' Sebastian said. 'You want to hear some music?'

We retired to the compartment we were sharing with Rupert and his producer, Holly Williams, a fluent Chinese speaker who, like many of the ABC cameramen I had met, had escaped from a small town in Tasmania. They had just tried the same thing at the other end of the carriage and been driven back like us. Sebastian began to play the first of twelve Pink Floyd CDs he had brought. He also started smoking something that smelled like a definite contravention of Chinese regulations.

'Sebastian!' I whispered. 'There's a policeman standing outside our door.'

'Chill man, they don't know what it is,' he murmured, passing it over.

Sixteen hours later, still locked up, we arrived in Golmud for the official start of the media tour.

As Stanley boomed orders through his megaphone for us to gather on the platform, we slipped away to interview workers getting off the train. All were heading to the railway construction project. We quickly rejoined the media group in case we'd been spotted filming 'illegally'.

Stanley herded us onto a new set of buses, which took us to the hotel for the first event on the itinerary ... a banquet. It was midday. Officials from Golmud arrived to reinforce the Beijing minders and Xining Waiban. After two hours of watching them eat, it was time for the filming highlight of the day — a press conference in the hotel conference room with a dozen local-government officials.

All wearing identical suits, they sat at a long table behind matching bottles of mineral water, which remained unopened. Smiling young women, called *xiao jie* (little mistresses) and wearing matching red gowns, walked up and down the length of the table serving tea. As usual, the speeches were along party lines. 'All the ethnic groups in Golmud live together in great harmony and prosperity,' proclaimed Vice Mayor Xia Jaiqiang.

Next item on the itinerary was: *18.00 Banquet hosted by officials of the Golmud Municipal Government.*

I told the minders I was unwell and sneaked off with Sebastian to try to find Tibetans to interview. It was not easy. Ninety per cent of the town was Han Chinese. Eventually we found a teahouse serving Tibetan truck drivers. Burly men in cowboy hats sat around smoking and drinking with the owner, a middle-aged Tibetan woman named Yangzung.

These were the first Tibetans we'd met on our own and communication was tricky. None of them except for Yangzung spoke

Mandarin. I spoke to them in English, Sebastian translated my questions into Mandarin, Yangzung translated Sebastian's Mandarin into Tibetan, they answered in Tibetan, which Yangzung translated into Mandarin, which Sebastian translated into English while filming.

They clearly didn't see themselves as living in harmony and prosperity. The largest of the truck drivers, a thick-set, bullish man named Jayanima, told us there were too many Han Chinese here now. 'The Tibetans have small faces,' he said, meaning that they have no social status, 'and the Han have big arses.'

Jayanima and his friends were not the skinny, gentle, chanting New Age Tibetans of Hollywood movies. They were pugnacious truckies who looked like they enjoyed a drink and a fight. They also seemed unafraid of Chinese officials. One of the few jobs available to Tibetans was to drive Chinese goods on the three-day journey across the mountains to Lhasa. The railway threatened to take away their livelihood.

'When the railway is built it will destroy the grassland where herding is done,' Jayanima said. 'It will make our lives harder. They will take away mineral resources from here. It'll be like that. There is no benefit for the Tibetans.'

I then asked him, via Sebastian and Yangzung, what he thought of the exiled Tibetan leader, the Dalai Lama. He held up both thumbs. 'He's this kind of lama,' he said, smiling. 'I definitely believe in the Dalai Lama. It would be good if everyone spoke Tibetan again and the Dalai Lama came home to Lhasa.'

The next day we were scheduled to film the site where work had begun on extending the railway line to Lhasa. But the program had the entire group on the verge of mutiny. There was to be a 90-minute drive to the railway construction site for a one-hour briefing, followed by a 90-minute drive back to Golmud for a banquet. We told the senior minder, Mr Lu, that we had not come all the way to the Tibetan Plateau to spend half of each day eating. After a long debate, he reluctantly agreed that on this one occasion we would take a packed lunch.

At the construction site, we were treated to a long press conference giving technical details:

1. There will be 29 train stations, 90 kilometres of bridges, and 3126 railway arches.
2. There will be 16 trains each day carrying 8 million tonnes of cargo annually.
3. More than 80 per cent of the railway will be built at elevations of more than 4000 metres.
4. The tracks will have freezer units to ensure that the permafrost doesn't melt in summer.

We were allowed only a few minutes to film construction before we were ordered back on the bus to go to the next stop, a shed full of engineers. After concerted pleading, Mr Lu agreed to let the BBC and us go ahead in one of the minders' cars so we could film pieces to camera away from the mob. But when another crew complained that we were getting special treatment, Mr Lu told the driver not to stop. I thought he was joking but the car began racing back to Golmud at high speed, the driver refusing to let us out to film any scenery. When he was forced to stop for petrol, Sebastian and I jumped out and began filming a mountain. Horrified, the minder ran in front of the camera, shouting that Mr Lu had forbidden any filming. 'You work for Mr Lu,' I shouted back. 'I don't!'

Eventually I intimidated him into moving out of frame, and we completed our illegal shot of the mountain. It felt like a great victory.

Later, back at Golmud, I buttonholed Mr Lu, saying that I wanted to interview someone about the railway. All of the officials had discussed technical details but said they could not comment on why the railway was being built. Mr Lu appeared taken aback by my request. 'Why do you want to discuss the railway?' he asked.

'I thought that's why we were here,' I answered.

He thought about it and suggested I contact somebody in the Railways Ministry in Beijing.

'Wouldn't it make more sense if we spoke to somebody here, seeing this is where it's being built?' I asked.

'That will not be possible,' Mr Lu said.

Fortunately yet another press conference was scheduled at Golmud, with Qinghai's deputy governor, Bai Ma. He agreed to be interviewed afterwards. Bai Ma was a Tibetan who had risen through the Communist hierarchy to his current post. He maintained that the railway would mean Tibetans could trade their goods outside Tibet and grow rich. 'The Qinghai–Tibet railway will bring happiness to the Tibet people,' he said. 'It is called the "Happy Line". It will bring happiness.'

I asked if it might also bring hundreds of thousands of Han Chinese.

'Han people wouldn't dare to live on the Tibetan Plateau,' he said. 'They couldn't adapt to the climate. What would they eat and drink?'

We were in a town on the Tibetan Plateau that was 90 per cent Han Chinese. Bai Ma was deputy governor of an ancient Tibetan province that was already majority Han. His boss and most of his colleagues were Han. But he just kept smiling and saying that no Han Chinese would ever come here.

The tour was almost over. We had shot kilometres of tape of press conferences, train and bus interiors, and the backsides and elbows of journalists, cameramen and photographers who'd got in the way. We had a few shots of men with shovels, and an illegally obtained but exclusive shot of a mountain. I doubted it would prove riveting viewing.

Back on the train for the sixteen-hour return journey to Xining, the officials now said we were welcome to film anywhere on board. But since we were going east, the train was, of course, devoid of migrant workers. 'What about the regulation banning us from filming?' I asked Stanley.

He strained a laugh through a tight smile.

Relations between the minders and the media were growing increasingly poisonous, but Stanley appeared to have no concept of why we were dissatisfied. The next morning he brought us the train guest book for us to write our comments in. We were clearly meant to say something nice about the service. Holly wrote in perfect Chinese, 'Not bad, apart from police locking us in the carriage.'

Stanley grabbed the book in horror and tried to rub out her comment. Realising he couldn't erase ink he began tearing Holly's comment off the page. Then, realising he was illegally damaging railway property, he stopped, slammed the book shut and stared at Holly, speechless with rage. On the verge of tears, he ran out of the compartment. A moment later, he ran back in and shouted, 'You are a very low quality person. You should leave China as soon as possible.'

There was one last item on the tour itinerary: a visit to the Kumbum Buddhist Monastery outside Xining. It was one of the most important Tibetan monasteries in China, and a showpiece of state-sanctioned religious freedom. Officials regularly brought visitors here to show how Buddhism was flourishing.

There was another aspect of the monastery that was strictly taboo for discussion. Kumbum was just near the birthplace of the Dalai Lama. Ever since he fled Lhasa, the god-king has held a special place on the Communist Party's hate list. Tibetans are permitted to practise Buddhism but they are not allowed to acknowledge any place in religion or society for the Dalai Lama. In official parlance, he is an 'evil splittist'.

A gripping handbook, titled *Tibet's March Toward Modernisation*, published by the Information Office of the State Council of the People's Republic of China, sets out the sinister intent of his splittist group.

> The Dalai Lama clique represents the backward relations
> of production of feudal serfdom, the retrogressive religious
> culture of the theocratic system and the interests of the
> dying privileged few of the feudal serf-owner class.

And that's not his worst crime.

The Dalai Lama clique and international hostile forces
slandered the peaceful liberation of Tibet and the
expulsion of the imperialist forces from Tibet as 'China's
occupation of Tibet'.

In 1998 the abbot of Kumbum Monastery fled to the United States after concerted pressure was put on him to denounce the Dalai Lama in favour of a Chinese-appointed rival. Officials appointed a more compliant committee of lamas to run the monastery in his place. But many of the young monks resented the interference and were furious that the monastery had become a sightseeing destination for Han Chinese. Hundreds of tourists were able to wander up and down the main pathway through the monastery, or even hire out traditional clothing from a stall, dress up as Tibetans and pose for 'hilarious' photographs.

It was impossible for us to speak to the monks walking past. The laneways were full of undercover police, instantly recognisable by their tough build, close-cropped hair and rough slacks and shirts. But Rupert, who spoke fluent Mandarin, managed to talk briefly with two young monks in a quiet alcove. He asked them what they liked about being at the monastery.

'The weather's nice sometimes.'

'What else is nice?'

'Not much. It's best to be deaf and mute here.'

Rupert asked what they thought of the tourists.

'There are too many tourists, it's a mess.'

The other monk added disdainfully, 'They are all Han.'

They asked Rupert if he'd ever met the Dalai Lama and were thrilled to find that he had. They said they hoped the Dalai Lama would come back one day. It seemed they hadn't got round to reading *Tibet's March Toward Modernisation*.

The officials led us into an ornate room for a briefing with the ruling committee of lamas. Several of them sat cross-legged behind a long, low table wearing long red and yellow robes. Another, who was wearing a

Mao suit, was introduced as a Living Buddha. They spoke Tibetan and some Mandarin but no English. A tour guide with a megaphone translated their greetings for our benefit, then invited questions.

'What reverence do you have for the Dalai Lama and what place do you think he should have in Tibetan society?' I asked.

A pin dropped loudly.

The interpreter and the lamas went into a huddle, whispering in Tibetan. We kept recording. The conversation was later translated as follows:

> Interpreter to lamas: 'Dalai Lama. What now?'
> Lama: 'You answer, Living Buddha.'
> Interpreter to Lamas: 'What kind of place does the Dalai Lama have in Tibetan society?'
> Lama: 'I see. We only know he is a, eh ... Let's say, we only know about this lamasery, nothing else.'
> Man in glasses: 'Say as we discussed.'
> Interpreter: 'We only know about our monastery.'
> Man in glasses: 'Things about our monastery.'
> Interpreter: 'The rest we don't know much.'
> Man in glasses: 'Just say whatever you like.'
> Interpreter (in English): 'We only know the circumstances about this monastery, about the others we know a little.'
> Reporter: 'The Dalai Lama comes from this monastery so I think it's a natural question to ask.'
> Interpreter (in Tibetan): 'She says the Dalai Lama is from this monastery. Like you said, you only know about this monastery so it's normal for you to answer this question.'
> Lama: 'Get up, get up.'
> Man in glasses: 'Hmm, all right.'

They rose and walked out. Without explanation, the press conference was over. Mr Lu's face was rigid with anger. I told Sebastian to keep filming while I walked up and asked Mr Lu if the monks had been threatened. He looked from me to Sebastian in fury, genuinely affronted that we would dare to turn the camera on him, and accused me of threatening the Chinese Government. But he was soon distracted by another public relations disaster. Just outside, the Chinese-American photographer, Chien, who'd been bitten by the Muslim woman, was being punched by a Tibetan monk.

It seemed he'd once again been mistaken for a Chinese tourist. Like the truck drivers in Golmud, the monk was not a Hollywood-style Tibetan. He was a mean fighting monk who'd had one too many cameras shoved in his face by Chinese sightseers. He punched Chien again and, when Chien punched him back, the monk grabbed his camera and started garrotting him with the neck strap. Another monk came running over and starting punching Chien from behind. Three television cameras were now recording the brawl. Finally everyone had a story. This was not how the Foreign Ministry had intended the tour to end.

The bus was unusually quiet as we drove back to the hotel. The atmosphere at the final banquet was icy. As I sat between Chinese officials studiously ignoring me while they toasted everybody else in the room, I thought my standing with officialdom couldn't possibly sink any lower. Then I remembered I was going to India to interview the Dalai Lama.

Tenzin Gyatso, aka the fourteenth Dalai Lama, aka Ocean of Wisdom, aka Evil Splittist, was 23 when he disguised himself as a soldier and fled across the Himalayas with tens of thousands of followers. He was now 66 and was having even less luck getting back into Tibet than I was.

His temporary base in northern India had become the permanent home of his government-in-exile. Once a tiny hill station, Dharamsala was now a large town crowded with private residences, monasteries, nunneries, government offices, meditation retreats, hotels, astrology centres, restaurants, bookshops and souvenir stores. It had become a magnet for Tibetan refugees, religious pilgrims, supermodels, Buddhist Hollywood stars and unwashed backpackers. Dharamsala was part

Buddhist shrine, part New Age Mecca, part glamour destination and part tourist hell.

For me, it was something far greater than the sum of all those things. It was a place we could film that didn't have any Waiban.

The Evil Splittist's office had scheduled us in for a one-hour interview on 31 August to discuss the new railway, warning that if we missed the appointment he would not be available again for several months. It took three days to get there, flying via the former Soviet republic of Uzbekistan — China had stopped all direct flights to India after a border war in the 1960s — and driving for twelve hours from Delhi. But I felt energised by the sense of freedom that came from not having minders.

The security check at the Dalai Lama's headquarters was rigorous but the officials were friendly and polite. They ushered us into a room as elaborate as the ruling lamas' hall in Kumbum. We set up our gear, waited five minutes and the Dalai Lama walked in. He looked at me with a mischievous smile, walked up and clasped my hand. A minute later we were sitting down and giggling about Chinese officials. I told him about the walkout at the Kumbum monastery and he shrieked with high-pitched laughter.

'So what they actually want is that a Buddhist should at the same time be absolutely loyal to the Communist Party,' he said and chortled again. 'So sometimes they are making every effort to achieve some impossible thing.'

I'd always considered the Californian/New Age/crystal-rubbing adoration of the Dalai Lama to be just another annoying manifestation of a shallow, celebrity-obsessed culture. But sitting in the reflected light of the world's number one Tibetan mystic I couldn't help but share it. He positively lit up the room with charisma. No wonder the old men who ran China hated his guts. The Evil Splittist may have been a celibate monk but he had more charm and sex appeal than the entire Politburo.

He gave us a funny and persuasive interview about the perils of the Tibet railway, concluding that it would hasten Tibet's 'cultural genocide'.

Sebastian and I used up the remaining five minutes of our allotted time getting happy snaps with him on his couch. I was already imagining hanging a large blow-up in the bureau for the time when the Waiban came round to complain about my story.

And I thought of Madame Ren Xiaoping from the Chinese embassy in Canberra. Perhaps we weren't going to be friends after all.

The day after my audience with the Dalai Lama, Sebastian and I stopped off in Uzbekistan to report on its tenth year of independence from the Soviet Union. The celebration of this anniversary was not a momentous event in world terms. Even so, the authorities must have been disappointed by the world's response. The only foreign media who turned up were a woman from Chile and Sebastian and me.

It turned out to be an interesting if obscure story — the government was cracking down on dissidents, claiming they were Islamic terrorists sponsored by Osama bin Laden in neighbouring Afghanistan. Dissidents insisted this was just a trumped-up excuse to crush democratic opposition. After ten days in Uzbekistan I tended to agree. There was no sign of religious fanaticism and I couldn't believe a nutter like Osama bin Laden holed up in Afghanistan could seriously threaten any other country.

At the end of the shoot, Sebastian flew to Sydney for a holiday, but I decided to stay on for a day or two in the capital, Tashkent, before heading off on holidays with Kim to Spain.

The next night I went to a popular bar to see some Uzbeks I had met on the shoot. Something felt wrong as I walked in. Everyone was gathered in front of the TV screen watching a live relay of CNN but with a frenzied Uzbek commentary. A caption on the screen said: 'AMERICA UNDER ATTACK'. A building that looked like one of the towers of the World Trade Center was on fire. And then it started falling down.

Chapter 24
Kabul and Tora Bora, Winter 2001–2002

Jackistan

'You ain't gonna fuckin' believe this. You are *not* gonna *fuckin'* believe this!'

We looked up to see Jack standing in the doorway, dressed in his usual sunglasses and US Special Forces–style uniform, holding a Russian assault rifle.

'Fuckin' peacekeepers, fuckin' Kraut peacekeepers! They tried to take my fuckin' gun!'

Jack was a 46-year-old ex-Green Beret with a short, stocky build, a Tom Selleck moustache and a sharp military haircut. He went under the name Jack for 'security reasons', but also enjoyed cultivating an air of mystery and seemed to prefer his pseudonym to what we later found to be his real name, Keith. He had become such a regular visitor to our house in Kabul that he'd effectively moved in, bringing vast quantities of Pepsi, Snickers Bars and, on one occasion, ammunition. Every evening, Jack heralded his arrival with an expletive-filled account of his day.

Today it seemed that he and his Afghan militia had been wandering back to their van when a German peacekeeping unit asked them to hand in their weapons. The new post-Taliban Government had a policy of disarming the mujahideen roaming the capital. But nobody had counted on trying to prise a weapon from a paid-up member of the National Rifle Association. After a testosterone-filled standoff, the Germans had apparently thought better of it and let them on their way.

It was another small victory in what, for Jack at least, had been a highly successful war. But he was now glimpsing the end of a dream. 'Jesus,' he said sadly. 'Gun control in fuckin' Kabul!'

It was Afghanistan's world-beating lack of gun control that had first brought Jack here shortly after September 11. Like many retired Special Forces soldiers, he had volunteered to return to the fold in any capacity after watching the Twin Towers collapse. Just how he got here was never quite clear but Jack's version had him flying into the opposition-controlled north of Afghanistan on a Pentagon mission.

His job, as he explained it, was to help bring in humanitarian aid drops and to find out why so many Afghans were getting sick from eating them. In the early days of the bombing, the parachuted food aid had not been the public relations triumph the US had expected. Reports filtered back of Afghan villagers being crushed to death when the food crates dropped on their homes and of other Afghans losing limbs trying to collect crates that were inadvertently dropped in minefields. More alarmingly for the Pentagon, many who survived the humanitarian drops were showing signs of poisoning after eating them. The Taliban were suspected of foul play.

Jack said he flew in from Tajikistan under the auspices of a 'humanitarian aid group' to help sort out the mess. He told us he soon solved the poisoning mystery by noticing something that had eluded the finest minds of the Pentagon. Each food parcel contained a drying sachet with a warning not to eat it that was incomprehensible to illiterate Afghans — who were eating them.

Mission accomplished, it should have been time for Jack to go home. But he hadn't come all this way not to kill some Taliban.

Fuck that! thought Jack.

So he'd hung round the Northern Alliance frontline in his Special Forces-style uniform. One day he showed the mujahideen how to redirect their wildly inaccurate mortar fire. Within moments they were excitedly slaughtering Taliban in the trenches opposite and Jack was a hero. Or at least that's what Jack told us. One thing led to another, and Jack eventually became a military adviser to the Northern Alliance, who had by now taken over most of the country. Whether they realised he was just a civilian with absolutely no official status was also never quite clear.

And now Jack had moved into the ABC bureau in Kabul and was showing no sign of ever leaving.

We had met Jack not long after Sebastian and I were sent to Afghanistan to cover the aftermath of the new War on Terror. We'd missed most of the fighting thanks to taking holidays the day before the Twin Towers collapsed. But we were expected to make up for it by spending the next two months based in Kabul, which had just been liberated from the Taliban.

The city was at once depressing and uplifting. The wintry gloom made the bombed-out city look even less habitable than when I was here in the summer of 1997. Armed militias of the Northern Alliance patrolled the streets, suggesting that the gun-toting brutes of the Taliban had simply been replaced by rival gun-toting brutes. Yet there was an unmistakeable air of optimism. The streets seemed to be coming to life after a long hibernation. Men sat on street corners fashioning homemade satellite dishes from flattened tins of cooking oil for their once banned televisions. Shops again played music, Pakistani trucks were bringing in consumer goods, restaurants and cinemas were opening, and children were even flying kites — one of the many sinful activities outlawed by the Taliban.

It was hard to imagine that just weeks earlier the same streets had seen mass rallies denouncing US bombing and vowing to destroy the Taliban's enemies. Afghan allegiances had always been fluid. Warlords changed sides regularly for fun and profit, and civilians had learned that pragmatic acceptance of whoever had the most guns was the best way of surviving.

As much as people had tired of the excesses of the Taliban, they had good reason to be nervous about the Northern Alliance. Most of its commanders were former mujahideen who had fought among themselves after defeating the Soviets. Kabul suffered no damage under

Soviet rule and relatively little was caused by the Taliban. The leaders of the Northern Alliance bore most of the blame for the ruination of the city. Even so, most people seemed happy with how things had turned out. After 23 years of conflict, the fighting was finally over. People wanted peace above all else, regardless of who could bring it. For now, Kabul was unusually calm, which was good for locals but bad for journalists.

The big story had shifted to Tora Bora near the Pakistan border, where Osama bin Laden was believed to be making his last stand. B-52s were pounding the mountains and US Special Forces were beginning to sift through the caves where the al-Qaeda militants were holed up.

The problem was, we couldn't get there. The road from Kabul to Jalalabad, the town nearest to Tora Bora, was a no-go zone. Four journalists had been murdered on it less than three weeks earlier, including an Australian cameraman, Harry Burton. So the ABC had grounded us in the capital. I had almost given up hope of getting out of Kabul when a notice appeared in the hotel foyer, promising safe escort to Tora Bora. The price was ridiculous — $5000 per car. But with no other option I rang the number.

An Afghan named Syed answered and took my details. A few hours later, he and another man arrived at my store room. Unlike most Afghans, Syed was neatly groomed and wore Western dress. He spoke fluent English and had an air of quiet authority. However, something about him seemed shifty. He said the convoy was 'official' but was evasive about who was organising it and why it was so expensive. I was inclined to turn him down but I was intrigued by his companion — a muscular American in a black T-shirt and sunglasses who introduced himself as Jack.

Jack didn't say much and wouldn't really answer questions. But he hinted that there could be an 'American adviser' on the trip. This was getting interesting. I negotiated the price down to $1000 a person and said I'd think about it. Later we found that six other media groups had signed up for the trip, including *Newsweek* and the *New Yorker*. On the principle of safety in numbers, Sebastian and I decided to chance the trip and the Foreign Desk gave us approval to go.

The following dawn we assembled at a meeting point on the outskirts of the city and found Jack coordinating everything. It was heartening that all the other journalists were from magazines and press agencies, meaning that we wouldn't have to compete with other television crews for shots. On the downside, there was Jack's militia.

He'd taken a rag-tag group of Northern Alliance fighters and was trying to turn them into an elite protection unit for aid workers and journalists. And they clearly had a long way to go. There were about a dozen of them, most in their teens and early twenties. They were heavily armed with machine guns and rocket-propelled grenades but looked just as likely to shoot each other as to protect us from the Taliban. Standing within 50 metres of them made you feel instantly insecure. Even so, they were fewer than we'd been promised and some of the journalists were threatening to pull out. Jack explained he had to hire more guards along the way, at a town called Surobi. It was the price of passage from the local warlord. The road was supposed to be safe until there so we agreed to go.

We set off in a six-car convoy, a vanload of soldiers at each end and Jack scooting back and forth between them in a beaten-up sedan. At every prayer and pee-stop, Jack sent his soldiers off in pairs to scan the horizon, which they faithfully did until the moment he looked away, when they sat down and smoked.

The least motivated was Jack's interpreter, Zabi. Jack, who couldn't get his head around Afghan names, called him Joe. Zabi (or Joe) was about twenty years old (Afghans are rarely certain of their age) but looked about fourteen, with puppy-dog eyes and a fuzzy adolescent beard. He spoke only rough English and rarely had any idea what Jack was shouting at him, feigning comprehension by nodding and looking interested. He owed his position more to family connections than talent. All Jack's soldiers were from the Northern Alliance stronghold, the Panjshir Valley. But Zabi was from the same village as Ahmad Shah Massoud, the Northern Alliance leader who was assassinated just two days before the September 11 attacks.

We were fortunate to be travelling with a former Kabul University professor, Dr Iqbal, who had agreed to be our interpreter. His family was part of the exiled Afghan community in Pakistan, who were now coming back to try to rebuild their country. He was a reminder of the urbane, educated middle class which had dominated Kabul before the warlords and fundamentalists destroyed it. Dr Iqbal had a dream of building a railway line around Afghanistan to link the main Tajik and Pashtun cities: 'like an iron bracelet to hold the country together,' he said.

It would certainly be a hell of an improvement on the road. The potholes were even worse than I remembered from four years before and we had barely left Kabul when the van burst a tyre. There was little other traffic on the lonely dirt road. It was a perfect place for an ambush. I imagined the fear and helplessness that Harry Burton must have felt when his car was pulled over by gunmen.

When we arrived in Surobi two hours later, I instantly had a bad feeling about the place. Armed men loitered around the road. Some of the buildings had machine guns mounted on the roof. Most of the country had been pro-Taliban before the US bombing, switching allegiance only when it was obvious that the Northern Alliance was going to win. Judging from the sullen mood of Surobi, it was clear that our new bodyguards were recent Taliban.

By the time we arrived in Jalalabad, the main town near the battlefield of Tora Bora, it was dark. The streets were full of soldiers and military vehicles. Most of the hotels were full of media so Jack split us up. The guards took Sebastian, Dr Iqbal and me to a dirty concrete hostel with cold rooms and grubby mattresses. The other journalists got the last rooms in the relatively good hotel next door. We were about to meet them for dinner when Dr Iqbal whispered that we had a problem. Our guards, it seemed, were planning to murder us.

He had overheard the Surobi soldiers arguing with the Panjshiris about whether they should kill and rob us. The Surobis had somehow heard how much we had agreed to pay for the trip and felt they were being cheated. Their proposal was to demand that we pay twice the wages. If we disagreed, they could slit our throats on the way back through Surobi and take our money.

I passed this on to Jack. He was already having a stressful day and started throbbing in fury, first at Dr Iqbal, whom he accused of telling the Surobis about the money, and then at the 'fuckin' Surobi assholes'. He stormed off with one of our group's translators to confront them. His message, he later told us, was roughly as follows: 'If you try to stop us passing we will shoot it out with you, and if I die, US Air Force planes will come and bomb your town into the ground and there will be nothing left for your children to inherit.'

Given the level of collateral damage caused by US bombing, it must have seemed a credible threat. The Surobis agreed to behave. Jack even insisted we go back to spend the night in the hostel, promising that the Panjshiris would keep an eye on us. 'No problem,' he said. 'It's cool.'

The only other option was sleeping in the car so we went back to our room and barricaded the door. But before I could go to bed, I had to call the ABC in Sydney to say I'd arrived safely. I couldn't get a signal from the room so I crept out past the soldiers to the hostel balcony. As quietly as I could in the dark, I set up the phone and satellite dish and dialled the Sydney Radio Desk. A muffled-sounding voice answered on an almost inaudible line.

'It's Eric Campbell calling from Afghanistan,' I whispered.

'Hello?'

'It's Eric Campbell calling from Afghanistan,' I whispered slightly louder.

'Can you speak up?'

'It's Eric Campbell,' I muttered. 'I've arrived in Jalalabad.'

'Good-o. What have you got for us?'

'I can't talk right now.'

'Hello?'

'I can't talk loudly.'

'Listen, we need something for seven and seven forty-five.'

'I can't talk now.'

'Hello?'

'Look, there are people wanting to kill us.'

'You're going to have to speak up!'

'Sorry, the signal's going,' I shouted. 'I'll try to call back.'

'I can hear you fine now. What have you got for us?'

I hung up, looked around nervously and crept back to bed. It was a sleepless night.

At daylight, with the street now bustling, I went back to the balcony to set up the satellite phone again. The day of travel meant that I hadn't been able to film but, as the ABC's only reporter in Afghanistan, I still had to file a story. One of the downsides of covering breaking stories on your own is how often you have to fudge it by writing something to accompany pictures you haven't seen of events you didn't witness. I dialled into a London web server, downloaded the news wires onto my laptop, wrote a television script based on what I could have read on the internet in Australia, recorded a voiceover and emailed it to Sydney. The Foreign Desk would edit it to news-agency pictures of overnight bombing.

Jalalabad felt very different from Kabul, where Afghanistan's various ethnic groups — Tajiks, Pashtuns, Hazaras and Uzbeks — lived side by side. Most of the population here was Pashtun, the ethnic group that gave rise to the Taliban. As in nearby Pakistan, the streets were full of motorised rickshaws and brightly decorated trucks, and the shops were full of Pakistani goods. This had been friendly territory for both the Taliban and al-Qaeda. Jack's Northern Alliance Panjshiris seemed out of place.

They were also running late. We waited for more than an hour before they were ready to leave for Tora Bora, minus the Surobi guards, who remained in Jalalabad despite being dismissed. But Jack made up for it with a bonus excursion along the way. He had found the address of the house where Osama bin Laden had lived in his Jalalabad days. It was an impressive compound just outside the city, with a huge metal gate decorated with stars. The abandoned interior had been ransacked but among the rubbish was some evidence of how the al-Qaeda leader's acolytes amused themselves. There were bomb-making diagrams and brochures for hi-tech radio transmitters.

Our arrival brought a crowd of curious onlookers. They were Osama's old neighbours and they were sorry he had left. 'People here think he was a very nice Muslim,' one man told us. 'He was a very kind man.'

The mood was much the same at Tora Bora. B–52s were still circling high overhead, visible by their vapour trails, but they had given up bombing. After weeks of bombardment, the mountains were pockmarked with craters and littered with unexploded ordnance but most of the al-Qaeda fighters were believed to have escaped, including bin Laden. The US was relying on the local soldiers to track them down. The Jalalabad militias were nominally allied to the Northern Alliance, but the foot soldiers clearly didn't have their hearts in it. We stopped a party of them returning from the 'hunt'. All they were interested in was collecting their pay and going back to their villages.

We headed back down the mountain towards Jalalabad to begin filing our stories but Jack had one more mission in mind. He wanted to pinch the metal stars from the gate of Osama bin Laden's compound and he wanted Sebastian to film the mission. 'Shoot it on night scope,' he said. 'It'll look fuckin' cool!' It didn't seem quite right to be looting private property, even if it belonged to the world's most wanted man, but it made for an interesting photo. 'I'm gonna give this to the Special Ops museum in Fort Bragg,' Jack said, clutching a star. 'They're gonna love it!'

Back in town we managed to move into the good hotel — without the Surobi guards who wanted to kill us. It was just as well, as we had to cut two television stories and a radio feature that night and wouldn't be getting any sleep. Sebastian was always happy to keep doing whatever was required, no matter how tired or dirty or uncomfortable we were.

All he needed was a constant supply of Marlboro Reds and a continuous soundtrack of Pink Floyd, CDs of which he carried with a Walkman wherever he went. But that night he seemed unusually tired and I wondered if age was finally catching up with him.

We finished cutting the pieces just in time for a quick breakfast before we headed to the satellite feed points that news agencies had set up in the rambling 1920s-era Spinghar Hotel. A small plaque on the entrance commemorated the cameraman Harry Burton and his colleagues. They had spent their last night in the hotel before they were murdered on the road to Kabul. A sign asked visitors not to bring in Kalashnikovs.

Jack had another treat for us at the Spinghar Hotel — an exclusive interview with the newly returned pro-American warlord Hazrat Ali. Dozens of news crews were camped out trying to get to him but he'd agreed to speak only to Jack's group out of respect for his being a military adviser to the Northern Alliance. The other crews were outraged as we walked in. They tried to follow, with CNN and NBC pushing their way to the front of the pack, but Ali's armed bodyguards shoved them out and closed the doors. 'What did I fuckin' tell you?' Jack said. 'I look after you guys.'

Ali was an ethnic Nuristani whose family had ruled much of the area like feudal lords until the Taliban drove them out in the early days of their revolution. At that time, most people believed the Taliban were liberating them from the corruption and brutality of the warlords. The Taliban's subsequent corruption and brutality diminished their popularity but not everyone was pleased to see the old order returning. Ali had been directing operations against Tora Bora and he had no doubt that some of the Pashtuns were deliberately letting his opponents flee. 'They are not all finished,' he said. 'Their bases are destroyed but they are still throughout the country.'

It wasn't even clear if many had been captured. The day before we arrived, Ali had paraded a dozen al-Qaeda militants before the media for a photo-op but not allowed them to speak. Jack now asked if we could interview some of the captives in Jalalabad's prison. Ali was reluctant but the Afghan sense of hospitality prevailed. He'd let three of us go in, so we settled on Sebastian to film it and the *New Yorker* writer and photographer to pool for the print media.

The prison was in an old brick fort that had seen better days. The guards ushered them inside the prison courtyard and locked the metal gates behind them. After a revolt by al-Qaeda prisoners in northern Afghanistan which left hundreds dead, the guards were understandably nervous about their inmates. But Jack clearly relished the chance for some face time with 'ass-wipe terrorists' and went in with them.

There were about 40 prisoners from Tora Bora in the fort, most of them locked in cells. Two men were allowed out into the garden to be interviewed. Both denied having anything to do with al-Qaeda. One of them, Fayez Mohamed Ahmed, claimed he was a 26-year-old businessman from Kuwait. He was wearing a traditional long, baggy shirt called a *shalwar kameez* with combat trousers. The other man, Nasir Abdul Latif, who was 36, wore a combat jacket but also claimed to be a businessman. He insisted he had come to Afghanistan to live under proper Islamic rules, not to fight.

Jack noticed that both men's hands bore small cuts that could have come from firing Kalashnikovs. The older man, Nasir Abdul Latif, eventually admitted having seen Osama bin Laden at Tora Bora. 'He was saying that you should believe in God, you should believe in me. We are living the jihad for the sake of Allah. We will win this jihad.'

After a few prompts, he became a businessman with considerable attitude. 'We came to fight Americans and we will fight them. We will fight them forever, up to the time that we destroy them totally.'

'He fuckin' said that?' Jack asked when he heard the translation.

Fayez Mohamed Ahmed, the Kuwaiti 'businessman', quickly qualified the threat, saying they only wanted to fight Americans who were fighting Muslims. Jack was unimpressed. 'America will come and get you,' he said in parting.

We headed back to Kabul for the inauguration of the new Afghan administration, motoring slowly through Surobi on the way. The guards' grudging agreement not to slit our throats was obviously as friendly as the town would get. Bearded Taliban types sat on the rooftops with Kalashnikovs, belt-fed machine guns and rocket-propelled grenades.

'I pity the poor fucker who stops here to buy an apple,' Jack said.

When we were safely back in Northern Alliance territory on a winding pass outside Kabul, Jack stopped the convoy, suggesting that everybody relax with a little shooting practice. He and his soldiers took turns firing across the gorge with glee, then offered us the rifles, laughing at our clumsy attempts to shoot. Everyone took happy snaps of each other holding weapons in one of the silly, matey rituals of war zones. Within minutes we heard the crack of gunfire overhead as soldiers further up the mountain joined in. It was not so much a threat as a kind of answering birdcall. After 23 years of conflict, gunfire had become part of the natural order. The new government faced an interesting future.

Al-Qaeda's Funniest Home Videos

We consider this our duty: to defend humanity against the
scourge of intolerance, violence and fanaticism.

— *Ahmad Shah Massoud, Defence Minister, Northern Alliance*

Massoud's troops were responsible for looting and rape after
they captured the Karte Seh section of Kabul from the
Taliban and Shi'a forces in March ... Massoud's troops went
on a rampage, systematically looting whole streets and raping
women.

— *US State Department Human Rights Report, 1995*

For a dead man, Ahmad Shah Massoud was becoming quite a celebrity.
The victorious Northern Alliance had hung portraits of its slain military
leader over intersections, in shop windows and on office walls. Soldiers
and schoolboys exchanged swap cards of his image. Commanders and
mullahs praised his saintly qualities.

I'd never quite understood the cult of Massoud, given that he was a
warlord who had been linked to various war crimes and atrocities,
including indiscriminate shelling of civilians. But I was in a small
minority. Visiting Western journalists had generally fallen under the spell
of Massoud's charisma, taking at face value statements he made on
women's rights and ignoring his fundamentalist past and the fact that he
had ordered women in his fiefdom to wear the burqa.

The French Left in particular had pursued a passionate love affair
with Massoud, *enchanté* by his ability to speak French, his natty woollen

cap cocked at *un angle* rakish, and his resemblance to that other militant style icon, Che Guevara. The adulation did not appear affected by Amnesty International and Human Rights Watch reports on Massoud's forces engaging in *le* raping *et le* looting.

I was more cynical than some colleagues, perhaps because Kim had experienced Massoud's feminism first-hand. Seven months earlier, she had filmed a documentary in Afghanistan on the long-running war and conducted one of the last interviews with Massoud. Confronted with a female journalist, he refused to make eye contact with her or even acknowledge her presence, addressing all his answers to her male interpreter.

Several thousand women had bitter memories of the last time Massoud's mujahideen had ruled the capital, when they were subject to constant fear of kidnapping and rape, one of the reasons many had initially welcomed the Taliban.

So it seemed a little odd that the inauguration ceremony for Afghanistan's new government of national unity had a giant portrait of Ahmad Shah Massoud hanging over the proceedings. The Northern Alliance might have seen him as a natural symbol of the new Afghanistan but I wasn't sure why the rest of the nation would see a Tajik warlord as their unifying symbol of choice. Not that it really mattered what anybody else thought. Even in the new government of national unity, the Northern Alliance was calling the shots.

The UN had brokered the makeup of the interim government to rule until elections could be held and it was probably as good as could be expected. All the main ethnic, religious and political groups were represented (excluding, of course, the Taliban). Even a couple of women and a sprinkling of exiled intellectuals were awarded minor posts. But the Northern Alliance had the most guns on the ground and that had ensured they were awarded the most powerful ministries.

We joined the crush of bearded men in Massoud-style *pakul* hats trying to squeeze into a large concrete hall to watch the inauguration ceremony. All traffic was stopped for several blocks and stony-faced

British peacekeepers stood guard outside, fingers poised over the triggers of their machine guns. Not every faction was happy with the ministries that had been doled out and the atmosphere inside was both triumphant and tense, like a giant wedding where the families don't get along but are trying to be nice for the day. Which was just as well, given that many of the guests had private armies.

Sharing the stage were leaders of factions who not so long ago had been trying to kill the people sitting next to them. The Uzbek warlord Abdul Rashid Dostum was there, waiting to be sworn in as deputy defence minister. Years earlier he had been defence minister in the pro-Soviet regime. Nearby was Abdul Rasul Sayyaf, an exceptionally homicidal Islamist who was now a powerbroker in the Northern Alliance. Both men had shelled Kabul when it was controlled by Massoud and his allies, killing thousands of civilians. But today they were joining hands to build a new tomorrow — either that or biding their time until they could start the shelling again.

The great hope for a new Afghanistan was the interim chairman of the new government, Hamid Karzai, a Pashtun doctor who had fought the Taliban in their stronghold of Kandahar and was independent of the Northern Alliance and its various warlords. He was the UN's choice as leader, but it took days of pressure to persuade the nominal president and Northern Alliance figurehead, Burhanuddin Rabbani, to agree to recognise him. At the climax of the ceremony, Rabbani formally stepped down from the position he had held in name only since the Taliban ousted him in 1996. I couldn't help wondering if the transition would have gone as smoothly if the unyielding Massoud were still alive.

Karzai's first press conference, held a few hours later, attracted hundreds of journalists. The presidential guards gave most of us a cursory security check but took extra pains to search the female journalists, feeling their breasts and buttocks for concealed weapons.

The multilingual Karzai said all the right things for a Western audience, stressing the need for peace, rule of law and equality, and even outlined his program in French to a persistent French reporter. '*Liberté, egalité, fraternité,'* he said helpfully. But there were strong doubts about how far his power extended beyond the presidential palace. (In fact, it didn't yet extend even that far. Rabbani had occupied a wing of the palace when the Taliban fled and was stubbornly refusing to leave.)

We had just found new digs ourselves and, like Karzai, were discovering we had limited control over the place. To escape the horror of the bombed-out Inter-Continental Hotel, we rented a house in Wazir Akbar Khan, a relatively upmarket suburb of tree-lined streets with two-storey concrete houses behind walled compounds. It had long been a favoured address for warlords and other merchants of death, and was therefore one of the few places in Kabul relatively untouched by the civil war, since warlords tended not to shell themselves.

A venerable, half-blind commander lived opposite, surrounded by a small army of uniformed guards. He took a disapproving view of Westerners moving in and sent word by messenger to our door that Sebastian and I were not to use our balcony, as we might see women in the adjoining courtyard. Kim had just arrived in Kabul to shoot a documentary on Afghan women. To appease the commander, I introduced her to everyone as 'my wife'. But we overstepped the mark by hiring a young Afghan woman named Fereshte to do our laundry. She was excited to have her first job since the Taliban ordered women indoors five years earlier. However, the commander deemed it unacceptable for an Afghan woman to work in our house and ordered that we dismiss her.

The house came with six servants, working as guards, cooks and cleaners on salaries of $50 a month. Five of them were relatives of our new interpreter, Hamed, a slick young entrepreneur who had found the house for us and was turning it into a personal cash cow. While he paid his relatives a pittance, Hamed charged $200 a day for his own services and leased his car to us for $150 a day, paying the driver a salary of $35 a month. I wanted to sack him, but interpreters were in such demand that some news groups had persuaded English-speaking doctors to abandon their posts in hospitals to work for them. That left school students — who would accost us outside the gate. 'Hello, English, very cheap, $100, please sir, hello!'

Hamed treated the staff as his personal servants, clicking his fingers to have them bring him tea. They didn't seem to do much else and it was apparently not part of their job description to do anything for Sebastian and me. The only one who worked hard was the cook, Fayez Mohammed, a sad-faced and extraordinarily hirsute man who laboured away in an unspeakably dirty kitchen. The others sat around on cushions looking glum, occasionally getting up to let in visitors or jumping up to serve Hamed.

The lack of bomb damage was the house's main attraction. It had concrete floors, almost no furniture, only occasional electricity and no hot water (in fact, no *cold* water except from a well in the basement). The only heating was from small wood stoves. We were perpetually cold and dirty and the staff seemed miserable, but with a negligence born of exhaustion I left the running of the house to Hamed. I was too tired and busy to concentrate on anything but the work.

The day began at six with cold bucket showers by candlelight, after which Sebastian would fire up the generator to power the edit suite. As the room filled with the odour of petrol fumes, we would cut a television package by nine to allow for the time difference with Australia. After an hour's round trip to the satellite feed point in the Inter-Continental Hotel, we would eat breakfast and go out filming for the day. At night I would cut radio news pieces and features and often end up with a live radio cross at one-thirty in the morning. Then I'd sleep for four hours and start again.

The great frustration was that most of the news was happening outside Kabul in places we couldn't get to — last-ditch battles with the Taliban near Kandahar, starvation looming in Bamiyan, infighting in Mazar-e-Sharif, arrests of al-Qaeda suspects in Jalalabad. No matter how much we filmed in Kabul during the day, we would often have to ditch it the next morning in order to send voiceover for agency pictures of distant events we knew nothing about. Many of the stories could have been filed far more easily in Sydney. While I was desperate to get original material that could lead the news bulletins, Kabul remained steadfastly quiet.

But that was about to change, thanks to Jack.

We met up with him again at a Christmas party at the Inter-Continental Hotel. Christmas wasn't a big event in Muslim Kabul, but for godless Western journalists it was an excuse for a piss-up. An American television producer had managed to smuggle in a case of vodka on an aid flight, and invited some of us to share it. We gathered by the satellite feed point, standing on the mouldy carpet under flickering fluorescent lights, trying to summon up Christmas cheer and ignore each other's BO — many journalists had stopped washing entirely rather than persist with cold showers on freezing mornings.

Jack wandered in, still wearing his sunglasses indoors at night, and greeted us as long-lost buddies. 'How the fuck ya doin'?' he asked and launched into an account of his latest exploits. We were about to leave to beat the ten o'clock curfew but Jack appeared to be settling in for a long drink. 'Don't worry, I've got the fucking password,' he said. 'Hey, where you staying? I might have a story for you.'

Two days later he came around with a box of grubby Video-8 cassette tapes and an equally grubby portable player. It was more than six hours of al-Qaeda home movies. They were nothing like the usual al-Qaeda vision of masked men marching and staging exercises which were used as recruitment videos. In these tapes, the militants weren't wearing masks and they were doing what appeared to be genuine training in assassination and bombing. Some had even filmed their families — one tape showed an infant boy and his young sister carrying automatic rifles. The militants had obviously never expected the footage to be seen by outsiders.

It was possibly the most comprehensive view of al-Qaeda training that anyone had seen and potentially one of the biggest stories of the war. Jack told us one of his soldiers had found the tapes in a village that foreign militants had used as a training camp. We were almost touched

251

he'd brought them to us first. For someone who continually threatened to kill people, Jack seemed to have a soft side for people he liked. But he also needed us. We were the only TV crew he knew well enough to trust. And without our help, he'd have no way to transfer or edit the footage into a form that could be sold to broadcasters who, unlike us, had money.

Sebastian stayed up all night to dub the footage, which he cut down to a 50-minute highlights reel. It was extraordinary stuff. The village school had become a university of terrorism.

There was a hostage-taking lesson on a rooftop, with the trainee terrorists barking at the mock hostages in English. Human-size cutout targets were placed in various situations and blown to pieces by gunmen. There was a carjacking and even a practice assassination of political leaders at a golf course. A trainer showed a map of a city on a whiteboard outlining how an ambush would be carried out. He went on to explain how the assassins would then assemble at a certain point where they would be given passports and visas to travel to Yemen.

It was uncomfortable having these tapes in the house, especially as I didn't trust Hamed to keep them secret. Captured al-Qaeda and Taliban videotape had become a valuable commodity among the mujahideen, who were selling it both to media groups and to the US military. This footage was potentially worth hundreds of thousands of dollars. Sebastian and I were nervous about it being seized at gunpoint if the Northern Alliance found we had it.

Jack offered to sleep at our place 'for a few nights' to make sure there were no problems. His weapons came with him, including a Kalashnikov and a pistol. As we watched him move his paraphernalia into the spare room upstairs, it occurred to me that he might be a difficult house guest to extract.

To confirm the footage was genuine, we made two trips out to the village of Mir Bacheh Kowt where Jack had said the al-Qaeda tapes were shot, to see if we could match the landscape and buildings to the tapes. Given Jack's penchant for self-promotion, I also needed to make absolutely sure that he hadn't staged the footage. This would have been all but impossible, as many of the people on tape looked and spoke Arabic — a death sentence now the Northern Alliance was in control. But the definitive evidence would be the snowline. One part of the video showed heavy snow on the mountains behind the buildings. Winter had just begun but as yet no snow had fallen, leaving only a thin cover on the mountains surrounding Kabul from the previous winter. If we could find the same location and there was still less snow than in the footage, it would be proof the tapes had been shot long before Jack arrived or the Taliban had fled the region.

Mir Bacheh Kowt was a 40-minute drive north of Kabul along a half-destroyed road, the same road on which Tim and I had been stoned by the Taliban's Vice and Virtue Police four years earlier. The Taliban had poisoned the wells and the villages had been destroyed as the frontline shifted back and forth between Kabul and the Panjshir Valley. We drove through now deserted remnants of mud villages that had been caught in the crossfire. Then we saw the mountains behind the village. Sure enough, they were almost bare of snow, meaning that the footage could not have been shot in the warmer weeks since the Taliban had fled.

The villagers in Mir Bacheh Kowt waved al-Qaeda detritus at us, hoping to sell it as souvenirs. A charred copy of the Koran, ammunition casings and even man-shaped shooting targets were among the offerings. They told us that the Taliban had ordered them to leave three years earlier to make way for the foreign fighters. They had just returned to the dilapidated remains of their homes to find they had been used for target and bombing practice.

The village school was in a two storey-building I recognised from the tapes. It had been the main training centre. It was eerie to walk through the rooms where Arab and Pakistani militants had been learning to kill and maim. The walls were pockmarked with bullet and mortar holes from live-fire exercises. A blackboard still had a chalk diagram showing the correct shooting stance for close-quarter assassination.

The militants had used the entire village as a training range, blasting each building with machine-gun fire and rocket-propelled grenades. Some buildings were still filled with live shells. Ragged children followed us around the village and toyed with the al-Qaeda debris, playing happily with Zeppelin-shaped grenades. A man with one leg pointed to a row of buildings and told us not to go near them. 'Mines,' he said, gesturing at his stump.

If the US military knew of the base, it had certainly not investigated it. Wandering around, we found an extraordinary range of terrorist debris, including instruction manuals, notebooks filled with what looked like chemistry lessons and an Arabic translation of a US taskforce paper on counter-terrorism.

It seemed the Pentagon was less than delighted that Jack had found the tapes first. Jack had visions of Donald Rumsfeld or even George W. Bush hailing the discovery of the footage as an important breakthrough in the fight against terrorism. Every night he would stand on our balcony muttering animatedly into his satphone as he tried to call important figures in the Pentagon. But it was obvious that the military regarded Jack with deep suspicion, if not as a total whacko.

Media interest in the tapes made up for any hesitancy on the part of the Pentagon. Using the highlights reel Sebastian had edited, Jack was hawking the story around the US, Japanese, British and German network producers in Kabul. He created a bidding war, playing rival networks against each other, quoting figures of many tens of thousands of US dollars for exclusive rights. Everyone was incredulous that part of the deal was that the footage would be broadcast in Australia (on the ABC) first. The response of the Fox News producer was, 'Australia! Who the fuck lives in Australia?' — suggesting a limited knowledge of his boss, Rupert Murdoch.

I still had a nagging doubt about Jack. He'd refused to give me his real name, hinting that it was classified. Some journalists suspected he was a con artist. Producers back in the US, Japan and Britain wanted to know more of his credentials before paying him the money. They also wanted to know where it was going. Jack insisted it was all for charity. Speculation came to a head in a dramatic incident on New Year's Eve.

We were invited to a party at the house of a *Newsweek* reporter. All was fine until a reporter from the US military magazine *Stars and Stripes* who shared the house recognised Jack as someone he'd interviewed years earlier. The problem was, he used Jack's real name and mentioned where he'd seen him last — in prison. Jack exploded in rage and punched him out before storming back to our place, where he then vowed to have a Northern Alliance commander kill the reporter.

'The motherfucker!' Jack shouted. 'I'm going to tell General Bariolai tomorrow he's a spy and get him shot.'

We managed to calm him down and made him promise not to take revenge. The next day Jack told us about his time in prison but insisted he'd been framed.

'I was in Lithuania in the early '90s tracking down nuclear smugglers,' he said. 'The FBI wanted me to hand over my sources but the Lithuanians wouldn't let me. They knew the FBI had been infiltrated by spies. So they [the FBI] threw me in jail. I wouldn't talk though. Then two of the agents who testified against me were caught for spying for the Russians.'

Jack had a flair for exaggeration but this sounded like pure fantasy. I did an internet search on his real name and found he'd spent three years in prison for swindling $200,000 from companies involved in an exhibition of military goods. Bizarrely he was also suing the film director Steven Spielberg over the film *The Peacemaker*, starring George Clooney as a Special Forces colonel fighting nuclear smuggling. Jack claimed that the George Clooney character was based on his personal exploits in Lithuania in the early 1990s.

It was tempting to simply dismiss Jack as a fantasist and con man. War zones were magnets for Walter Mitty types claiming military prowess and mysterious pasts that were 90 per cent imagination. But the intriguing thing about Jack was how much of what he said checked out. He definitely *had* wrangled himself a position as military adviser to the

Afghans. We had seen enough of his dealings with Hazrat Ali and other Northern Alliance officials to be sure of that. He had extraordinarily good contacts in the new government and was able to get us any interview or access to any location we wanted. US journalists bidding for the footage were able to confirm that he had served in Special Forces. Above all, the tapes of the al-Qaeda training camp were genuine. We had confirmed that from the detritus left at Mir Bacheh Kowt and the accounts of the villagers.

After a couple of uncomfortable days, I decided that it was safe to go ahead with the story — the footage was just too good to ignore. But first I had to wait for the networks' bidding war to end. Jack wasn't charging us to use the footage but insisted we hold off on running it until just before it was broadcast in the US so as not to lower its selling price. After what seemed an eternity of wrangling, it finally came down to a contest between CNN and the US program *60 Minutes*. It was settled when the *60 Minutes* producers announced they would send Jack's hero, Dan Rather, out to do the story. Jack moved into the CBS house during the four days of filming but, after several fights with the producers, he was told to leave and came back to us. We ran the story three nights before the tapes aired on *60 Minutes* in the US.

The tapes caused a major media sensation. Everybody tried to follow them up. More broadcasters paid huge sums to Jack for the rights to screen the footage. But the Pentagon and the White House remained resolutely silent when normally they proclaimed every new al-Qaeda tape as further proof of the ongoing need to fight the War on Terror. It seemed nobody in Washington wanted to say anything to talk up anything that came from the man called Jack.

Jack was nevertheless delighted with his newfound fame and was suddenly flush with cash. He brought all his remaining belongings into our house, along with industrial quantities of his favourite junk food. His militia arrived each morning and milled around on the street outside. Our makeshift ABC bureau became known as Jack's official address. Wazir Akbar Khan, our leafy upmarket district, had a new warlord in town.

House Rules

After a month or so in Kabul, what passed for daily life was starting to feel normal. It no longer seemed strange to have a 'Green Beret' living in the house, or a militia hanging out in the front yard, or to be existing on four hours' sleep per night while living in what felt like a refrigerator. We were even growing accustomed to having one of the country's dirtiest cooks. Fayez Mohammed was growing steadily grubbier as the assignment wore on and, on the few occasions I wandered in, the kitchen looked even more frightening. But I was too tied up with work to pay much attention to it.

Kim was the first to notice the food building up on Fayez Mohammed's shirt. He always wore the baggy shirt and trousers known as *shalwar kameez*. To the extent that I thought about it, he always seemed to wear the same colour. What I hadn't noticed was that it was actually the same outfit. Kim finally broached the subject with him and found out that Fayez Mohammed had lost his luggage on the trip here from his last job in Peshawar and had been wearing (and sleeping in) the same clothes for five weeks. The grime on his shirt had progressed from crumbs to solid chunks to recognisable dishes from the night before. He'd been too embarrassed to mention his plight and I'd been too distracted to notice. Hamed, of course, hadn't bothered to do anything about it.

Some of the media were now scaling back their coverage and demand for interpreters was falling. We bade farewell to Hamed and hired an English-speaking medical student named Walid who was saving up to pay for his future tuition. In contrast to Hamed, he seemed genuinely concerned about the welfare of others. At twenty he had known nothing but war all his life yet had a remarkably sunny personality and an infectious sense of optimism. He came from a large family of boys and was the only Afghan I spoke to who actually wanted to have a daughter. Few Afghans even count their daughters when they tell you the number of their children.

Through Walid I finally got to know about some of the men who were working for us. There was Najibullah, a night guard who had studied in Russia, and was later wounded in the war against the Soviets. He walked with a bad limp and I found Walid was giving him some of his own pay so he could get a taxi to our house. Until then Najib had been spending almost his entire salary on getting to and from work, leaving almost nothing for his wife and four children.

Walid was happy to work for a fraction of what we had paid Hamed, allowing us to increase the others' pitiful wages. One of our staff, Mia, was an engineer and his skills should have been in demand to help rebuild his devastated country. But there were no engineering jobs available so he had no choice but to chop wood and clean toilets for foreigners. We doubled all their salaries, which was as far as our ABC budget could go, but it still felt like exploitation.

Walid set about reordering our dysfunctional household, organising a tailor to make new clothes for Fayez Mohammed and mobilising the other staff to help clean the kitchen. He also set minimum hygiene standards, introducing hot water and detergent to the cleaning process. Most importantly for Fayez Mohammed, Walid drew up a staff roster that gave everyone a day off a week.

Fayez Mohammed's turn for leisure came on Thursdays. He was by nature a sad man and missed his family terribly. He despaired for his country and abhorred the gunmen who ran it, shaking his head morosely as he listened to the Kabul news each night, saying, 'Afghan people, stupid people.' But as each Thursday approached, his mood brightened. He would leave early in the morning and not return until dark, sampling the full delights of post-Taliban Kabul. He would always see a Hindi film in the newly reopened cinema, enjoying the once forbidden sight of unveiled women dancing and singing. He would go to a restaurant for lunch, savouring the rare pleasure of someone else cooking for him. But mostly he just walked the streets, saving his money for his family stranded in a refugee camp in Peshawar.

Jack had no sympathy for Fayez Mohammed. As far as he was concerned, Fayez was a terrible cook who had no idea what good food was. Jack was determined to educate him in the superiority of American cuisine.

When you buy meat in Afghanistan you pay for a kilo and get a hunk of meat, innards and bones. It's used in soup or cut into small pieces for kebabs. But Jack craved steak. He came back to the house one day waving a bag of meat triumphantly. 'It's taken me two hours to teach these idiots how to do a real cut of meat,' he declared. 'But just look at this.' He handed the bag to Fayez Mohammed. 'Here, this is how it's supposed to be.' Fayez was naturally obliging but he was terrified of Jack's weaponry and couldn't understand his American drawl. He took the bag and thanked Jack.

A few hours later Jack came into the dining room in a steaming rage. 'He's fuckin' ruined it,' he shouted at us. 'Come and look at this.' We went outside to the charcoal burner that that Fayez used to cook kebabs. Jack's steaks had been reduced to tiny cubes on kebab sticks. He had to be physically restrained from shaking Fayez, who had no idea what he'd done wrong.

Once his temper cooled Jack promised to make the household a meal they wouldn't forget. It would be a real American meal. Fayez and the rest of the staff would be his guests.

A couple of days later he arrived home laden with shopping bags from Chicken Street. Next to Flower Street in downtown Kabul, the Chicken Street shops stocked Western foodstuffs at exorbitant prices. You could buy Kellogg's cornflakes, Mars Bars and Heinz baked beans. There were also English-language bookshops, carpet merchants and souvenir stores where you could pick up replica guns from the British–Afghan wars, gunpowder holders, whips and knives. The shopkeepers' businesses were booming for the first time in years.

Jack unpacked his bags, boasting that he'd just spent $400. Fayez Mohammed's eyes widened in disbelief. That was more than he would spend to feed our household of ten for a month. Jack had bought Pepsi, Fanta, oranges, a chicken, some cuts of meat, Oreo biscuits, mayonnaise, cheddar cheese and crackers, and various other items of Americana. He set about preparing his meal, ordering various staff to chop oranges, to which he added Fanta and bootleg Tajik vodka. 'Fruit punch,' he announced, offering Fayez a glass. Fayez had never drunk alcohol and quickly became tipsy. This was just as well considering what Jack was about to do to his kitchen.

Within half an hour there was a large flood on the kitchen floor and smoke billowing from the oven. The oven door was hanging by one hinge. Fayez stood in the doorway wringing his hands and muttering helplessly. Smoke from the now almost cremated chicken filled both floors of the house. At ten o'clock Jack announced that dinner was ready.

The blackened chicken was the centrepiece and Jack set about dissecting it with a ten-inch knife from his leg holster. He had been drinking Fanta and Tajik vodka for three hours and was a worrying sight but finally it was time to eat. The chicken tasted like burnt roadkill.

Hours later, as he stood washing the dishes in the remains of his kitchen, Fayez Mohammed shook his head sadly. 'American people, stupid people,' he said softly.

The only person who could make Fayez Mohammed laugh was Sebastian. His eyes would light up whenever Sebastian came home and slapped him on the back and asked, 'How ya doin', bro?' He would make special treats for him, which Sebastian forced down out of politeness, and listen to his music while Sebastian explained the intricacies of Pink Floyd riffs. I often wondered how much he understood, given his limited English and Sebastian's unique way of talking. But it was obvious that Sebastian had become his first foreign friend. Like the rest of us, Fayez Mohammed grew increasingly worried by Sebastian's apparently worsening health.

By early January, Sebastian was coughing constantly. Each morning he found it harder to get up, exhausted from another sleepless night. He was missing his wife, Carol, and son, Wesley, and just wanted to go home. We began to make arrangements to get him out.

It was no easy task. The twice-weekly UN flights to Islamabad were heavily booked and there was no guarantee that the plane would take off. Bagram airbase in the Shamali Plains was surrounded by mountains, and whenever the sky was even slightly cloudy, flights were cancelled. Some people had been waiting for weeks, driving out to the airbase several times before finally making it onto a flight.

Despite the odds, we managed to get Sebastian back to Carol in Beijing. The house felt empty after he'd left and Fayez Mohammed grew even more depressed. Every time the satellite phone rang he would come running, asking, 'Sebastian? Sebastian talk me?' No one who ever met Sebastian could forget him.

For all the political change in the country, few women in Kabul had dared to remove their burqa, the shuttlecock-shaped, tent-like garment they had become accustomed to wearing over their clothing. Most of them remembered how the mujahideen had behaved before the Taliban threw them out. As a 1995 Amnesty International Report put it:

> Women and girls all over Afghanistan live in constant fear
> of being raped by armed guards. For years, armed guards
> have been allowed to torture them in this way without
> fear of reprimand from their leaders. In fact, rape is
> apparently condoned by most leaders as a means of
> terrorising conquered populations and/or rewarding
> soldiers.

The Northern Alliance's professed position, of liberating women from Taliban tyranny, was enunciated regularly by the smooth, suit-wearing foreign minister Abdullah Abdullah. But in reality little had changed for women in Kabul and even less in the rest of Afghanistan. The Taliban had removed the last traces of secularism from most of the country and the 'new' order was in no hurry to bring it back, at least for women. Cigarettes, videos and music were reappearing in the villages. Women's faces were not.

Dr Sima Samar was the minister for women's affairs in the new government, courtesy of the UN-brokered deal. The government didn't bother to provide her with an office for such an unimportant ministry. She worked from her new home, a suburban house in Kabul.

A fellow exile and friend of Dr Samar's took us to her house to meet her. It was unguarded and we walked straight in. She was sitting in the lounge room, a small, demure woman with thick glasses, wearing traditional Afghan dress and talking to two male visitors in Dari. She seemed tense and reserved, even with her friend, but invited us to stay while she continued her meeting.

Dr Samar had a formidable reputation that belied her unassuming manner. She had fled Afghanistan for Pakistan after her husband was arrested during the Soviet occupation. In Quetta she had campaigned for women's rights in the face of fundamentalist opposition and opened a hospital for women, also setting up a humanitarian organisation called Shuhada, meaning martyr. Through Shuhada she had built four hospitals and ten clinics inside Afghanistan, along with many schools. She had continued to live in exile in Pakistan until now.

Dr Samar hadn't sought the job of women's minister and knew the risk of making even a mildly feminist statement. She had refused to give any interviews to the newly established Kabul TV station, knowing that her opponents could seize on her comments as un-Islamic. She was almost as guarded when I began filming an interview with her, acutely aware that those who disagreed with her would somehow find out what she said, even if it was only shown in Australia.

'The Taliban are not gone, not all of them,' she told me. 'They simply change their hats.'

While the Taliban had favoured turbans, everyone was now wearing the woollen *pakul*, à la Ahmad Shah Massoud.

Just 100 metres away from her house lived the man who scared her most. Abdul Rasul Sayyaf's large house stood on the opposite corner, guarded by a heavily armed militia. His men loitered around the street with their guns, in full view of Dr Samar's house — a constant stream of visitors in Toyota Landcruisers marking Sayyaf as an important man.

Sayyaf was a Wahhabi extremist who led a Pashtun militia linked to the Northern Alliance. Their reputation for brutality went back a long way. A Human Rights Watch report accused his forces of murdering up to a hundred civilians in just one night of raping and looting in Kabul back in 1993. There had been a raft of allegations of war crimes ever since, all of them denied by Sayyaf.

I requested an interview and was led into an antechamber to meet him. He emerged from a back room flanked by aides and welcomed me in fluent English, inviting me to sit on the ground and take some tea. Sayyaf was an imposing man with white hair and a Santa Claus beard. He had been a professor of Islamic studies before becoming a warlord and almost evoked the image of a grandfatherly academic. But there was something chilling about him. While he was now a senior figure in the Northern Alliance, his religious views were indistinguishable from the Taliban's. He didn't bother with the politically correct rhetoric of Abdullah Abdullah, and insisted that women should stay in burqas, out of schools, out of jobs and out of sight.

'If you go to a society where Islamic law is in force you'll see that women have comfortable lives, they are not tired and bothered like in other societies,' he told us. 'Women are so happy, so satisfied.' He said that strict Sharia law was the only option for Afghanistan. 'All of them want to live under the umbrella of Islamic law, therefore there is no chance for any law or any constitution except Islam.'

But many women were not happy or satisfied. Kim had become friends with a woman named Fauzia, whom she met on the UN flight from Islamabad. Like Dr Samar, Fauzia was an Afghan returning from Pakistan, where she and her war-crippled husband and four children had been refugees. She was working for the World Food Program based in Kabul, while her husband looked after the children in Pakistan.

Fauzia's job was to set up and monitor women-run bakeries throughout Kabul with the aim of eventually extending the program to other cities. Most of the women who worked at these tandoori bread ovens were illiterate and had lost their husbands in Afghanistan's endless wars. Ranging in age from 20 to 60, most were struggling to provide for large families and all were grateful for the opportunity to get out of the house and earn their own money, even if the amount was a pittance. The bread was distributed free of charge to locals on presentation of a kind of ration card.

With Kim, Fauzia was quite outspoken about politics. She said she trusted no one in the new government to seriously tackle women's issues, as there was too much at stake. Too many people agreed with the mujahideen and the Taliban's hardline stance for anyone to risk trying to change the situation for women too much. 'In reality,' she said, 'most men do want their womenfolk at home and hidden from the gaze of all other males.'

I was trying to shoot a news feature on women in the new 'liberated' Afghanistan and Kim mentioned that Fauzia might be willing to be interviewed. She agreed and arrived at our house at the appointed time, wearing her burqa. She kept it on in front of our male staff and only removed it when she was alone with us. She was a large middle-aged woman and seemed quite relaxed in the presence of a male foreigner. Apart from Dr Samar she was the first Afghan woman I had spoken to since re-entering Afghanistan who didn't cover her face.

Fauzia spoke excellent English and had strong, clear convictions about women's rights. Before we turned the camera on, she chatted animatedly, confirming what she had already said to Kim alone. I asked if she would mind if we filmed an interview. 'No problem,' she said. As soon as the camera was rolling, though, her whole attitude changed. Suddenly she was vague and noncommittal.

Knowing the risks, I decided not to push her too far and wrapped up the interview. When we finished she mentioned that her great-aunt had been the second wife of King Amanullah, the King of Afghanistan in the early twentieth century. She showed us an old sepia photo of a woman in a flapper costume, a wispy knee-length dress with shoulder straps, and a string of beads around her neck. 'See how things have changed. Back then, educated Afghans were very liberal,' Fauzia told us. 'I wonder if she would ever have imagined that 80 years later I would be afraid to show my face on the streets of Kabul.'

A lot of things were happening on and off the streets that would have shocked Fauzia's great-aunt. One day Walid told me that a man he knew of had a couple of Taliban prisoners in his basement. 'They are Pakistanis,' he said, 'and he is trying to contact their families back in Pakistan so he can sell them back.'

It was tantamount to running a private prison and ransoming the inmates. Walid assured me many people were doing it. I thought this would be a great story and asked Walid to find out if the man would let us film his prisoners. Walid came back to me saying he wanted $500 to film each one. 'He's worried that if they're seen on TV it might affect the price,' Walid said.

I suddenly realised I was considering paying a kidnapper to show me his captives. Five weeks earlier I would never have contemplated it. But in the craziness of Afghanistan it seemed normal. It was almost easy to forget it was also wrong. 'Tell him to forget it,' I said.

Jack couldn't see the problem. Checking out our cellar, he said, 'This would make a great place to keep prisoners.' I assumed he was joking.

Tens of thousands of refugees were now returning to Kabul, many for the first time in two decades, but it was a hard homecoming. A third of the city had been reduced to rubble in the civil war and up to half the population was reliant on food aid for survival. The NGOs (non-government organisations) distributed as much food as they could directly, but anything that went through the government was likely to be sidelined to relatives and cronies. We watched a Russian food convoy unloading at a central warehouse as police beat back women trying desperately to get something for their families. They complained bitterly that all the grain, ghee and other items would disappear into the hands of officials and their families. It wasn't entirely true: one part of the convoy's load would end up with foreign journalists.

The Russian aid people had a sideline in smuggled Tajik vodka. The day the first convoy arrived in Kabul, the trucks assembled in a field for a publicity shot. Kim chatted to the drivers in Russian. They were all comprehensively drunk but in that peculiarly Russian way of still being able to function normally. They had been drinking solidly on the journey, fortifying themselves for the hairpin bends on the mountain roads from Tajikistan. It wasn't long before the Russians became the main conduit for vodka. It was smuggled in empty ghee tins; eight low-grade bottles wrapped in newspaper in every tin. The Russian Emergency Services Ministry office was just around the corner from our house. Jack became a regular customer for 'humanitarian aid'.

Alcohol was the most sought-after commodity for foreigners. It was about the only one of the Taliban-era vice prohibitions that still hadn't been lifted. A couple of the restaurants sold homemade whisky on the sly and there was a steady trickle of Pakistani bootleg, but not nearly enough to meet demand. The one period of plenty had been just after the US Marines arrived in mid-December to reopen the American embassy. They found a huge cache of Budweiser that had been abandoned when the last diplomats fled in 1989. I drank one on New Year's Eve. It was passable for the first five sips, then you hit the sludge. They were selling for $15 each.

Jack came up with a revolutionary idea for entertainment in Kabul — a Beef, Bourbon and Burqa Bar. His plan was to open a

Thai-style alcoholic bar with strippers taking off their burqas and everything underneath. 'Jack, you will be shot dead the first night,' I warned. But he wasn't fazed. He appeared to have no concept that even in Afghanistan there were limits to what a foreigner could get away with. He also saw no problem in selling alcohol in a country with the highest number of weapons per person in the world. Fortunately, it was one of Jack's long-term schemes and remained in the conceptual stage.

Kabul did have one entertainment spectacular that had made a huge comeback since the Taliban's ouster — quail fighting. Once a week scores of bearded men in traditional dress gathered at an indoor pit to watch and bet on it. We arrived as the first fight got under way. Expecting blood and gore, we found two tiny quails hopping around and occasionally taking a peck at each other. In the front row, the next contenders were being primed for battle. Their owners took the quails out of small sacks and tapped their heads to annoy them.

It was the most ridiculous sport I'd ever seen but the atmosphere was electric. Huge sums of money were changing hands as the quails scratched around in the dirt before giving another indifferent peck to their opponents. One man was betting a Toyota Landcruiser on the outcome. Victory was determined by the other quail running away.

The manager apologised that we had come on a bad day. 'You should come back next week,' he said. 'None of the big-name quails are here today.'

By now Jack had begun to realise that Joe/Zabi did not always translate what Jack was intending to say to his troops. One day he brought home a new interpreter who introduced himself to us as Rafi. Rafi was about twenty, with carefully slicked-back hair and combed eyebrows. He spoke remarkably good English with a slight Scottish accent but there was something odd about it. When we offered him a drink, he said, 'One coffee, very black,' adding, 'shaken, not stirred'. It suddenly clicked. I asked Rafi how he had learned his English. Sure enough, he had spent countless hours watching and absorbing James Bond movies and learning Sean Connery's one-liners by rote.

Rafi didn't get on with Jack's soldiers, who appeared to regard him as a pansy. Zabi, who remained in Jack's employ, loved waving his gun around but Rafi was one of the few men in Afghanistan who seemed uncomfortable with weapons. His great dream was to be a movie actor.

Jack also had visions of stardom and gave Zabi a small digicam to film him. Jack was planning to piece together a documentary about his exploits in Afghanistan. Zabi's filming was as bad as his English, the shots waving aimlessly from the ground to the sky, with an occasional fleeting image of Jack's back. When Rafi expressed an interest in learning to use the camera, Jack was more than happy to let him have a go. But when he went to look at Rafi's first efforts, he was furious. Rafi had discovered that the flip-out screen on the side of the camera could be rotated, meaning if you filmed yourself it was like looking in a mirror. Instead of filming Jack, Rafi had recorded half an hour's footage of himself, swirling the camera round, puckering his lips and preening in the monitor. Jack wanted to kill him.

Jack's militia was starting to get out of hand. We had grown used to Jack's expansive presence and idiosyncrasies, although Kim was losing patience with him smoking for hours in the toilet and leaving cans of Pepsi and Snickers wrappers around the bowl. But his soldiers had begun treating the bureau as a clubhouse. Despite our constant objections, they were also starting to bring in weapons. On one occasion, we saw Zabi struggling to carry a large wooden crate upstairs to Jack's room. I asked him what was in the box.

'Bullets,' he said panting.

Zabi in particular had decided he had the run of the house and began giving orders to the staff. One night he banged on the gate to be admitted while the guard was praying. It is forbidden to break off prayers so the guard stoically ignored Zabi's demands. By the time he had finished, Zabi had worked himself into a fury. When the guard opened the gate, Zabi attacked him.

Within seconds there was a full-scale riot on the front lawn between the household staff and Jack's militia. We ran out and pulled them apart as best we could. Eventually our shouting and pulling calmed them down. But Zabi was still trying to throw punches at the bleeding guard as I held him back.

From that point on the soldiers were banned from setting foot in the house. Kim also set new ground rules for Jack: no smoking, no threatening to kill the staff, no talking while we were working and definitely no storing ammunition or weapons in the house. It was that or leave. It was clear that Kim in full flight was the only person in Afghanistan who scared Jack. She made him stand to attention and recite the rules.

Before long Kabul had been transformed. The streets were choked with traffic, the markets were full of Western consumer goods and Western consumers. The international community was moving in en masse — NGOs, UN staff, peacekeepers, engineers, consultants, diplomats and journalists. They crowded the new restaurants springing up around town and renovated their homes, offices and embassies. Prices soared and entrepreneurs made plans for mobile phone networks and internet cafés. The exoticism, mystery and edginess I had long associated with the city were disappearing under safe, comfortable and dull internationalism. It was time to get back to the real Afghanistan.

Chapter 27
The Hindu Kush, January 2002

Indiana Jones and the
Temple of Bamiyan

Back in the 1970s, before the wars began, hippies used to pour across Afghanistan on the overland trail to South-East Asia. They would collect marijuana, which grew wild beside the roads, drink tea in guesthouses, sleep safely in village hostels, accept lifts from strangers and head up the old Silk Road to the most extraordinary place in the country, the ancient city of Bamiyan. At dawn they would climb up an old fort to watch the first rays of light fall on massive Buddhas carved into the cliff face, and mutter meaningful things about eternal love and peace.

These days hippies would need a flak jacket and an armoured car to be sure of driving across Afghanistan safely. And if any made it to Bamiyan, they wouldn't see the Buddhas. The giant statues, rising five and ten storeys high, had stood for more than 1400 years. But seven months before being overthrown, the Taliban declared the Buddhas an affront to Islam and blew them up.

Even without the Buddhas, I was determined to get to Bamiyan. It had the mystical allure of Timbuktu — with the advantage of being just up the road from Kabul. Sydney had grudgingly approved a short field trip, warning me that the war coverage budget was already well into the red. A few journalists I knew had managed to get over the snow-covered pass to Bamiyan and, while the road was appalling, they were in awe of what they'd seen. It might also be a good snapshot of what was happening outside 'liberated' Kabul.

Bamiyan lies in the centre of Hazarajat, a mountainous territory inhabited by the Hazara people, a group quite unlike other Afghans. Hazaras believe they are descendants of Genghis Khan's Golden Horde, who conquered Afghanistan in the thirteenth century and intermarried with the indigenous Tajik and Turkic people. They have Mongolian features and, like the neighbouring Iranians, follow the Shia branch of Islam. The majority Sunni Muslims in the rest of the country have long regarded Hazaras with suspicion. The Taliban saw them as heretics and punished them without mercy.

The Taliban had fled six weeks earlier and the area was now back under the control of a powerful Hazara warlord named Karim Khalili. He had battled the Sunni Tajik militias at various times during the civil war but was now united with them in the Northern Alliance. His political movement, Hezb-i-Wahdat (Party of Islamic Unity), had an office in Kabul and assured us the road to Bamiyan was now secure.

Back at our house Walid said he was less confident, warning that there were few villages on the road and therefore long stretches where we could be at the mercy of bandits. It was impossible to know for sure. The security situation had improved and UN vehicles and aid groups were driving through the north without hindrance. I felt we should organise one Hazara guard to be on the safe side. But Jack had other plans. 'I might just come along and keep an eye on you guys,' he said.

Jack was determined to make his protection service a going concern and he'd found a Brazilian crew willing to make use of it if they could share the cost with someone. They were also keen to go to Bamiyan, but for a different reason — they were following someone who was even crazier than Jack was.

Christina Mezquita was a producer with TV Globo trapped in an assignment from hell. She had been sent to Afghanistan not to report on the war but to record the journey of a middle-aged experimental video artist named Omar. His filmmaking technique consisted of shoving his camera up the nose of anything that moved. He would follow every person who caught his interest, wandering around the room after them or walking a pace behind them down the street. He would loom over anyone doing anything at all, holding his camera at close range to their hands or faces without a word of introduction or explanation. After a week filming everything in Kabul, Omar had decided he wanted to video the Buddhas — or whatever was left of them.

Our plan was to leave by seven at the latest to avoid driving at night. But by nine, there was still no sign of the guards. An hour later they arrived in force. I had expected that Jack would only bring a handful but, with two film crews watching his enterprise, he was determined to put on a show. There were twelve of them, carrying the heaviest armament I had seen in Afghanistan.

Turning his best side to the camera, Jack assured us we would be well covered for any emergency.

'We've got Kalashnikovs, RPGs, six extra rockets and a PK machine gun. That should be enough. I think we could probably take on about 50 Taliban, as long as they have good direction on what to do,' he said, winking.

The soldiers faffed around, fumbling with bullets and ammunition belts. As usual they showed a complete lack of interest in their work and a determination to gouge as much as possible out of Jack.

'More ammo!' Jack ordered. 'When I go to war I take a lot of bullets.'

The replacement cameraman for Sebastian had recently arrived from Australia and this was our first assignment together. Michael Cox was relatively new to international work but was taking it all in his stride, even adjusting to finding an American mercenary living in the ABC bureau. He just wasn't expecting a Brazilian postmodern video artist to be getting in every shot.

Omar seemed to have no awareness of anyone else and continually walked in front of our camera. After spending more than an hour loading all our equipment, we seemed no closer to leaving. Omar was still shooting kilometres of tape, waving his camera over the ammunition and machine guns and tracking up the soldiers' uniforms to their mystified faces. It was hard to imagine what he could possibly do with all the footage but he explained he had an innovative editing technique. 'I turn my back when the tape is playing so I don't see the pictures,' he said. 'When I instinctively feel the moment is right I say, "Cut."'

And so Omar filmed everything, and the TV Globo crew filmed Omar, and we tried to film anything except Omar. Finally our overloaded and overarmed convoy lumbered out of Kabul. Omar had decided to film the entire journey, holding the camera out the window as we drove through town. He had brought 100 one-hour DVD tapes for the three-day trip to Bamiyan, but in desperation the TV Globo crew filming him had hidden 50 of them to restrain Omar's shooting.

We had only driven for 30 minutes when we passed a landmine-clearing team on the Shamali Plains, a little before the town of Charikar. This was reputed to be the most heavily mined stretch of land in the world. The Afghan mine-clearers were just a bit further on from the old terrorist training camp at Mir Bacheh Kowt. Returning refugees were setting up tents in the few areas cleared of mines.

The clearance team told us they were about to blow up a tank mine. It was likely to be spectacular footage so we decided to film it from a distance, locking the camera off while we retreated behind a line they designated as safe. Omar, however, thought it wasn't close enough. Ignoring the shouts of the mine team, he wandered an extra 200 metres closer and refused to budge. Eventually they decided to blow it up anyway. Omar emerged unscathed and unconcerned at the power of the blast. Despite making a 'video installation' about a war zone, he appeared to have absolutely no understanding of war's dangers and only the loosest relationship with reality in general.

There were soon other dangers beside landmines. Running westward from Charikar, the road to Bamiyan snaked up into the mountains following a gorge carved out by the Ghorband River. The dirt road was in terrible condition, narrowing to one vehicle-width with a crumbling sheer drop to the river below. This was followed by a two-hour zigzagging ascent to the Shibar Pass at an altitude of more than

3000 metres. Sections of the road were covered in ice, making it doubly perilous. Our van at least had an experienced driver. The TV Globo crew were in the van behind us with Zabi at the wheel. Christina had hired Kim as an assistant to try to make sense of what Omar was doing. As they careered around the slopes Kim asked Zabi how long he had had his licence.

'I don't have a licence,' he said.

'Well how long have you been driving?'

'This is my first time.'

The soldiers insisted on stopping every hour to pray, pee, smoke or eat, so we had barely covered half the distance by the time night fell. We drove the most dangerous leg, across frozen streams that crisscrossed the mountain pass, in pitch-darkness. It was nearly ten when we arrived in Bamiyan. It had taken us more than ten hours to cover less than 240 kilometres. The town was completely dark, except for an illuminated poster of the warlord Karim Khalili.

Jack's militia had proved to be unnecessary, but the unexpected arrival of a dozen heavily armed soldiers caused a minor panic among the sentries. After some hostile exchanges, the mood relaxed slightly and we were taken to one of Khalili's houses to spend the night. The soldiers were sent to one room, where they immediately began fighting over the two mattresses and blankets provided. The foreigners were led to a more comfortable room with cushions and a wood stove. There was a common pit toilet outside, piled up with frozen turds.

It was a tight squeeze for the eight of us in the foreigners' room, especially as Omar had brought an enormous suitcase with a special oversized pillow. Zabi and Rafi came to our room and insisted they should sleep with us, saying the other soldiers had taken their mattresses and blankets. Jack told them to be 'fuckin' men' and ordered them back to sleep on the concrete floor. We invited Walid to stay with us, but he was concerned the other Afghans would ridicule him. Jack ordered one of the soldiers to give him a mattress, leading to another round of complaining and fighting.

Eventually the noise of the soldiers' squabbling died down and I drifted off to sleep. A few hours later I was woken by Jack treading on me as he crept towards the fire. I feigned sleep, along with everyone else in the room, as Jack noisily stoked the almost extinguished fire, muttering 'motherfucker', 'sonofabitch' and 'motherfucking sonofabitch' at its unresponsiveness. Omar was taken with the moment and came stumbling over in the darkness with his camera.

'Let me document this,' he said.

'Are you fucking crazy?' Jack whispered.

'No, you are crazy.'

For once, they both seemed right. Ever true to his art, Omar continued to film Jack stoking the fire then stepped on my head as he walked back to his giant pillow.

Just before dawn Michael and I climbed on to the roof of the house to shoot the first rays of light on the cliff top opposite. It was bitterly cold. We could see the glow of small cooking fires in the blackness but no sign of the remains of the Buddhas. Behind us we could just see the outline of a sentry on a mudbrick fort.

Moments later the sun rose on a landscape of almost biblical majesty. The huge alcoves in which the Buddhas had stood seemed tiny compared with the enormous, bright orange cliffs into which they were carved. Snow-capped mountains towered above them. As the sun came up and the shadow gradually retreated across the ground, the valley came to life. We watched the distant tiny figures of old men on donkeys walking through patchwork fields and children playing in the ruins of the old mud town.

Bamiyan had once been a bustling Silk Road city, with traders coming from Rome, China and India. It had been a centre of Buddhist study and worship until the tenth century, with monks living in cells carved into the rock and pilgrims coming from distant lands to see the giant statues. It had taken until the twenty-first century for Afghanistan to become backward enough to destroy them.

We climbed back down from the roof to find the soldiers bitching about money. With astonishing hide, they were claiming they needed $20 each to buy breakfast — approximately the average annual wage of the locals. 'This is a very expensive place,' Zabi explained. They claimed to have eaten all the food and drunk all the water we had brought for them for three days. When we checked our van, we found they had drunk all our water as well. There was nowhere to buy bottled water in town. We now faced the choice of boiling water or going thirsty. We gave the soldiers some money just to make them go away.

Driving down to the valley, we walked to the base of the cliff, crossing a frozen stream where women were chipping the ice to wash their clothes. The women didn't cover their faces like the Sunnis; they wore brightly coloured scarves and dresses which contrasted starkly with the dusty brown of the valley. The smell of baking bread drifted down from the cliff face which, in the area around the shattered Buddhas, was pockmarked with monastic cells. Hazaras had lived in them for centuries, but the numbers had swollen drastically since the Taliban's shelling destroyed the town. Extended families were crammed into each cave with whatever livestock had survived the fighting. As we climbed up, a donkey emerged from one of the openings followed by a small boy. The place was as miserable as it was beautiful.

The horror of Taliban rule was etched onto people's faces. The Sunni Taliban had persecuted the Shias relentlessly because of their variant faith. When the Taliban seized part of Hazarajat in January 2001, they rounded up all the young men and executed them. Women and older men were beaten. A woman named Kobra showed me her ripped ear lobe where a Talib had torn off her earring as a sinful adornment. Her thumb was deformed from a beating they had given her.

She began to weep as she catalogued her family's suffering. 'We have nothing. Everything was burned by the Taliban. We are all poor people and we are farmers. The Taliban beat me and broke my thumb and took my child from my arms and threw him away. Now he is paralysed. He is at home now. They beat my husband on his chest. When he coughs, he bleeds. Now he is in hospital. We don't have enough money to treat him here.'

Her 'home', where her child lay paralysed, was a tiny, smoke-blackened cave right beside the old site of the larger Buddha. All that remained of the statue was the 50-metre-high alcove in which it had stood. The Taliban had used mortars to blast the main body of the Buddha and then exploded dynamite charges to remove any trace of its form. But they hadn't had time to destroy the centuries-old carved adornments in the temples and monasteries hewn deep into the cliff.

As we climbed a rock staircase, we came across Jack looking as if he was auditioning for *Raiders of the Lost Ark*. Wearing desert fatigues and with his Kalashnikov slung over his shoulder, he was exploring the crevices of an ancient temple, followed by three of his Afghan soldiers. He seemed strangely quiet, as if the overwhelming sense of history and pointless destruction had brought out his sensitive side. Jack had repeatedly told us he was a Buddhist, having joined an order popular with US Special Forces in Thailand that had a 'kick ass' philosophy. I asked him what he felt about the Taliban destroying the Buddhas.

'It really makes you sad that people could be so destructive and negative,' he said thoughtfully. 'I just wish I could have had a mortar on the hill behind them and blown the motherfuckers away before they fired the first round.'

That was as sensitive as Jack got.

By the time we climbed down to the base of the cliff, a Red Cross truck had arrived to distribute food. The Red Cross was one of the few aid groups that risked coming to the area, but it lacked the resources to feed more than a small proportion of the people. Several hundred had come from surrounding villages, some walking for three or four days across the mountains, to try to get sacks of wheat or flour. The Red Cross had a strict rationing system to ensure that people who'd received food in the previous distribution six weeks earlier hadn't come back for more. It meant that women like Kobra were turned away. 'They told me it wasn't my turn,' she said. 'I asked them if we could wait in the line and they said, "No, go away."'

In desperation the people were turning to the warlord Khalili for help. Jack took us to meet him in a mud fort in the centre of the old town. Khalili sat in a courtyard carpeted with green blankets, holding audience with a group of elders squatting on the ground in front of him. He greeted Jack warmly then asked us to wait while he dealt with his other visitors. Khalili was a Hazara version of the Pashtun warlord Abdul Rasul Sayyaf — tall, imposing and heavy-set, with white hair and a bushy silver beard.

While Human Rights Watch had accused his forces of routine torture and execution, many now saw him as their only possible saviour, entrenching and legitimising his return to power as he filled the vacuum left by the Taliban. Today Khalili was in benevolent grandfatherly mode, hearing the elders' appeals for food, shelter and money.

'We have 60 crippled people who were disabled after they were stuck in the snow,' one venerable man in a turban said. 'I hope first in God and then in you. If no one helps us our life will be even worse so now we have come here to ask for your help.'

It was a feudal setting, with a sentry in traditional dress patrolling the mud ramparts of the fort to protect his lord. But a few things were jarringly modern and out of place. Like the green blankets. Jack pulled a label off one of them which was marked 'US Federal Prisons Industry'. Khalili's other guards by the gate had brand-new weapons and uniforms. 'American uniforms, Iranian weapons,' Jack whispered.

Khalili eventually consented to a short interview. I asked him what help he was getting from foreigners.

'The number of troops is not high,' he said dismissively. 'We have a group of eight Americans and four or five British troops.' That meant Special Forces and SAS. 'They came before the fall of Bamiyan and they have remained here still to cooperate with us. Since the Northern Alliance captured Bamiyan, they have been engaged with aid distribution to civilians.'

The only glimpse we'd had of Special Forces (apart from Jack, who was long retired) had been a convoy driving at high speed through a village near Tora Bora. They were instantly recognisable as the white guys trying to look undercover by growing a beard. Everybody in Bamiyan knew exactly where the Special Forces base was. After leaving Khalili, it took us just five minutes to get directions to it. A young boy pointed down the road to the base entrance. The Hazara guards waved us through when they saw we were Westerners.

We stopped as soon as we could see the headquarters, a large house about 150 metres away overlooking the remains of the Buddhas. A few commandos were standing around outside the building. Michael got out of the van with his camera and started rolling. Our intention was to get some quick shots and go.

Within seconds a young American soldier appeared at the gate about 50 metres away. He seemed perplexed to see us. 'Who are you guys?' he shouted.

'It's OK, we're from Australian television,' I shouted back, as if that meant something.

'Yeah, well you can't film here.'

'We're just getting some general shots of the area, we won't be a second.'

'Hey, put the camera away!'

'Oh, OK, no problem, absolutely.'

The commandos outside the house had seen us and begun moving towards us.

'Let's go, guys,' I said. We started climbing back into the car as I waved at the guard and smiled. 'Thanks a lot, bye,' I shouted.

The commandos were now running towards us.

We had just shut the doors and our driver was starting the engine when the commandos surrounded the van. One of them pulled out a pistol and dragged the driver out with the gun to his head. Another hauled Michael out. I had locked my door so a third commando reached round from the front and opened it and dragged me out, throwing me off the road into a field next to the others.

'Hands in the air, motherfuckers!' a commando shouted. We raised our hands as the Hazara guards surrounded us, pointing their rifles at our heads.

There were six Americans in all, pumped up, breathing hard and very, very angry. They all had beards except for a skinny, sandy-haired soldier who seemed to be the most excitable of them all.

I explained we were only journalists. That seemed to make them angrier. I had an uncomfortable feeling that things were about to get completely out of control. 'Look, let's all bear in mind that whatever happens next will be on the public record,' I said.

'Are you threatening me?' the skinny soldier shouted.

'No,' I said. 'You're threatening us — with guns.'

Michael managed to ease the tension. 'I know you guys are well trained,' he said to the Americans. 'But the Afghans aren't. Would you mind if they pointed their rifles down?'

An American with a dark beard, who appeared to be the senior officer, nodded to another soldier who told the Hazaras to lower their rifles. We kept our hands in the air.

'What did you film?' he asked me.

'I don't think we filmed anything before you stopped us,' I said.

'You're going to have to give us the tape.'

'Look, I'm not authorised to do that. I'd have to get permission from Sydney,' I said.

'So call them.'

'I can't. It's three in the morning. There's no one there.'

'Then we're taking the tape.'

I had little negotiating power against a dozen armed soldiers but I had one potential bluff. 'Look, I can't stop you taking the tape,' I said. 'But it's also got an interview we just did with Karim Khalili.'

That stopped them. It was one thing for US soldiers to shake down Australian journalists at gunpoint but quite another to offend the host warlord.

'All right, your cameraman comes to the van with us, shows us what's on the tape, and we erase the footage of the base.'

'I can't do that without authorisation from Sydney.'

'OK, bottom line!' he shouted. 'That tape is not leaving this base.'

'What about the interview with Mr Khalili?' I asked.

This was turning into a more complicated situation than they first imagined. Short of threatening to shoot us, they couldn't force us to erase the footage and they couldn't seize the tape without taking the interview the warlord had granted us.

Eventually we made a deal. It was much better than I expected. They would allow us to film a US humanitarian aid drop they were bringing in that night, provided we didn't show their faces. In return, Michael would show them what he'd filmed and erase it in front of them.

I agreed, hoping they wouldn't notice that the interview with Khalili was on a different tape.

A few hours later two commandos arrived at our guesthouse, telling us to get moving. We piled into the van in darkness and followed them up to the airstrip. They were in full camouflage gear. The senior officer welcomed us and said we had three minutes to set up. Their attitude had changed from aggression to hometown hospitality. As Michael organised the camera, the sandy-haired, beardless commando called me aside. 'I'd just like to apologise to you,' he said. 'Things got a little out of hand back there. I don't normally like to shout at people, I like to be nice to people.'

I said, 'No problem,' and thanked him. These were nice guys when you got to know them. Not that I had the faintest idea who they were.

Right on cue, a military transport plane appeared overhead and in total darkness disgorged ten large pallets by parachute. Michael and I jumped on the back of the commandos' three-wheeled motorbikes and we raced off towards the drop. The supplies included grain and blankets — utter necessities for the locals struggling to survive the winter. A crowd of villagers had assembled beside the airstrip hoping for a share of the drop. The Hazara guards were holding them back.

One of the Americans pointed his light towards the crowd. 'See the people lining up?' he said. 'They're here to scavenge anything the soldiers don't get.'

The need for aid was desperate. 'Not long ago we had the largest HA [humanitarian aid] drop in history,' another soldier said. 'Right here in Bamiyan. It was huge. One hundred and five tonnes.'

'So where does it all go?' I asked.

'The wheat we turn over to Mr Khalili and he distributes it,' the commando told me.

Suddenly it all made sense. Rather than helping the Red Cross to distribute aid, the US military were helping their favoured warlord. That's how the blankets got to his compound. Khalili had returned home to a power vacuum and quickly established himself in his old position by demonstrating his influence to his people. There was no need for him to contest any imposed democratic order. The US was simply restoring the old order which the Taliban had removed.

As we drove back to Kabul, past the rusting tanks and ruined villages of decades of war, I felt the familiar ache of disillusionment I had felt in every war. It should have been possible to build a new Afghanistan. The West could have sent peacekeepers to disarm the warlords; I was sure the Afghan people would have welcomed it. But the US wasn't fighting the War on Terror for the Afghans' sake and it was already gearing up for Iraq. It was far easier to re-instal anti-Taliban warlords than to have the costly distraction of fostering genuine peace.

Khalili may have been a sonofabitch, but he was now America's sonofabitch. Such was liberated Afghanistan.

Chapter 28
Jalalabad, February 2002

Osama's Lucky Escape

Bottom line. Jack hadn't come here to eat Snickers. He'd come to kill Taliban. But weeks of relatively soft living and junk food were blunting his edge. 'In the States I normally only eat a couple of cucumbers and a tuna sandwich,' he'd often say through a Hershey Bar. Now he was threatening to burst through his uniform.

He'd become one of the best customers of sweets and soft drink at Kabul's main shopping stretch, Chicken Street. Homesick for Americana and with a tendency to excess, he'd arrive at the house laden with snacks, steaks and booze for nightly bingeing.

Under the surface, however, Jack was desperate for military glory. And fate had given him a rare second chance to be a hero.

Somewhere in a small village on the mountains around Jalalabad, an Afghan spy had been biding his time for twelve years. He had worked for the CIA in the holy war against the Red Army, in the days when Osama bin Laden and the US fought on the same side. The Americans had left in 1989 when the Soviet Union withdrew, and their 'intelligence asset' had been abandoned. The spy had then watched the peace descend into civil war and chaos, followed by the coming of the Taliban extremists and their Arab overlords. And he'd waited and waited for the Americans to come back.

The first American he'd seen was Jack.

It was during the first trip we did with Jack to Tora Bora. An elderly Pashtun man came to the hotel to speak to the 'Special Forces soldier'. Jack had met him in his room, borrowing a camera from

Sebastian to record the meeting secretly. What he learned was potentially as big as the al-Qaeda tapes. The man was aware of a group of senior al-Qaeda militants who had escaped Tora Bora and hidden in a village near his own for the winter. At great personal risk, he was prepared to follow their movements in the coming weeks and report to Jack on when it would be possible to attack them. For security, he would only deal with Jack.

Jack could do nothing with the information immediately but it became his main mission. He was going to turn his protection corps into real soldiers and come back 'to blow the motherfuckers away'. As he'd often tell us while unwrapping another Snickers Bar.

Despite the weight, Jack could still do a convincing impression of a formidable soldier. He would regularly demonstrate assault techniques as we tried to work, usually with Zabi as a reluctant prop. One night before we banned Zabi from the house, Jack used him to demonstrate three ways of disarming someone pointing a pistol at you. Each involved grabbing the revolver from Zabi's hand before he could fire it and slamming him against the wall. He insisted on making me hold the gun as well. I was in no position to judge the finesse of his technique but Jack was not a man you'd want coming at you after dark.

The trouble was, his soldiers seemed about as capable of taking on al-Qaeda as I was. There were now twenty Afghans in Jack's militia and he had worked hard to train them over winter, promoting anyone he thought had leadership talent and even designing new uniforms for them. But they remained unruly, whining, scamming and lazy.

However, time was now running out for Jack to put his plan into action. If he waited much longer the snow could melt and the militants might slip away into Pakistan. Jack knew he needed help and knew just who to turn to.

The Jalalabad warlord Hazrat Ali had an ambitious nephew called Sami. We'd met him on the Tora Bora trip one night after he'd returned from the front. He was still in his early twenties but commanded 600 men and seemed competent and self-possessed. Jack decided to head back to Jalalabad with his motley militia and get Sami on board the glory train.

He also invited us to film with him. Kim was busy finishing her documentary in Kabul but I had time for one last trip before I flew back to Sydney and it seemed it could be a unique story. As well as reporting news, I was trying to put together a long feature for *Foreign Correspondent*, which was prepared to pay for a field trip, as the story needed a dramatic centrepiece. Yet there was an obvious ethical dilemma — was Jack planning a battle just for our camera? He insisted that that had nothing to do with it. After all, the whole point of the war was attacking al-Qaeda.

'You know, I've always been lucky,' Jack said. 'Now, I don't think Osama bin Laden is in that village, but just imagine if he *was* hiding in that village,' he continued, clearly imagining that he might well be. 'I mean the fucker is somewhere in that area. It's near Tora Bora, that's where he was last seen. Can you fucking imagine if he was in this village?'

I imagined it was about as likely as finding Princess Diana, but following a crazy American on a hunt for bin Laden was bound to be interesting. We could always just tag along for the ride and see what happened.

Jalalabad was very different from when we were last there. Life had returned to normal, or at least what passed for normal in this part of Afghanistan. The media were gone, the streets were choked with traffic and the markets bustled with merchants if not buyers. Michael, Jack and I moved into the Spinghar Hotel, which was now empty except for us.

The next day we found Sami Ali outside the city at a meeting with other commanders. Hundreds of his men loitered with their guns. There was no longer any meaningful role for such large numbers of gunmen but there were no other jobs for them. The size of a militia denoted the power and position of a commander or warlord. Disarming it would be a sign of weakness.

Sami remembered Jack and was immediately interested in his proposal. But he didn't seem quite as competent and self-possessed as I recalled him being at our previous meeting. In daylight he looked more like a pimply kid whose uncle had given him an army, which in fact he had.

Before any firm plans could be made, Jack had to make contact with the 'asset' to find out which village the al-Qaeda militants were staying in. This meant sending word to a go-between who had to find the man and bring him to Jalalabad. With at least another day to kill, I decided to spend some time with Sami.

We found him at his uncle's house, which was also his house. As well as being Hazrat's nephew, he was also his son-in-law, having married his cousin, Hazrat's daughter. With no war to fight they were both bored. Hazrat lounged on a cushion, surrounded by satellite phones, which he idly pushed around with his bare feet. Sami sat on the carpet next to him, pouring tea into a glass and then back into the pot. Hazrat showed brief interest in being interviewed by the foreigners, and told us there was a desperate need for the world to send him money so he could buy medicine for the hospital.

'The hospital is in a worse condition than the jail,' he said. 'The doors are broken, people are sitting in cold rooms.'

But he soon grew tired of the questions and went back to toying with his satellite phones. Sami, who didn't feel like being interviewed, idly clinked his cup. After half an hour of awkward silences, punctuated by servants bringing in dates and sweets and fresh pots of tea, I asked if Sami could show us his barracks. He yawned, stood up and left the room, which the interpreter told me was a sign we were going.

We followed Sami to the street behind the compound, where two shiny new Toyota Landcruisers were parked. They looked and smelled as if they had just been taken out of a showroom. The seats were still covered in plastic. I asked where the cars came from and Sami grunted something about them being flown in from Dubai. Then he ordered his servants to take off the plastic. Sami, it seemed, was going for a spin.

He climbed into the driver's seat of the first car and Michael, Jack and I climbed in behind him, not sure what Sami was intending. I looked back to see a vast entourage of soldiers, servants and hangers on getting ready to follow. Sami revved the engine and raced off. The other Landcruisers and four more cars fell in behind us.

I assumed he was taking us to the barracks but within a few minutes we had left the city and were racing across the desert. Sami pressed a switch and a CD of techno-pop started pumping through the sound system. He pulled the visor down to check his appearance in the mirror, adjusted his hat and gunned the engine. We were now on a rough dirt road and, even with the car's expensive suspension, we were bouncing wildly. I asked the interpreter if he could find out where we were going. He tried but Sami just grunted. A few minutes later he mumbled to Jack. I asked the interpreter what he said. 'He say to Jack, "Why you no bring me satphone?"'

Jack tried to make an excuse in reply but the car lurched violently and he was bounced into the roof. Sami drove on unconcerned as Jack yelled in pain. It wasn't just that he'd injured his head. More seriously, he had broken his sunglasses. He stared at the smashed lenses in disbelief, while Sami gunned the car past a herd of camels.

'Jesus faarking Christ! I've broken my fucking sunglasses. I don't fucking believe it! My favourite fucking sunglasses. The only fucking sunglasses I can shoot with!'

I had never seen Jack so upset.

Shuddering, thumping, rocking and bouncing at high speed down the dirt track, we eventually arrived at a village.

'This is my village,' Sami said as he rocketed down its narrow street. He didn't mean he lived here. He meant he owned it.

He skidded to a halt outside a large half-built residential compound. This is what he had brought us to see. It was to have been Sami's new residence in what was effectively a feudal holding. But the Taliban had seized the village and halted construction.

'I built these two houses,' he whined. 'I bought the plans for these houses from overseas and they destroyed them. They destroyed them all.'

Sami appeared to believe we should see this as a terrible crime. Michael was bruised from trying to hold the camera in the car and looked like he was about to hit him. 'How much more are we doing with this arsehole?' Michael asked.

'Just enough to get us back,' I said.

We piled back in the car and braced for the return journey. It was even worse than the ride out. The car may have been new but it felt as if Sami had trashed its suspension on the first drive. Jack hardly said a word, silently mourning the death of his favourite sunglasses.

Back in Jalalabad, Sami decided to take us to his barracks, a mere five hours after we'd first asked him to. He called out to some soldiers to line up for inspection. Most of them stared vacantly into the distance, looking about as lethal as Jack's militia.

Finally Sami agreed to be interviewed. I asked him how long he intended to be a commander.

'I would like to be a businessman,' he said. 'This is my country, people tell me to go to London, this country or another country. I'm not going anywhere. This is my country. If I am killed in my country I don't mind. It would be good for me to become a businessman.'

His answer made no sense. But I had a feeling he was going to make a lot of money no matter what he did.

Michael and I went back to the hotel wondering why we had come. He was uneasy about the whole trip, fearful that a bunch of halfwits were about to shoot up a village just to get on camera. I was starting to feel the same.

'Nothing's happened yet,' I said. 'Let's just meet the spy. We can always bail out.'

We didn't have long to wait. The next morning, Jack's 'intelligence asset' turned up at the hotel and with great secrecy met us in Jack's hotel room. If it were known he was giving information about al-Qaeda, he would certainly be killed. He was nervous about having an Afghan interpreter present but there was no other way to communicate. He confirmed the al-Qaeda men were still in the village but cautioned that we would have to wait a few days.

'I must go quietly into the village to find out which houses they are in,' he said. 'It must be done carefully so they don't know of my inquiries.'

'Now hang on,' Jack said. 'It has to happen tomorrow. These guys are heading back to Australia.'

'It cannot be tomorrow. If I do not find where the men are and there is shooting, it may kill the innocent.'

'These guys can't wait,' Jack insisted. 'You have to find out today. We've got to go in there tomorrow.'

Michael and I sat in stunned silence. What we'd half feared, and been reassured about, was true. This was all being planned for us. Michael looked at Jack in disgust. I was suddenly glad I was leaving Afghanistan.

'Do what you want Jack,' I said. 'We're going back to Kabul.'

Jack appeared genuinely hurt that we were leaving. He couldn't understand why we didn't just film him attacking the village. But it didn't matter. As we loaded our gear in the van, Jack's soldiers told him they weren't going to fight unless he gave them more money. It seemed as though they had never intended to fight anyway.

We drove back to Kabul on our own, deliberately driving ahead of Jack's heavily laden convoy, preferring to chance the dangers of the road than spend any more time with his militia. Jack was apologetic when he arrived back in Kabul and I decided there was no point in staying angry. For all his talk, nothing had actually happened. Nobody had been hurt. Jack was full of threats and bluster but deep down he seemed harmless. And he had helped us out with some extraordinary stories.

We flew out of Kabul a couple of days later and Michael went back to Australia. Jack sent a few emails in the following months, talking about his exploits tracking down al-Qaeda and even rescuing earthquake victims. Then I lost contact.

I did well out of the al-Qaeda tapes story, winning one of the main television journalism awards, a peer-selected Logie. A few weeks after the win, I was browsing through a bookshop when I saw a photo of Jack and Zabi on the front cover of a self-described bestseller. It was a book he had co-authored on the war in Afghanistan, full of tales of a legendary figure called Jack. I laughed and felt relieved. Jack had finally found his glory and nobody had been hurt.

Or so I thought. In July 2004, Jack was arrested in Kabul and charged with imprisoning and torturing Afghans. He had found another house with a cellar and put it to use, kidnapping people he deemed suspicious and interrogating them for days. One of them was an Afghan Supreme Court judge. It ended with Afghan and US troops raiding his private prison.

At Jack's trial he denied mistreating the prisoners and insisted that the Pentagon had been fully aware of what he was doing. He produced tapes of him talking to senior Pentagon officials. NATO admitted taking part in raids with him but insisted he had conned them into thinking he was with Special Forces. The US Government disowned him. It was just after the scandal of US soldiers torturing Iraqi prisoners in Abu Ghraib, and the last thing any American officials wanted was to be tied to Jack.

More surprisingly, the Afghan Government cut him adrift as well. The Northern Alliance commanders he had befriended and advised claimed they had had nothing to do with him. I wasn't sure if Jack ever had authority from the Pentagon but I knew for certain how close he was to senior Afghan officials. After a farcical trial, in which he was stopped from presenting most of his evidence, he was sentenced to ten years imprisonment and sent to rot in an Afghan jail.

Jack really had seen Afghanistan as a place with no rules, where American heroes could take down bad guys in a battle between good and evil. He turned out to be an expendable pawn in the murky War on Terror he had imagined he was fighting.

Chapter 29
Xinjiang Province and Beijing, May to July 2002

Learn from Ancient China!

Madame Zhang Qiyue looked at me like something unpleasant she had stepped in.

'You come from a young country,' she said. 'You have come to an ancient culture. You should *learn* from that culture.'

I felt like saying I would be happy to learn from it if the hundred police shadowing us would let me speak to anyone. But Madame Zhang was ready to put me on a plane back to Beijing if I argued with her again. As well as being a rude and ignorant provincial, it seemed I was also unappreciative.

'You have not shown *any* gratitude for the opportunities you are being given here,' she said, with genuine affront. 'You have been extremely discourteous.'

I was in the middle of the worst trip I'd ever been on, courtesy of the Chinese Foreign Ministry. This was Waiban hell.

'Xinjiang' means New Territory in Chinese. Except half the people there call it East Turkestan, meaning the eastern land of the Turks, meaning they don't want to be part of China. There had been an armed uprising as recently as 1990 and underground Islamic resistance groups have been active ever since. As a result, Chinese officials are even more paranoid here than they are in Tibet.

Bordering the northwest of Tibet, it's China's largest province but the area and its conflict are almost unknown in the West. Xinjiang has never had a cuddly figure like the Dalai Lama to interest celebrity-hungry Westerners. What it does have are large numbers of Central

Asian Muslims who feel they have nothing in common with China and dream of living in a separate state. And the authorities were determined to make sure we didn't get to speak to a single one of them.

The Foreign Ministry had sent its most senior media bureaucrat to ensure the trip went smoothly. Madame Zhang was head of the Information Department and effectively the voice of China, enunciating government policy at a weekly media conference for Beijing-based correspondents. An outstandingly capable official in her forties, she occupied a deservedly high pedestal in the diplomatic hierarchy, from which vantage she was now lowering herself to deal with a serial miscreant.

The purpose of the tour was to convince journalists that China's long-running crackdown on Muslim separatists was another front in the War on Terror. But in typical Foreign Ministry style, it was refusing to let us see anything remotely connected to the issue.

We had spent four days driving vast distances across the desert to endure mind-numbingly boring press conferences with Chinese party officials. We had seen innumerable folk-dancing exhibitions and handicraft displays but had not been allowed to meet a single ordinary person. We had spent the previous night changing from taxi to taxi in a vain bid to shake more than twenty police cars tailing us to stop us speaking to any locals. And I had spent the whole time arguing with Madame Zhang and trying to sneak out to film anything we weren't supposed to.

'I suggest you think about your behaviour on the rest of this trip if you wish to continue to enjoy these opportunities,' she warned in a tone I had not heard since high school.

I nodded as politely as I could, wondering why I had ever come to China. Instead of plunging into another culture, I had wound up stuck in a foreigners' compound, only ever travelling with control-freak officials. After months away on holidays and in Afghanistan, I had lost all tolerance of the mindless rules and make-believe world of Waiban officials.

Worst of all, Sebastian had left China. Kim and I had come back from Kabul to find his coughing and exhaustion were even worse. He was barely able to work but he brushed it off as a cold he couldn't shake. It was a month before he agreed to see a doctor. I rang him after his appointment and asked stupidly, 'Are you going to live?' He forced a laugh.

'The X-ray showed there's something on my lung. But no need to worry, bro, we'll just get another test. It's going to be cool.'

It was the first time I had heard him sound frightened. Further tests confirmed the worst. He had cancer.

Sebastian had been a chain-smoker most of his life but I couldn't believe he was gravely ill. He had always coasted through misfortune, eternally unscathed and optimistic. He joked he would kill the tumours with Jack Daniels. But first he had to fly to Singapore for chemotherapy.

'Oh man,' he said. 'Bloody Singapore. Don't know what's going to kill me first, the cancer or the boredom.'

His wife, Carol, who had become Kim's closest friend in Beijing, followed him with their three-year-old son, Wesley. It was as if a light had gone out.

The ABC sent a freelance cameraman, Justin Hanrahan, to fill in temporarily. He had been looking forward to working in China but was finding it as frustrating as I was. Early on in the Xinjiang trip, I made the mistake of losing my temper with Madame Zhang, suggesting it might be constructive to ask us what we wanted to film rather than giving us pre-packaged programs which were of no interest to us.

She stared at me icily. 'We have long experience in providing for the needs of foreign media.'

'I think journalists are capable of working out what they need and getting it on their own,' I countered.

'It is normal practice that Foreign Ministry officials in many countries assist journalists in the way we are helping you,' she replied.

'It's normal practice in Iraq, North Korea and Libya, but they're not exactly shining examples to follow.'

Her eyes narrowed. 'You will be given all the opportunities you need.'

I wasn't the only reporter trying to buck the rules on the trip, but Madame Zhang had targeted me for special attention. It seemed my behaviour in Qinghai had irrevocably marked me as a troublemaker. The story on the Qinghai railway to Tibet had not gone to air yet because of a backlog of War on Terror stories. But I knew I would be in even deeper trouble when it did.

It was almost tempting to keep arguing with Madame Zhang, despite her warning. The worst that could happen was expulsion. I could leave China in a blaze of martyred glory. But as much as I hated working here, the last thing I needed now was to be told to leave. The reason was Kim.

Not long after we came back to Beijing, she began to feel something unusual was going on. She went to a Chinese pharmacy to confirm her suspicion but found that all the labels were in Chinese. She performed an elaborate mime to the giggling salesgirls who finally worked out what she wanted. Early the next morning she took her purchase into the bathroom. A minute later, she came out with an odd look on her face and showed me a strip with two stripes.

'What does that mean?' I asked.

'It means I'm pregnant.'

A long pause followed.

'.......... Wow .... Umm .... Wow ....'

It was an emotion quite unlike anything I had ever felt: a mixture of overpowering shock, euphoric joy and primal terror. We had been planning to start a family some time in the future but hadn't counted on it happening so quickly. We both had shoots lined up for several months. Kim was about to film a documentary on heroin addicts in Moscow. We knew a baby was going to change our lives radically. However, Kim was sure things wouldn't have to change overnight.

'Don't worry, they take a long time to cook,' she said.

'Phew ....' I agreed. 'Umm .... Whee ....' I added.

So, as I left for Xinjiang, Kim flew confidently off to Russia. She spent seven hours throwing up in the Aeroflot toilet, threw up after the car trip to the city, threw up every time she woke, and spent the next two weeks fighting morning sickness and chronic exhaustion while filming drug deals and hanging around until dawn in seedy apartment blocks with junkies sharing needles.

She returned to China shattered and drained. We realised that we had to be certain of staying here for at least the next nine months. It was unthinkable to try to move countries again before the birth. Beijing wasn't necessarily where we wanted to be but it was home. We just couldn't be sure for how much longer.

The Chinese Government rarely expels journalists outright — but sometimes it doesn't renew their visas. My multiple-entry visa would expire on 20 December, the day our baby was due. There was any number of technical reasons the Foreign Ministry could use to wave goodbye. And as much as I was trying to be on my best behaviour, the trip to Xinjiang had only cemented my position as their least favourite reporter.

There was just no way to get a story out of the tripe they were serving up to us other than by making a feature of their clumsy attempts to control our filming. We filmed undercover policemen shadowing us, police cars tailing us, minders putting their hands over the camera lens and Madame Zhang ordering us to stop filming unauthorised interviews. On the last night in Xinjiang I suggested to the undercover police that they come out for a drink with us rather than following ten paces behind. In a rare sign of Chinese police humanity they agreed and suggested a bar we could go to. I told them we'd follow their car and the senior policeman looked aghast.

'No, no!' he said. 'We must follow you.'

Two weeks after I came back from Xinjiang, the ABC broadcast my story on the Tibet railway and I got the phone call I had been dreading. It was the Foreign Ministry media office saying that Madame Zhang would like to see me.

A lowly official met me at the entrance and escorted me wordlessly through an enormous lobby into a small reception room. I sat down in an uncomfortable traditional Chinese chair, studying the huge plastic chandelier above me.

The room temperature dropped sharply as Madame Zhang walked in accompanied by her deputy. 'We have just watched a tape of your story on the visit to Qinghai,' she began as her deputy scribbled notes. 'We think you were very rude to Mr Lu on that trip and you have distorted facts. This will be the first of our conversations to address those problems.'

I nodded silently and started taking my own notes.

'First of all you said that Tibet was invaded. Perhaps you do not know that Tibet has been a province of China since 1247. You have not read the history. Imagine if I was to say to you that Australia was invaded by the British and the British continued to occupy it. You would not like me to say that.'

I thought briefly of saying that actually Britain did invade Australia. A large and sudden influx of armed men rowing ashore, raising the flag for England, shooting the locals and staying for good would have trouble passing for 'peaceful liberation'. Instead, I thought of where we were going to have our baby.

'You talked about large numbers of Han Chinese moving in,' she continued. 'The November 2000 census shows the population of Tibet is 2.616 million, out of which 91.2 per cent are Tibetan and only 5.9 per cent are Han, which includes temporary workers but doesn't include Tibetans working outside Tibet. If you count them, Tibetans are 95 per cent, which is the same percentage as in 1951, even though the population has more than doubled. In 1951 there were 1 million people approximately, now there are 2.6 million.'

An urge to challenge those statistics welled up inside me, forced its way to the front of my mouth and attempted to prise open my teeth, but I held it back.

On it went. I had deliberately tried to antagonise her officials, especially Mr Lu, after they had done so much to assist me. I had treated them very unfairly. I had clearly come to China with old, hackneyed ideas. I was unwilling to learn. My reporting lacked objectivity and my conduct was unacceptable. 'We have to consider whether the ABC will be able to go on any more trips like this,' she added.

'Does this mean just me or also my colleague Tom O'Byrne?' I asked.

'No, we are not threatening you with anything, but you need to consider your behaviour.'

So it was not to be expulsion after all. It was going to be probation. 'Well, you've given me a lot to reflect on,' I said.

Madame Zhang smiled and relaxed back into her chair. The meeting was over.

I left the room wondering what the first punishment would be. I arrived back at the office to find they had blocked the ABC website. This meant it couldn't be accessed anywhere in China. It wasn't the first time the Public Security Bureau had closed our website. But the fact that the shutdown coincided with the reprimand suggested that the issue of my reporting had gone well above the Foreign Ministry.

I raised the issue with the Australian embassy, which promised to make inquiries. Some diplomats appeared annoyed that they were unable to access the website but I sensed it was more because they had relied on it for footy results. The website remained blocked.

The Chinese embassy in Canberra, meanwhile, stepped up the pressure, complaining to the ABC that my reports were not conducive to 'friendly Sino–Australian relations'. It lodged formal complaints about the reports on the Tibet railway and Xinjiang. Neither pointed to any specific errors of fact but argued there was no reason to criticise China's actions, as they were bringing great prosperity to those areas.

Shortly afterwards the Foreign Ministry announced it would at last take an organised tour to Tibet. I didn't bother applying. Tom did. His application was rejected.

The message I took from all this was that my reporting life in China would be short and unpleasant if I continued to do critical stories. If I didn't buckle, the authorities would punish my colleagues and limit the ABC's presence in China.

Many foreign journalists in Beijing did tone down their reporting to avoid trouble with the authorities. Some were China scholars who had drifted into journalism and saw less reason than most to be critical or antagonistic. Some simply played the percentages — if they were going to be here for a long time, they couldn't afford to jeopardise access to interviews, tours or 'sensitive areas'.

There was no shortage of fearless reporting, particularly in newspapers and from some TV groups like the BBC. But the foreign media community in general was a tamer beast in Beijing than I'd seen in any other news centre. Officials were rarely grilled at press conferences. Reporters usually tried to creep around restrictions rather than confront them. Some broadcasters' stories were 'balanced' to the point of being neutered. Examples of repression, which we all knew to be true, could be presented as merely 'claims' that the authorities denied.

Even so, I hadn't interviewed anyone or aired any criticism that officials hadn't seen or heard from other journalists before. I wondered if my worst crime had been repeatedly highlighting the minders' attempts to stop us reporting freely. In doing so I had made the criticism personal in a culture where face was everything.

By now Kim and I had been living together for more than three years. But the Chinese authorities didn't recognise our *de facto* relationship. For Kim to keep living with me in China, she had to get a new tourist visa every month, which meant leaving the country. This had been a nuisance but possible while she had been travelling for work. Soon it was going to be impossible. Once she was more than 30 weeks pregnant she wouldn't even be allowed on a plane.

Kim was exhausted, grumpy and confused when I called her on her latest trip in Moscow. She had gone out to do an interview, realising only later that she was wearing house slippers. 'Let's get married,' I proposed. Six weeks later we were on our way back to Sydney for our wedding.

It was a relief to have a break from China and I kept being reminded of how long I'd been away. It had been years since I'd even spoken to some of the friends I asked to the wedding. Worse than anything, my mother was too sick to come. Her health had been deteriorating for several years while I had been travelling around the world, leaving it to the rest of my family to care for her. I started wondering if a life lived overseas was worth the personal cost.

Armed with a marriage certificate, Kim finally got a Chinese residency permit. The expiry date for her multiple-entry visa was the same as mine — 20 December, when we were expecting the birth. People kept asking us where we were having the baby. The answer was always: 'Beijing, we think. Unless they throw us out.'

On the way back to China, we stopped off in Singapore to try to see Sebastian. The tumours had spread and he was enduring another massive round of chemotherapy. I rang him in the morning but he was too sick to get up and told us to call later. At lunchtime I called again and he told me he had collapsed after trying to walk.

'Just take it easy, bro,' I said. 'We'll see you soon in Beijing.'

For the first time, I wondered if I would ever see him again.

Chapter 30
Beijing and Shenzhen, August to December 2002

The Party's Over

I came back from Australia determined to focus on aspects of China other than boorish Communists. It was an intriguing and fascinating place, and I had barely scratched the surface of it. But politics kept intruding into every story.

I went to Shanghai to do a story about a finishing school for women, only to find that the dean was a party official who insisted it was a perfected refinement of Marxist principles of equality. I went to China's first outdoor rock festival billed as 'China's Woodstock' to find 500 helmeted paramilitaries from the People's Armed Police keeping order, and Communist censors vetting the song lyrics in order to cut out any political criticism. I went to an arts festival where Australian street puppeteers weren't allowed to perform on the street in case they threatened 'social stability'. Every story I did wound up making the authorities look ridiculous and I wasn't even trying.

On one level it was surprising that the world's largest and most successful dictatorship was so utterly insecure. The economic improvements it had overseen were truly breathtaking — none more so than in the city of Shenzhen, just across the border from Hong Kong. In 1978, when it was chosen as a 'special economic zone' to experiment with capitalist reform, Shenzhen was a sleepy fishing village of 30,000 people. It was now a city of seven million that made Hong Kong look like a backwater.

We flew there to do an economic story and I found myself staring in disbelief at what had been achieved in just one generation. It was a mega-city of soaring office blocks and frenetic construction sites. A cynic might argue that it was achieved despite the Communist Party rather than because of it. Freed from the sloth of socialism, the Chinese had simply revived the entrepreneurialism that the party had tried to repress. Even so, it was more impressive than anything I'd seen in 'democratic' Russia.

The local Waiban were happy to give us a guided tour of Shenzhen's main attractions: the giant shopping malls, the stock exchange, the observation tower on the tallest building. But, as always, officials tried to stop us seeing anything that conflicted with the image of stable prosperity.

Shenzhen's back streets were full of slums crowded with peasants from the countryside. They worked twelve-hour days in Dickensian conditions so they could send money back to their villages to stop their families starving.

China's rapid economic growth had made the coastal trading cities rich but had left most of the countryside in dire poverty. More than 100 million peasants had already drifted to the cities looking for work. They had few enforceable rights and were ripe for exploitation.

Telling our minder we were going back to the hotel, we instead drove to a hostel where I had arranged, through an underground labour group, to meet a worker activist. Liu was waiting for us on one of the concrete walkways that ringed the hostel floors. A 30-year-old peasant from Sichuan province, he was dressed incongruously in a neat shirt and slacks, a contrast to the hundreds of men who stood on balconies in shorts and singlets.

Liu seemed excited by the chance to tell someone his story, even a foreign media crew that couldn't possibly help his cause. He showed us around the tiny one-room apartments where he and his fellow workers lived. I was surprised that at least two families shared each room, with up to eight people living, washing, eating and sleeping in less than 25 square metres. Liu explained that the hostel belonged to the construction company they worked for. They had to live here to get the job, then pay almost all their wages in rent. The only way they could afford to eat was to split the rent with other families.

'If you don't work it's terrible,' Liu said. 'Only if you work can you eat.'

It wasn't the bad living conditions that angered Liu, or the pitifully low pay or the dangerous conditions they worked in. It was that the company had cheated them. A few months earlier it had sacked Liu and 220 other workers and refused to hand over the pensions for which each worker had paid 8 per cent of his or her wage. The explanation was that the company had subcontracted their labour to a shelf company with no assets. There was nothing Liu or the others could do.

'We complained but officials did nothing. We went to court and the company paid off the judges. Our money went into their pockets,' Liu said, disgusted.

As they fought for some measure of justice, the workers were still paying rent to the company that had sacked them and stolen their entitlements.

It was a brief glimpse of the utter powerlessness of workers in the workers' paradise. And we were lucky not to be arrested for seeing it. The next morning we were summoned urgently to the Shenzhen Waiban office. The minder, Miss Niu (meaning Cow), was nearly trembling with anxiety and rage. 'What were you doing at the workers' hostel yesterday?' she demanded.

Someone had obviously snitched but we'd left before the police came. 'What hostel?' I asked.

'You were seen filming there yesterday!'

'We filmed a market, we were just getting some general shots. But we didn't film in any hostel.'

'So you didn't do any interviews?' she asked, almost smiling with relief.

'No, nothing,' I said. 'Just some pictures of the market.'

Miss Cow exhaled. She wasn't going to lose her job, after all, for the unpardonable crime of allowing the masses to speak unsupervised to journalists.

'I look forward to seeing your story,' she said.

The authorities were utterly paranoid about foreign media reporting worker unrest. We all knew there were strikes, protests and worker riots almost every day across China but journalists would only ever hear of them much later.

The cover-up made it easier for Western governments and investors to ignore the issue. On 1 May, to coincide with International Labour Day, Amnesty International published a damning report on China's labour practices. It detailed police crackdowns on peaceful worker protests and the imprisonment without trial of labour leaders.

The same day, Australia's then opposition leader, Simon Crean, arrived in Beijing for an official visit. As well as being leader of the Labor Party, Crean was a former president of the peak trade union group, the ACTU (Australian Council of Trade Unions). I asked him for a reaction to the Amnesty report.

'I'm not aware of the report.'

'Will you be raising any concerns about the imprisonment of labour leaders and suppression of labour protests?'

'I'm not aware that these are issues that people want raised,' he responded.

Crean was in the awkward position in which all visiting politicians to China find themselves. Public criticism of the dictatorship means a frosty reception and nothing to show for the visit. Innocuous praise and sidestepping of human rights questions brings warm banquets, promises of mutual cooperation and the odd major trade deal. Not surprisingly most Western politicians choose to pucker up and think of the money.

It was even harder for a lowly opposition leader to make a mark. Crean was invited to speak at a faculty of the Beijing People's University. A large banner said in English: 'Warmly welcome Simon Crean, MP, leader of the opposition'. But below it the Chinese characters said: 'Warmly welcome Simon Crean, leader of the Labor Party'. Chinese political terminology simply didn't have a word for 'opposition'. After three days of polite but low-level talks, Crean announced that the main achievement of his trip was the beginning of ongoing consultation between the Australian Labor Party and the Chinese Communist Party.

The Chinese Government had no such awkwardness dealing with another former Labor leader, Bob Hawke. He was held in high esteem by the Communist leadership and was on friendly terms with the heads of government. Yet as prime minister he had been fiercely critical of the Tiananmen Square massacre. The day after the mass murder, Hawke had wept on television as he described the scene. 'Anti-personnel carriers and tanks then ran backwards and forwards over the bodies of the slain, until they were reduced to pulp,' he said sobbing. 'Afterwards, bulldozers moved in and pushed the remains into piles that were then incinerated by troops with flamethrowers.'

By 2002, however, the ex-prime minister was a consultant advising Australian companies on doing business in the Middle Kingdom. His tone on China had softened markedly. I caught up with him in Tianjin, a large trading port near Beijing, where he was keynote speaker at a conference about China joining the World Trade Organization (WTO). His address was characteristically bullish.

'Never before has such a significant economy grown at such high rates for such a long period of time and at the same time lifted so much of its population out of absolute poverty,' he enthused to a hall of business leaders and Chinese officials. 'In two decades China has accomplished what in other countries took centuries.'

Like Crean, Hawke had been head of the ACTU before entering parliament. I asked the former champion of workers' rights about China's suppression of labour rights.

'You're wanting to impose on China standards of the West that took ... more than a hundred years to acquire,' he growled. 'Now, I don't think we should be expecting China to change overnight in that regard.'

Without low wages and primitive working conditions, China could not have transformed its economy so quickly or become such a competitive exporter. While Western companies in China often provided good pay and safe workplaces to their own employees, they all benefited from the low prices of their suppliers. The last thing Western businesses wanted was for China to push up costs by leap-frogging to Western standards.

The WTO forum in Tianjin at which Bob Hawke was a keynote speaker was one of the more remarkable cheer sessions for China's raw capitalism. Limousines pulled up at the grand entrance disgorging Chinese tycoons and Western business executives. Important speeches were interspersed with sumptuous banquets with guests waited on by willowy young women in tailored pink suits. The mood inside was overwhelmingly upbeat. Outside, truckloads of riot police armed with truncheons and water cannon surrounded the conference building.

The star of the conference was former US president, George Bush Senior, now one of the most fervent Western supporters of China. He arrived with his wife, Barbara, and a bevy of bodyguards on the final day of the meeting. As the only foreign television crew at the conference, we were allowed to stand in a roped-off area to film him entering. But I had to swear to the Chinese officials that I would not try to ask him any questions or say anything as he walked past.

President Bush Senior stopped in front of us looking chipper and surprisingly sprightly for his age. 'How are you doing?' he asked. Remembering my promise, I smiled inanely and said nothing. The ex-president waited a moment for me to ask something and I stared awkwardly into the distance. He looked puzzled and walked on.

A few minutes later we were invited to film him meeting Vice-Premier Li Lanqing. Bush greeted him like an old friend.

'China's changing so fast,' he said. 'I don't think I can keep up. I'm 78 years old. It's goin' all the time.'

Bush had been the US envoy to China in the mid-'70s, when the Cultural Revolution was winding down and America didn't even formally recognise the Communist state. As president, his occasional

Cold War rattlings had concealed a long-held belief that America should make money from the commies.

In his speech to the conference's closing banquet that night, he made it clear his policy had passed down the Bush dynasty:

> With China's WTO accession, I know I speak for our
> president, which I seldom would do. [Laughter from
> audience.] His mother does it but I don't do it. [Smile
> from Mrs Bush, more laughter from audience.] But I
> know I speak for him, his cabinet and many, many more
> in the US when I say that we welcome the chance to
> move in the same direction and make up for the lost
> opportunities of the past.

George and Mrs Bush Senior departed to enthusiastic applause and a burst of fireworks. Everyone else headed off to make more money.

Marxism-Leninism in China had been replaced by McDonald's-Leninism. While the state retained the Leninist structure of one-party dictatorship and subjugation of all institutions to the party, it had traded socialism for global consumer capitalism. Even so, the party pretended that nothing had changed.

As November approached, the state media was gripped with excitement, counting down the days until the Sixteenth Communist Party Congress. Posters of hammers and sickles were festooned around the city. Television started running back-to-back revolutionary films. Every night, TV news showed a different city discussing how the forthcoming congress was 'Galvanising the Chinese masses to redouble their efforts to develop a well-off society in an all-round way!'. Breathless reporters interviewed enthusiastic 'workers' about how Jiang Zemin-thought and Marxist theory were helping them 'Strive towards ever greater prosperity!'. Banners with uplifting slogans like 'No New Communist Party, No New China!' adorned streets.

I could not imagine a single adult among China's population of 1.3 billion actually believed this. Most ordinary people I spoke to away from minders thought the party was corrupt, incompetent and brutal. They tolerated it grudgingly because they feared chaos and wanted prosperity. As long as the government could keep the economy ticking along, the Communists had a chance of avoiding the fate of their former ideological brethren in Russia. Economic reform was a matter of political survival.

There was no shortage of bright young things trying to join the Communist Party but that had nothing to do with wanting to assist their comrades by reform from within. While the Communists had a personal interest in raising living standards, the party was also an elite club bringing power and connections without accountability — in short, a progressive Russian mafia with Chinese characteristics.

It was hard to get excited about the party congress because it was as stage-managed as Chinese opera. Everybody knew that the senior party officials, including the leader, Jiang Zemin, would be stepping down in favour of their handpicked slightly younger protégés, who would implement precisely the same policies. But one scheduled change seemed highly significant if only for its symbolism. The congress was going to rubber-stamp amendments to allow entrepreneurs to join the party.

It had been happening unofficially ever since the party leader Deng Xiaoping unleashed capitalism in the late 1970s. Party members set up businesses through their wives or children, pulling strings to make sure they were profitable. Now the party was planning to twist its ideology even further to enshrine capitalist cadres.

We flew south to the city of Changsha to profile a typical business tycoon. Zhang Yue ran a huge air-conditioning factory selling industrial chillers to sixteen countries. He was barely 40 and was estimated to be China's 27th-richest man. He was also one of its most obnoxious. We followed him around his factory as he hurled abuse at his workers, publicly humiliating anyone he thought had made a mistake. He made them live in dormitories on site, allowing them to see their families only on weekends. We waited two days for him to take us up in his private helicopter to view his sprawling and tasteless domain, an industrial complex with a fake French chateau and a giant pyramid. We filled in time driving up and down in his chauffeur-driven ten-metre Cadillac. Zhang Yue was just the kind of get-up-and-go rich bastard the party felt it needed. However, he couldn't be bothered joining.

'Any businessman that gets involved in politics doesn't have enough business to do,' he told us dismissively, before breaking off the interview to make phone calls.

Back in Beijing, the Chinese media's excitement about the upcoming congress was reaching fever peak. Every day brought more examples of how towns and cities across China were looking forward to it with joy, exhilaration and enthusiasm! Newspapers ran articles about how excited foreign journalists were about the historic congress! Radio programs kept mentioning how some foreign bureaus were even sending in extra people to cover it!

A few days before it began, a crew from state television dropped in to interview me about my excitement. I wondered why they had picked me but the reporter turned out to be Yu Tingting, the woman who had interviewed me in my first week in China, at the re-education camp. Her first question was: 'What do you think of the Communist Party and the job it is doing for China?'

I paused. A few months earlier I would have happily said it was difficult to see how much longer the party could cling to power, given its unpopularity and corruption — ensuring that the interview never went to air. Instead, I took a deep breath and thought of the baby.

'Obviously the Communist Party is the most important institution in China,' I said. 'Now that it is more oriented toward business than it was ten years ago when it was, um, it had a different interpretation of socialism, um, that creates many economic opportunities for countries like Australia. So there will be a lot of interest in what happens in the congress because that will set the agenda for how China will be run for the next five years.'

It was unadulterated bollocks and it was all over the evening news. I saw myself in English on CCTV 9 and translated into Mandarin on CCTV 1, 2, 3, 4, 5, 6, 7 and 8. It played in every news bulletin for the next two days. I was once again an integral part of party propaganda.

'Fucking disgraceful,' was the cheery assessment from Rupert at the BBC. But all of a sudden the Foreign Ministry minders started being friendly to me. And for the first time in months I stopped worrying about being expelled.

The congress was an even bigger non-event than the media were expecting. We were allowed to film the opening ceremony and were then shut out until the closing ceremony. The day after that, we crowded onto a media podium to watch the announcement of the party's new standing committee. Half an hour later, some dull-looking men in dark suits walked out, indistinguishable from the dull-looking men they were replacing. I didn't feel like I was witnessing a moment in history: the unveiling of the new leaders of a quarter of humanity. It just felt like another empty ritual.

I was increasingly aware that I was covering a story of marginal news interest while a momentous story was building outside China. Iraq was moving inexorably towards war. I was feeling as isolated from the real story as I had been during the first Gulf War, when I had been sitting in Australia planning stories on caravan parks for a travel program.

'Just be glad they don't want you to go,' Kim told me. 'You're going to be a father, remember.'

But I couldn't get it out of my mind. I felt I had been sidelined, my experience wasted on trying to get around ridiculous restrictions. When the ABC's Foreign Desk sent out a planning list for covering the war my name wasn't on it. I was indignant and rang the Head of International Operations, John Tulloh, to complain.

'We assumed you wouldn't want to be going anywhere right now,' he explained.

'Well I do. I'm a senior reporter,' I said pompously. 'If it happens, I want to be part of it.'

Kim was furious when I told her what I'd said. 'What is wrong with you? Why do you want to go off to another war right now?'

I wasn't sure. I just did. It was like being an athlete and wanting more than anything to go to the Olympics.

'Wouldn't *you* want to go if you could?' I asked.

'No, I wouldn't!' Kim said. 'We're having a baby.'

We booked into ante-natal classes at Beijing United Hospital, a Western-style medical centre for rich Chinese and for Westerners with company insurance. Most of the doctors were American, British or foreign-educated Chinese. We focused on getting ready for parenthood and I tried not to think about Iraq.

Our baby came a week early. Kim and I had gone for a six-kilometre walk in the snow followed by a Thai curry, wondering vaguely if it were true that curry and exercise brought on contractions. It was. I timed the contractions as Kim darted round the house with a rush of pre-natal energy. She insisted on cooking an elaborate Spanish omelette at eleven at night. 'This will take a long time and you'll get hungry,' she said.

She was wrong. Minutes later Lao Zhang was driving us to the hospital. Our son was born three hours afterwards. He came out howling, wrinkled and bug-eyed. Then he peed on me. It was love at first sight.

We called him Nicholas, wanting him to have a name that was international. His Chinese name was Pu Niku. I spent every day at work wondering what he was doing and every night carrying him around in one hand trying to make him stop crying. I felt exhausted and wonderfully happy. I had a wife I loved and a son I adored.

But I still wanted to go to Iraq.

Chapter 31
Salisbury and Parvizkhan, February to March 2003

Get Me to the War on Time

A month later, I was standing in a gas chamber at a British Army base near Stonehenge learning how to survive a chemical weapons attack. The advice was that we had nine seconds to put on the mask. That was nine seconds to:

- Recognise you are being gassed ('Look for people keeling over in the distance').
- Breathe out.
- Find your chemical weapons pack (keeping your eyes tightly shut).
- Open it.
- Take your mask out.
- Remove your spectacles.
- Place the mask over your head in the correct fashion.
- Fasten it.
- Check the canister is attached.
- Breathe in deeply.
- Shout 'Gas, gas, gas!' for the benefit of your colleagues.

On the first rehearsal, I was dead about fifteen seconds before the 'Gas, gas, gas!' part. But I improved enough on the second try to move on to the next steps:

- Put on your chemical weapons suit, gloves and boots.

- Check the wind direction ('Try the back of your neck for that').
- Move out of the way of the invisible cloud.

If you hadn't supplied your driver, interpreter and armed guard with gas masks, it would then be prudent to lock yourself in the car and lock them out, in case they tried to snatch your gas mask before dying.

Survival courses had become compulsory for any media people planning to cover the Iraq war and this course was standing room only. There was the usual unfathomable multitude of BBC producers, correspondents and technical staff. There was also Dana Lewis, an NBC correspondent I knew from Moscow. And there was Robert Fisk from *The Independent*, a fervent critic of the coming conflict whose every question was a statement. 'What if you have to give first aid to someone who has been tortured by US soldiers?' he asked in the first-aid segment. 'What if you're contaminated with nuclear fallout from one of 200 nuclear warheads Israel is known to possess?' he asked during the class on radiation sickness.

It was still the stage when the war wasn't a certainty and every journalist was saying 'God forbid' but privately imagining their by-lines and pieces to camera in Baghdad. Even an army course reinforcing how ghastly it might be couldn't completely dispel the frisson of excitement and expectation.

I was still on the reserves list, as the ABC's Jerusalem and Moscow correspondents already had visas for Baghdad. Then I started talking to Dana Lewis. He was planning to cover the war from the Kurdish opposition enclave in Northern Iraq.

'We're thinking that could be the best story,' he said. 'You're going to have American troops there, Kurdish troops, you're going to be able to move freely. And you're going to have the Iraq dateline without having the crap bombed out of you in Baghdad.'

Back in Beijing the next week, I rang the Foreign Editor, Bronwen Kiely, about NBC's plans. She had also begun to think about Northern

Iraq as another base for our coverage. It could be part of the main story and much safer than Baghdad. A week later she asked me to get a visa, telling me I might be working with a freelance cameraman named Paul Moran who had worked in Northern Iraq before.

I didn't know Paul but I rang him a few times over the coming weeks to check if he'd been issued a visa. Paul was originally from Adelaide but was living in Paris with his Serbian wife, Ivana. Like me he had just become a father for the first time, with a baby girl called Tara.

From the outset, the odds were against us getting in at all. Northern Iraq was a de facto separate state protected by NATO air patrols and the only way in was through Iran. For months, the Iranian authorities had been deluged with visa applications from foreign journalists. By the time we lodged ours in January, the Iranians were in no mood to be accommodating. I agreed to pay a 'fixer' in Tehran an exorbitant fee to speed up our application.

'I hope you don't get it,' Kim said.

A week later my mother died.

I listened in shock as my father rang me with the news late at night. My mother had been sick for years and we had expected the worst for months. But it was still the saddest news I had ever heard. I found myself sobbing like a child as I packed to fly to Sydney. I wanted to take Kim and Nicholas so my son could at least be at the funeral of the grandmother he had never even seen. But he didn't have a passport yet so the authorities wouldn't let him leave China.

I was the only Westerner on the crowded overnight flight from Beijing to Guangzhou to Melbourne to Sydney. The passengers around me looked concerned but kept their distance, not wishing to disturb the red-eyed foreigner staring out the window and trying to hide his tears.

A few weeks after I returned to China, Sebastian came back to Beijing for what a doctor claimed was a secret miracle cure. He must have known it was hopeless but he had nothing to lose by trying. The Singapore doctors had told him the tumours were spreading and there was nothing more they could do. He looked cheerful when I saw him in hospital and we talked about stories we'd do when he was well. But a few days later he suffered a stroke and collapsed into semi-consciousness. The doctors advised his family to expect the worst. They flew in from Singapore to be with him.

I was grieving for my mother and morose with worry for Sebastian. But I kept pushing for the visa. Twice a day I would ring the Iranian embassy, go through a ritual of polite greetings and check if our visas had been approved. Each time the staff would apologise and assure me they were doing everything in their power. The fixer in Tehran warned me time was running out. In ten days the Iranian border would close for the Muslim festival of No Ruz, meaning New Day, when Iranians and Kurds mark the beginning of the religious year. It would not reopen if the bombing started. He said he was doing all he could but we must continue to put pressure on the embassy.

I rang Paul in Paris, mixing up the times and calling him at three in the morning.

'No worries,' he said in his laconic Australian accent. 'I'm up anyway feeding the baby.' We joked about fatherhood and sleep deprivation. Paul said he'd hassle the embassy in Paris about his visa application. 'Now what gear do you want me to bring?' he asked. 'Bring it all,' I said.

ABC headquarters needed Sebastian's camera kit to send to one of the other war crews. The only way to get it out in time was to hand carry it through Customs. I booked the first available flight to Australia and went to see Sebastian to say goodbye.

I wasn't prepared for the deterioration since I'd last seen him. He could no longer speak and could barely open his eyes, but he seemed to understand everything. And he was crying. For the first time there was no pretence that all would be well. The most vibrant man I had ever known was trapped inside himself, waiting to die.

I went home to pack, feeling sick and overwhelmed. Kim decided she would bring Nicholas, now nearly three months old, back to Australia with me. We had only just got his passport, and Kim didn't want to be alone in Beijing if there was going to be a war. I was in the office sorting out gear when John Tulloh rang.

'We've lost Sebastian,' he said. 'He passed away twenty minutes ago.'

I sat silently for a few moments. There was no time to mourn. It was three hours to news time and John wanted to run a short tribute. I called the staff together and told them Sebastian had died and asked if they could scour the office with me to find photos of our friend. We fed them down the line to Sydney and began organising a wake for the following night at Durty Nellies, Sebastian's favourite fake Irish pub that served genuine Guinness. I asked the others to drink to him for me. A few hours later, Lao Zhang drove us to the airport to start the journey to Iraq.

For the second time in six weeks, I flew to Australia in the aftermath of death. I left Kim and Nicholas at the international terminal in Sydney and caught a domestic flight to Canberra to plead with the Iranian embassy. It was my last possible chance to get a visa in time to get to the war. It was the Thursday before No Ruz and the embassy was about to shut for a week. The UN negotiations had ended and bombing was imminent.

The embassy's second secretary was sympathetic but, by the end of the day, he had still not received a telex from Tehran to issue me a visa. 'I am very sorry,' the diplomat said. 'There is nothing more I can do.'

I caught the evening flight to Sydney and told Kim the news. 'It means I'm not going to Iraq,' I said. She smiled with relief.

I felt both relieved and dejected. The ABC would send me somewhere else like Jordan or Israel. I would be safe but I would be missing the main story. I rang Paul in Paris and told him to unpack his bags.

The next morning, completely unexpectedly, everything changed. The second secretary rang to say approval for my visa had come overnight. Even though the embassy was closed, he was prepared to issue the visa. I could scarcely believe it. I couriered my passport down to Canberra and booked a Sunday flight to Tehran. I rang the fixer in Tehran, who said Paul's visa was also approved.

'But it's Friday in Paris,' I said. 'The embassy is closed.'

'Tell him to fly to Istanbul,' he told me. 'I have a good friend in the consulate who will issue a visa on Sunday.'

It was an extraordinary turnaround. Our luck had changed at the very last moment. And our fate was sealed.

Chapter 32
Kurdistan, Northern Iraq, March 2003

Collateral Damage

A chicken-wire fence was all that stood between the war and me. It had taken four days to get here, paying off Iranian officials and running the gauntlet of the Revolutionary Guard, which controlled the unofficial border crossing to Northern Iraq. It was the last afternoon before the border closed for the Muslim New Year and US bombers were already fuelling up to attack.

The guide the fixer in Tehran had given me came out of the commander's prefab hut smiling.

'Mr Eric, the final permissions have come through!' he said. 'I wish you a very successful trip.'

Northern Iraq, also called Kurdistan, was an unrecognised state controlled by two rival Kurdish factions in opposition to Saddam Hussein. As such, I wasn't officially leaving Iran — I was just going into territorial limbo — so the guards didn't stamp my passport.

They simply opened the gate and I walked across a dusty field to a small building with an unfamiliar flag. A man with a Kalashnikov slung over his shoulder and a cigarette dangling from his mouth directed me inside. It had turned into a beautiful spring day. For the first time in weeks I began to relax. I had made it just in time for the war.

The building was a guesthouse belonging to the PUK (Patriotic Union of Kurdistan), which controlled the eastern half of the enclave. A man who spoke no English gestured to me to wait in a lounge chair in front of a large TV set screening Baghdad television. A young boy brought me a cup of tea. Nobody even asked to see my passport.

Eventually a group of Kurdish youths who spoke broken English drifted into the room to watch TV. They all had moustaches but no beards and wore Western dress. They laughed and jeered as propaganda images of Saddam Hussein flashed across the screen, miming shooting him in the head. 'A few more days, he is dead!' one of them said to me.

Paul crossed the border two hours later, having raced there from Paris through Istanbul and Tehran. I had never met him before and he made a strong first impression, standing on the back of a truck, surrounded by boxes of camera gear, looking steady and relaxed. He saw me and smiled.

'Welcome to liberated Iraq,' I said.

'Yeah, only just,' he said. 'The guards almost confiscated my gear.'

I helped him unload a dozen cases of equipment as we talked about the respective bureaucratic hurdles we'd scrambled over. 'I told the guards about a soccer game I saw where Iran won by a point,' he explained. 'They're all football mad so they let me through.'

As we waited for a taxi to take us into the main town of Suleimaniyah, where most of the media were based, two American journalists arrived to collect extra gas masks they'd had shipped to the border. Saddam had often used chemical weapons against the rebellious Kurds (one attack on Halabja in 1988 killed 5000 civilians) and, now that they were allied to the US, the whole city was bracing for a retaliatory chemical strike once the US started bombing Baghdad.

'Don't even bother trying to buy a gas mask in Suly,' one of them said. 'Every single one has been sold.' He mentioned he was working with 'another Aussie', a *Time* magazine writer called Michael Ware. 'I'll tell him you're here,' he promised.

The taxi turned out to be a van with an armed guard. Security came as part of the fare. We drove a few kilometres down the road to where hundreds of Kurdish civilians had set up a makeshift camp in fear of chemical weapons strikes on their villages. Men were pitching tents and tarpaulins beside their cars while children played and women cooked over campfires in the waning light. Some were washing clothes in a nearby stream. It was almost like a holiday camp, except everyone was wondering what would be left of their villages in a few days' time. Paul ran around filming before our nervous guard called us back to get moving.

The cause of the worry was an extremist group called Ansar al-Islam, whose base was outside the city of Halabja near the road to Suleimaniyah. They were fighting a separate war with the secular Kurdish Government and had seized several villages, imposing Taliban-style rule on the residents. The US had claimed that the group was linked to al-Qaeda, reinforcing the justification for invading.

Paul didn't know any more about the group than I did but he seemed to have an encyclopaedic knowledge of Kurdish politics. He told me he'd made several trips here, including filming for the BBC during a brief civil war between the PUK and its rival, the Kurdish Democratic Party (KDP). 'I think we're going to be better off in the PUK area,' he said. 'It's a lot more secular and relaxed. The KDP are more hardline and a bit fundamentalist. You see a lot of women with veils. And they're not as easygoing about media.'

I had lucked out with Paul. He was capable, cheerful and instantly likeable. At 39 he had spent a third of his life overseas, living in Washington, Cyprus, Bahrain and Paris. He was both a cameraman and a documentary maker and, at his own expense, once spent a year making a film about refugees in Cyprus simply because he felt sorry for their plight.

We were both resigned to staying here for the duration of the war. The ABC had just evacuated its Baghdad bureau for safety reasons, meaning that we were now the only television crew for an Australian network inside Iraq. Another ABC reporter, Geoff Thompson, was embedded with a US Army unit in Kuwait but there was no certainty about where the unit would go during the invasion.

'There's a good chance we'll get to Baghdad first if the Iraqis' northern line crumbles,' Paul said. 'Baghdad's only about a four-hour drive from Suleimaniyah.'

Eventually the conversation turned to fatherhood. Like me, Paul had been a late starter. I told him how I'd dreaded not being able to go out late and sleep in. He told me his father's death had made him decide it was time. 'I nursed him until he died. That made me realise I had the strength to be a father.'

It was a strange remark for a journalist — personal and devoid of cynicism.

'How do you feel about the risk of being here?' I asked.

'I'm glad to be doing it,' he said. 'But I want to be as careful as possible.'

So we made a pact. We wouldn't hide in the hotel but we'd always stay at the tail end of the media pack, letting gung-ho reporters without children check out the dangers first.

We reached Suleimaniyah after nightfall and moved into the only hotel we could find with vacancies. All the decent hotels had been booked out for months by media networks waiting for the war to start. Even our small, out-of-the-way hotel was full of journalists lounging round the bar, wandering the grubby corridors, swapping stories or shouting into satellite phones in a dozen different languages. Every one of them had chemical weapons survival packs slung over their shoulders or within easy reach, gas masks peeking out beneath the flaps. Paul and I carried our packs with us wherever we went, even into the bathroom. As well as masks, we had chemical weapons suits, decontamination powder and syringes with vials of atropine for countering nerve gas.

Suleimaniyah was battening down for war. The next morning the roads were clogged with Kurds driving out of the city. Some people staying behind were sticking plastic sheets over their windows in a futile attempt to make their homes safe from gas. Bush's ultimatum to Saddam to leave Iraq was due to expire that night.

We managed to find an interpreter through the American journalists we'd met at the border. Handran was a short, chubby student who was working for the US radio network NPR. He told us he liked his boss but didn't like the money. 'He says he can't give me danger money,' he complained. 'I'm not going to risk getting killed for $50 a day.' It was poor form to poach another reporter's interpreter but I was desperate to start filing. I agreed to pay Handran extra for any dangerous assignments. Remembering the advice of the chemical weapons survival course, I also promised to buy him a gas mask.

That proved to be impossible. Just as the Americans had warned us, gas masks had sold out. The only thing doing a roaring trade was camping gear. Queues were forming outside camping stalls, families loading tents and groundsheets into their cars and heading straight into the countryside.

Despite the fears, I didn't speak to a single Kurd who wasn't glad the war was coming. Every person we interviewed was prepared to risk all to see Saddam overthrown. 'He has killed so many thousands of us already,' one man said. 'If he is not stopped, he will just keep on killing.'

The only foreign journalists getting a hard time were the French, who were seen to be anti-war. The Kurds seemed to hate them. 'Look at these fucking guys,' Handran said, pointing to a French crew in the hotel foyer. 'Why they love Saddam Hussein?'

'Handran, they're just journalists, they've got nothing to do with the French Government.'

Later a French journalist stopped me in the bar. 'Why you Australians want a war?' he asked.

The Kurds got their wish early the next morning. I lay in bed before dawn, switching the TV between Al-Jazeera and BBC World, watching the first bombing. Saddam's forces were just an hour away, opposite a village called Chamchamal. It was the obvious story for the first day of the war so we went to the main hotel where the media were staying to suss out the dangers of going down there. I found half a dozen journalists I knew from Canada, the US and Britain who advised it was safe to drive to Chamchamal but not to linger long in sight of Iraqi guns.

Smoke was rising from the village as we drove down, though it turned out to be from car tyres the Kurdish soldiers had set alight to mark the No Ruz celebration. Kurdish soldiers stood around smoking or squatting beside the roads, looking bored and frustrated. They told us they were keen to start fighting but their commanders had ordered them to wait until the US agreed they could advance. Many of them were *peshmerga*, traditional guerilla fighters, who knew every inch of the mountains and had their own informal way of fighting. They wore the Kurdish peasant outfit of baggy pants and jackets rather than standard uniforms, and toyed with worry beads, impatient with the delay and bristling to begin.

At the edge of the village, we could see Saddam Hussein's forces on the hills opposite. Away from the soldiers, the streets were eerily quiet: the entire civilian population had fled. Paul and I agreed to shoot a quick piece to camera in the open, along the lines of 'The Iraqi forces are just on this hill behind me . . .' We put on our flak jackets, set up the gear, then drove 100 metres down the road towards the frontline and jumped out. I fluffed the first take but managed to get it on the second go, signing off with 'Eric Campbell, ABC News, Northern Iraq. OK? Let's get the fuck out of here.'

The Kurds were banking everything on a US victory. After the first Gulf War, they had staged a revolt against Saddam, expecting the US to topple him. They paid a terrible price. On our way back to Suleimaniyah, Paul pointed out a village he had filmed on an earlier trip.

'There wasn't a single man there. After the uprising in '91, the Iraqis rounded up every male. None of them came back.'

I was going to ask him more about his trips to Kurdistan but the satellite phone rang. Unlike my experience in other war zones, I was now in constant phone range. The new-model satellite phones were handheld and worked like mobile phones, so you didn't have to stop the car and set up a satellite dish to make a call. The downside was that the newsroom could reach you at any time of night or day. But there was little to report, as the US attacks were focused on the south.

The story drought broke two days later. There was an unusual buzz in the foyer of the main media hotel as we walked in. Dozens of people were watching a giant television screen which was showing amateur footage of cruise missiles striking the Ansar al-Islam base near Halabja. US warplanes had pounded the area overnight in the first real action in Northern Iraq. It was tempting to check it out but it was already close to midday and I had told Sydney we were spending the day in town to do a feature. Just as we were about to leave, a voice called out, 'Is that you, Eric?'

It was Catherine Taylor, an Australian journalist I knew from Sydney. Neither of us had known the other was coming here. She was filing for *The Australian* newspaper and travelling with Russell Skelton from *The Age*.

'What are you doing today?' I asked.

'We're going to check out the base that had the air strikes.'

I thought, 'Oh shit.' It would be on the front page of all the Australian newspapers tomorrow but not on the ABC. I waved them goodbye and talked it over with Paul. He agreed the attack on the base was the better story. It was getting late but we'd still have time to film and get back before dark.

As soon as we left Suleimaniyah we saw other media cars heading down to the base, their windows and roofs covered with masking tape forming the letters 'TV', for dubious protection against snipers or US air strikes. We fell in behind an open truck with about 25 *peshmerga* standing in the back. Paul opened the car sunroof and stood up to film them. They saw his camera and started cheering and waving their Kalashnikovs in the air. Kurdish civilians clapped them as we drove through a crowded village, children running beside the truck and squealing. The air strikes had put everyone in a good mood.

We stopped at a PUK checkpoint for Handran to get information. He came back to the car and said, 'Oh boy, this is big. They hit Komala Islami too.'

KI was another radical Islamist group but it was formally allied to the PUK, even though it was suspected of aiding Ansar al-Islam. It wasn't clear if the Americans had bombed it by accident or just decided to wipe it out anyway, on the principle that any fundamentalist was a terrorist. The cruise missiles had killed dozens of people, including civilians.

The Ansar base was in the next valley, in a village down a side road from the main highway. We drove down to the turnoff, which was blocked by another PUK checkpoint. Soldiers and *peshmerga* had taken up positions on a hill opposite, their guns trained on the Ansar village about a kilometre away. We climbed up the hill to find a group of soldiers chanting a victory song and dancing. Their commander explained that the Ansar base was completely surrounded and most of the surviving fighters had fled into the hills. His men would move in soon to finish off any remaining militants.

A burst of distant gunfire sent us ducking behind a trench. The soldiers laughed, explaining that it was just *peshmerga* below firing in victory. But I realised we had stupidly left our flak jackets in the car. Handran went back to collect them while Paul and I kept filming, duckwalking around the trench to the amusement of the soldiers, who stood upright and relaxed. Some more journalists wandered through talking to the soldiers as we waited for our flak jackets. When Handran came back, I recorded a piece to camera, doing several takes until Paul was happy with the light. He looked at his watch. 'Time to get moving,' he said. It was a long drive back to Suleimaniyah and he was keen to start editing early.

We went down to the car, feeling better than we had in days. Finally, we were in the right place at the right time. Back at the checkpoint we quickly interviewed some Kurdish civilians who were fleeing the area in fear of more air strikes. The story was complete. We walked over to the car to go. Paul took off his flak jacket. I picked up the satphone to call Sydney. Something caught Paul's eye and he started filming again. I put the satphone on the ground beside me and took out my notepad to jot down some script. I noticed two Kurdish women standing across the road talking and laughing. I was vaguely aware of a group of journalists climbing into their cars and pulling out. Just as they passed us, some soldiers ran across the road about 10 metres in front of us. Instinctively following the action, Paul ran towards them filming. At that moment, a car screeched up beside the soldiers and stopped. An instant later it exploded.

The shockwave assaulted me, the noise slamming my eardrums, a blast of flames and hot air pushing me back. As if in slow motion, I watched the car disintegrate. Something round and spinning flew towards me, something like a steering wheel or a fan belt or hub cap. It sliced into my chest but bounced off the ceramic plate in my flak jacket. More metal hit my chest. Smaller parts found my skin, shards of shrapnel slicing into my right arm and face.

I ran behind the checkpoint hut, trembling, breathless, terrified. There was a deafening ringing in my ears. I looked down and saw I was soaked in blood, the white 'PRESS' marker on my flak jacket spattered with crimson. Overwhelmed with shock, I checked my limbs. They were bleeding but intact. I'd survived. Then I felt my face. Blood was oozing out of what seemed to be a hole in my forehead. I had never felt so frightened or helpless.

Movement started on the road — a soldier walking, dazed. I staggered back to the roadside, shaking. There was a mass of bloodied uniforms and limbs, the remains of the soldiers Paul had been filming. Another body lay on the road. Nearby were some Kurdish civilians. They were horribly injured, twitching in pain or shock. But I couldn't see Paul.

Some more soldiers came. I cried out, 'Cameraman, cameraman?' One of the men walked up and held out the blackened remains of a camera. It was Paul's. I yelled at him angrily. 'No! Camera*man*. My friend. My friend!' Another handed me a charred passport. It was Paul's. 'No. Where is my *friend*?' I screamed. But I knew where he was now. He was the body lying beside me that I hadn't wanted to see.

Paul could only have died instantly. He was terribly injured. I froze as I stood over him knowing I should do something, eventually kneeling down and holding his arm and saying his name. More soldiers had come by now. They told me I had to go and pulled me away. Everyone was scared there would be more attacks. I saw our driver. He was alive too. He was bleeding badly but still conscious. He gestured that we had to go.

The back window of the car had blown out, scattering shards of glass. I looked in the back for the first-aid kit in case I could help some of the others but couldn't find it. I went to pick up my satphone but it was melted, scorched by the blast I had somehow survived. The soldiers were now shouting and waving at us to leave. I felt I should stay with Paul or take him with me. I *knew* I should do that. But I couldn't summon the strength and drove off in shock and fear.

We found Handran 200 metres down the road. I jumped out of the car. He was bleeding from some cuts on his face but was otherwise OK. 'Where is Paul?' he asked.

'He's dead.'

'Oh, no, no!' Handran began to cry.

I felt nausea welling up in my stomach, ripped off my flak jacket and knelt beside the road. I stood up when the bile receded and noticed my reflection in the car window. My face was cut and bloodied but not disfigured. The driver shouted for us to go.

We drove in silence to a field clinic near Halabja. The enormity of what had happened was beginning to seep through the shock. Paul was dead. He had left a wife and baby girl. I thought of the people I would have to tell. The ABC would need to know first so they could contact Paul's wife in Paris and his mother in Adelaide. I would have to tell my wife I was OK. They had to hear first-hand before they heard it on the news. And I had no phone. This was not like an accident in the West where an ambulance and police would come and the authorities would take over. This was a twilight state at war. But no matter what I did now, it was skirting round the edges of tragedy. Nothing would ever make up for the fact that Paul was dead.

The soldiers guarding the small, makeshift clinic waved us through when they saw our injuries. The driver went in for treatment first. Two women stood at the entrance in tears. They were wearing Kurdish headscarves but when I heard their voices I knew they were American journalists. They asked me if Ivan had been killed. Ivan was the name of Handran's old boss at NPR. I told them, 'No, it was my cameraman; nobody called Ivan.'

The two American journalists I had met at the border were there too. The photographer put his camera down without taking a picture and helped me inside. Someone checked my injuries, scrubbed the cuts with disinfectant and bandaged my forehead and chin and right arm.

I walked outside and asked the women if they had a satphone. My hands were still covered in blood. I asked them to dial a number and waited for my boss John Tulloh to answer. It was about four o'clock in Kurdistan and near midnight in Sydney. I explained what had happened as best I could, trying to stay calm but failing.

I then rang Kim and tried to tell her what had happened — to assure her I was safe — but I could tell from her crying that I was making little sense. I rang John again, who told me he had rung Paul's wife, Ivana, but there was no answer.

I wandered round in a daze, avoiding the eyes of the other journalists in the hospital. I wanted to keep Paul's name and my name secret until John contacted Ivana, in case she heard on the radio that her husband was dead. It was better that nobody knew I was here, better that I didn't exist.

I slumped on the ground and closed my eyes, feeling as if I was sinking into a black pool and not caring if I was drowning. Someone's voice called me back. It was an Australian man shouting: 'Is Eric here?' I didn't want to answer but he saw my bandages and came to me, holding my shoulders and looking straight in my eyes.

'My name is Michael Ware. I'm going to help you.'

He gave me his jacket, saying it was to stop me going into shock. He told me to sit still and stay warm, saying he would take care of everything. I remembered dimly he was the Australian from *Time* magazine who was working with the Americans we had met. He was younger than I was but he already seemed hardened by the work he did.

I thought he looked more like a soldier than a journalist. He had a strong build, thick stubble and an intense gaze that made him appear absolutely focused.

A carload of Kurdish soldiers pulled up at the hospital. They had brought Paul's body in the boot. The American women told me not to look but I had to identify him. It was so wrong for him to be loaded in like baggage. Michael arranged for Paul to be brought back to Suleimaniyah in another car. I drove back with Michael. On the way I used his phone to tell my father I was alive and then let Michael take over everything. He found the Red Cross, the best hope we had of getting out of Iraq. 'We have one Australian journalist dead, another wounded,' he shouted down the phone. 'They need to be evacuated.'

We stopped at the main hospital in Suleimaniyah. All the victims of the bombing had been brought there, in varying stages of agony and mutilation. I lay among them for a while. Then a doctor who spoke some English took me to a private room upstairs.

A French crew tried to interview me but I told them Paul's wife didn't know what had happened yet so I couldn't do any interviews. They argued and Michael threw them out, shouting, 'This is non-negotiable. Fuck off!' An orderly smoked as he re-dressed my wounds. I thought, what the hell, and began smoking too.

More air strikes were expected on the Iraqi positions so Michael had to go back to the front to spend the night. But he told me I could have his room in the city's good hotel, where most of the journalists were staying. His translator drove me to my hotel to collect my things. For the first time an armed guard stood at the entrance. I couldn't face going into Paul's room and told reception I'd be back tomorrow. The manager said he was sorry about my friend.

In Michael's room I began to drink — scotch and red wine mingling with the Valium to deaden the pain. I rang Sydney and found they had finally reached Paul's wife, Ivana. I did an interview about what had happened, trying not to lose control when I mentioned Paul. I went upstairs to a Canadian crew we'd shared footage with, told them of

Paul's death, accepted their sympathies and shared stories and more wine. Back in Michael's room I sponged off the blood between my bandages, tore off my bloodstained clothes, threw them in the bin and got into bed. And then I wept for the friend I had known for just four days and for his six-week-old daughter who would never know her father.

Two days later I was back at the border post where I'd first met Paul. He was now in a coffin in the Red Cross car behind me. The two foreign Red Cross staff in Northern Iraq and the Australian embassy in Tehran had worked miracles to get permission to bring us back into Iran.

We were taken into the city of Kermanshah, where Paul's widow, Ivana, had come to meet us. Devastated, but bearing her loss with amazing strength and dignity, Ivana hugged me and said she was glad I'd survived. Then she went to spend her last moments with Paul.

For all our plans of being more cautious than anyone else, Paul was the first journalist killed in the war. It was a long time before I understood how I'd survived. The wounds I'd received weren't bad enough to cover me in blood yet I was drenched the second after the car exploded. The blood must have been Paul's. In running forward, he had placed himself between the bomb and me. He took the full force of the blast, which melted the satphone beside me and scorched the ground around me. In dying, Paul had saved my life.

Chapter 33

Going Home

Nothing was the same. I drifted through each day, feeling cut off from the real world and trapped in a new world created by a bomb. I saw the explosion when I woke up, when I closed my eyes and when I dreamed. I saw it when I told Ivana about how we went there, what we did and how Paul died.

We were staying in a hotel in Tehran, waiting for permission to take Paul's body from Iran. One of Paul's brothers, Gerry, joined us there. He was utterly crushed but, like Ivana, managed to keep functioning. The head of ABC News and Current Affairs, Max Uechtritz, arrived from Sydney to help with arrangements. Philip Williams, the London correspondent, had flown in with Ivana and stayed with us for the journey home. It took five miserable days to get the necessary permits and fly back to Australia. I turned 43 on the plane. I should have felt happy to be alive but all I could think about was death.

I broke down when I saw Kim at the airport. We hugged and wept. Ivana sat on a bench, crying and alone. Kim went to her and said, 'I'm so sorry for you.' Ivana embraced her and replied, 'I'm so happy for you.'

Kim and I stayed at my father's house in Sydney, not knowing what we'd do or how long I'd be off work. Kim looked after Nicholas — I was too vague and preoccupied to be of any use. I would try to bath him and then find my mind wandering to Iraq, forgetting what I was doing. I sat in front of the television each day watching news of the war, obsessively following each development, and combed the internet reading websites about Iraq.

An Islamist website named the Ansar suicide bomber as a 22-year-old Saudi national: 'The young mujahid Abdal Aziz al-Gharbi was a youth who graduated from university, but he decided to step forward for a great mission, the mission of prophets, that is jihad in the way of God. He went rushing to death.'

The man's identity meant nothing to me. I didn't wonder who he was or why he killed himself and strangers. He was not a real person to me, just a thing that happened; terrible and inhuman like the explosives.

More journalists were dying in Northern Iraq. A BBC crew that had been staying in my hotel drove into a minefield. The correspondent, Jim Muir, escaped unharmed but saw his cameraman, Kaveh Golestan, die. His producer, Stuart Hughes, lost a leg. Three days later another BBC crew was hit by US 'friendly fire'. The correspondent, John Simpson, was wounded. His interpreter was killed. The cameraman, Fred Scott, kept filming with his own blood dripping down the lens. He was a close friend of Sebastian's and had tried to get to Beijing to see him before he died. Instead he was sent to Iraq. Northern Iraq — the region that was supposed to be the safest place to cover the war from — had become obscenely dangerous.

Paul's funeral was held in Adelaide in the church where he had married Ivana. She spoke with composure, telling the mourners of the happiness they had known. 'The day after tomorrow will be our four-year anniversary. They were the happiest and most fruitful years of my life. My dearest Paul. You were forever in my heart, your spirit holds me and helps me to continue with my life.'

Five hundred people came for the service, dozens flying in from overseas, some from as far as London and Washington. I was awed by how many friends Paul had, by how many people loved him, by how much pain his death had caused in so many hearts.

Three days later I was flipping through a newspaper and saw a photo of Paul and Ivana under the headline: 'A RANDOM TARGET OR WAS THIS MAN A SPY?' I looked at it in disbelief.

The article claimed that Paul had 'worked undercover for a US public relations company which had been contracted by the Central

Intelligence Agency to run propaganda campaigns against Saddam's dictatorship'. I had no idea what it was talking about. The article went on to claim Paul's assignment in Iraq was to 'monitor Ansar al-Islam for the ABC'. I was stunned. The newspaper speculated that the suicide bomber had deliberately targeted Paul because of his 'undercover' work. It was absurd and patently false. The article even called Paul a self-described 'crusader' for the Kurdish people. Paul had worked with Kurds and Arabs in the Middle East for years, but I knew he would never have used a word as loaded as 'crusader'.

I rang Ivana, who sounded as if she was in shock. She insisted we shouldn't respond to the article, fearing any rebuttal would only fuel the story. I called a friend of Paul's who had worked with him in Kurdistan. He told me that they *had* been hired by a communications firm in the early '90s to train Kurds to set up an independent television station. Paul had taught people how to film and edit, and had produced public service announcements on landmines. Later he had found the money was coming from the CIA and left the project. Paul had continued to do freelance production work for the firm that had hired them on condition it wasn't for intelligence agencies. His friend had gone on to work for the US-funded opposition, the Iraqi National Congress, later giving Paul an exclusive television interview with an Iraqi defector. The defector claimed to have worked on storage facilities designed to conceal illegal weapons. His claims proved to be false.

I couldn't see anything wrong or sinister in what Paul had done. Giving media training to Kurds opposed to a homicidal dictator was hardly a crime. And every broadcaster had been running stories about weapons of mass destruction. We were all misled. But the combination of 'CIA', 'Iraqi defector' and 'murdered journalist' gave an easy and sensational local angle for war stories, and the dead can't be defamed. For months, more speculative reports came out, recycling the same innuendo. I felt as if Paul was being murdered again.

★ ★ ★

Kim and I moved down to Melbourne to stay with Kim's parents and I withdrew into myself. Kim had to take over everything, trying to mask her own strain as I brooded on Iraq and what had happened to Paul. I hated being in crowds, where I constantly felt uncertain and unsafe. I would jump at the sound of a car backfiring or a sudden voice behind me. Flashbacks of the bomb could come at any moment. At these times I would pretend that nothing was happening and try to keep talking — panting and stammering as I forced the images from my mind.

Meanwhile the dreams were getting worse. I would see the explosion, Paul dying and me not being able to help him. I started dreaming I was falling off a cliff, scrabbling on the edges and slipping into an abyss. I would wake in terror, go back to sleep and dream my baby son was being murdered. I began to fear sleep. I stopped going out in case I met people who asked me about Iraq.

The ABC sent me to trauma counselling, a standard treatment for accident victims but a process I saw as proof of my failure and weakness. I had always thought journalists who saw terrible things should deal with the problem and move on, like emergency workers or soldiers. If they couldn't, they shouldn't be in the business. But I couldn't block out the memories and I couldn't get back to normal.

'What's wrong with me?' I asked the counsellor. 'Soldiers see far worse than this and it doesn't stop them being soldiers.'

'You're not a soldier,' she said. 'You don't have to be.'

I had an operation to remove the shrapnel from my face and arm and watched the scars slowly heal, knowing they would never fully fade. Eventually I crawled back to life. The memories didn't fade but I learned to deal with them. I started feeling grateful, not guilty for surviving. I turned my anger over Paul's death into simple sorrow. I focused on my family and began to enjoy life again. And I started to think about the future.

I didn't want to go back to China. It was a place with too many bad memories, and now Sebastian wouldn't be there. I told the ABC I could only go to close down the apartment and ship our belongings home.

The question was, where was home? After seven years away from Australia I no longer felt part of the place.

There was a temporary vacancy in the bureau in Moscow. The ABC needed someone to fill in for a few months until it found another correspondent. It had once been a good place for me to start again. Maybe it was still. And Kim was excited. Like me, she felt as if Australia was a foreign country after so many years away.

In September 2003 we flew to Beijing and closed down that part of our lives. Then we boarded an Aeroflot flight with bad food and worse service and flew to Moscow's Sheremetyevo Airport. We queued at Immigration and handed a sullen official our passports, this time with the requisite photocopies of our visas. We waited an hour for our baggage and filled in endless forms before fighting our way through the crowds, clutching our baby boy, and driving through slush-filled streets to the dingy old apartment where we'd met. Looking out over the grey, freezing city we smiled. We were home in Absurdistan.